W9-AFI-912

Philosophy of Education

Philosophy of Education

THIRD EDITION

Nel Noddings

WESTVIEW
PRESS

A MEMBER OF THE PERSEUS BOOKS GROUP

Westview Press was founded in 1975 in Boulder, Colorado, by notable publisher and intellectual Fred Praeger. Westview Press continues to publish scholarly titles and high-quality undergraduate- and graduate-level textbooks in core social science disciplines. With books developed, written, and edited with the needs of serious nonfiction readers, professors, and students in mind, Westview Press honors its long history of publishing books that matter.

Copyright © 2012 by Westview Press
Published by Westview Press,
A Member of the Perseus Books Group

All rights reserved. Printed in the United States of America. No part of this book may be reproduced in any manner whatsoever without written permission except in the case of brief quotations embodied in critical articles and reviews. For information, address Westview Press, 2465 Central Avenue, Boulder, CO 80301. Find us on the World Wide Web at www.westviewpress.com.

Every effort has been made to secure required permissions for all text, images, maps, and other art reprinted in this volume.

Westview Press books are available at special discounts for bulk purchases in the United States by corporations, institutions, and other organizations. For more information, please contact the Special Markets Department at the Perseus Books Group, 2300 Chestnut Street, Suite 200, Philadelphia, PA 19103, or call (800) 810-4145, ext. 5000, or e-mail special.markets@perseusbooks.com.

Library of Congress Cataloging-in-Publication Data

Noddings, Nel.
  Philosophy of education / Nel Noddings. — 3rd ed.
    p. cm.
  Includes bibliographical references and index.
  ISBN 978-0-8133-4531-4 (pbk.) — ISBN 978-0-8133-4532-1 (e-book) 1.
Education—Philosophy. I. Title.
  LB14.7.N63 2011
  370.1—dc22

                              2011004102

10 9 8 7 6 5 4 3 2 1

To the memory of Lawrence G. Thomas,
who introduced me to philosophy of education.

CONTENTS

LIST OF FIGURES

PREFACE

Philosophy of education is the philosophical study of education and its problems. Unlike other branches of philosophy, it is rarely taught in philosophy departments. Just as philosophy of law or medicine is often taught (if it is taught at all) in law or medical school, philosophy of education is usually taught in schools or departments of education. Its central subject matter is education, and its methods are those of philosophy.

Traditionally, philosophical methods have consisted of analysis and clarification of concepts, arguments, theories, and language. Philosophers, as philosophers, have not usually created theories of education (or teaching, learning, and the like); instead, they have analyzed theories and arguments—sometimes enhancing previous arguments, sometimes raising powerful objections that lead to the revision or abandonment of theories and lines of argument. However, there are many exceptions to this view of philosophy as analysis and clarification. The classical Greek philosophers, for example, construed philosophy much more broadly and explored a host of questions that later philosophers—more narrowly analytic in their outlook—rejected as outside the scope of philosophy. Indeed, for the Greeks, "philosophy" meant "love of wisdom," and today we think of their discussions as part of an "immortal conversation." Many of us believe that philosophy went too far in rejecting the eternal questions, and there are signs that philosophers may once again invite their students to join in the immortal conversation.

Despite the dominant analytical view of twentieth-century philosophy, philosophers have sometimes created theories, and today many philosophers engage in constructive work. They introduce new language and suggest powerful alternatives to the standard uses of language. Some now even draw heavily on literature and empirical data in the form of teaching-narratives to make points that cannot be made in the traditional style of argumentation. Whether this work is properly called philosophy is part of an exciting contemporary debate.

Philosophers of education study the problems of education from a philosophical perspective. To do this, they need to know something about several of the standard branches of philosophy—epistemology (the theory of knowledge), philosophy of language, ethics, social or political philosophy, philosophy of science, and, perhaps, philosophy of mind and aesthetics. This is a formidable task, and in preparing an introduction to the philosophy of education, philosophers of education have often failed to satisfy teacher educators because the material has been too abstract and esoteric. Some of the liveliest contemporary treatments have all but abandoned what might be called the *content* of philosophy and concentrate instead on applying a clarity of thought (characteristic of philosophical method) to serious problems of education.

Here, for better or worse, I will introduce readers to the branches and major topics of philosophy and how they are relevant to problems of education, and I will also choose problems of current interest. The purpose is to acquaint readers with the rigor of philosophical argumentation as well as the complexity of issues in education.

The first four chapters provide readers with some knowledge about educational questions that have been important since the days of Socrates and address the ways in which philosophers have approached these questions. After a brief historical survey of such questions and their treatment prior to the twentieth century, I turn in Chapter 2 to the thought of John Dewey. This chapter continues the historical development, but it also sets the stage for current debate and introduces the methods of pragmatic naturalism. In Chapters 3 and 4, I discuss other methods or approaches used by contemporary philosophers of education: analytic philosophy, existentialism, phenomenology, critical theory, hermeneutics, and postmodernism. One cannot expect anything like a full treatment of these approaches, but my hope is to provide enough to enable students to read material from the various approaches with some understanding and appreciation and to recognize when writers are using the methods or content of a particular tradition.

After the introductory chapters, we will look at specific educational problems as they are studied philosophically—educational issues that fall under the general title of epistemology, ethics, philosophy of science, and the like. This arrangement is not entirely satisfactory even to me, its author, because I very much look forward to the day when sharp divisions between disciplines and subdisciplines will be broken down. However, as the exposition proceeds, I will try to point out the places where my own arrangement gets in the way of a full discussion of the problem at hand— where, for example, an issue that is currently treated as part of epistemology cries out for ethical analysis. Perhaps, by the end of the book, readers will see for themselves why rigid boundaries must be broken down. In the meantime, it may be instructive to consider what philosophers have accomplished within these boundaries and why so much remains to be done.

The second edition of *Philosophy of Education* added an entirely new chapter. Chapter 10, "Problems of School Reform," examines issues of equality, accountability, standards, and testing. The special features of the current school reform will surely change as the twenty-first century progresses, but the basic concerns will remain, and all educators should think deeply about them. Which of today's recommendations will function to maintain and advance our democracy? Which will promote individual growth? Are some currently popular ideas inimical to both great aims?

This third edition adds another chapter on topics of great current importance: multicultural education and cosmopolitanism. It considers the arguments for and against multicultural education, and it tries to sort out some of the confusions between multicultural education and ethnic studies, between cosmopolitanism and "exceptionalism," and between patriotism and citizenship.

The last chapter, "Feminism, Philosophy, and Education," summarizes the previous chapters from a feminist perspective. Philosophy texts in the early twentieth century often concluded with a chapter that presented a statement of the writer's philosophical convictions. The final chapter in this volume is written in that spirit. It should remind readers of the arguments discussed earlier, and it should provide stimulation for further exploration. In this edition, I have added a bit to bring readers up-to-date on the latest work in care ethics.

ACKNOWLEDGMENTS

My first thanks go to all the philosophers of education, cited and uncited in this book, who have influenced my thinking and contributed so much to generations of education students.

Special thanks go to Denis Phillips, Nicholas Burbules, and editor Spencer Carr, who read drafts of the first edition and helped me to eliminate misleading passages and clarify others. I owe special thanks also to the enthusiastic students at Teachers College, Columbia University, who used the first draft as a text and contributed significantly to its revision. My husband, Jim, also deserves thanks for reading the draft, locating typos, and, especially, for insisting that he enjoyed it thoroughly.

Since publication of the first edition, I have received helpful comments from Randall Curren, Amy McAninch, Nathan Nobis, Harvey Siegel, and Lynda Stone. Amy McAninch suggested revisions in my treatment of Values Clarification, and Harvey Siegel persuaded me to think more deeply on the issue of truth. Nathan Nobis wrote pages of suggestions that arose in his use of the text with students, and his efforts are much appreciated. I hope the changes have improved the text.

Nel Noddings

CHAPTER 1

Philosophy of Education Before the Twentieth Century

Philosophers of education are interested in analyzing and clarifying concepts and questions central to education. Long before there were professional philosophers of education, philosophers and educators debated questions familiar to contemporary philosophers of education: What should be the aims or purposes of education? Who should be educated? Should education differ according to natural interests and abilities? What role should the state play in education?

All of these questions are still asked today. The fact that they are still current discourages many students of education. Why study questions that never go away? If we cannot answer certain questions, why ask them? One answer to these sensible objections is that every society must answer them, not once and for all time but as well and conscientiously as it can for the benefit of its people and the future of the earth. In every age, the questions have elicited better and worse responses, and thoughtful people continue to examine the old responses, to generate new ones induced by changing conditions, and to reflect on current responses in the interest of making education as good as it can be.

Questions in philosophy of education are first and foremost questions about education, and most philosophers of education are employed in schools and departments of education. Their questions are philosophical in that they require philosophical methods for their investigation. For example, we cannot decide entirely by empirical methods—methods of experiment and observation—what the aims of education *should be*.[1]

Rather, we have to argue from certain basic premises or by positing certain likely effects of our choices. If we choose the latter approach, we can engage in empirical methods to show that our choices do in fact culminate in the predicted consequences, but we still need philosophical argumentation to persuade others that the consequences we seek should be valued.

One of the perennial questions in philosophy of education centers on who should be educated and how. As we will see, this question deeply interested Plato, and he began his discussion with an analysis of society's needs and the varieties of human talent. From an elaborate set of premises about the nature of real and Utopian societies and the nature of human beings, he derived his recommendations for education. In contrast, John Dewey (whose work we will study in Chapter 2) made his recommendations by asking what the consequences might be if we made certain choices.

Our current society answers the question, Who should be educated? with an almost unanimous Everyone. Our great debate is over *how* individual children should be educated, and the debate today is heated. Many educators insist that all children should have exactly the same education at least through grade twelve. Others, many in the Deweyan tradition, argue that education should be tailored as closely as possible to the interests and needs of individual children.

Sometimes questions of philosophical interest arise on the contemporary scene. Although such questions are not, by definition, perennial questions, they are usually rooted in issues that transcend the contemporary scene, and careful philosophical analysis can contribute to the ongoing policy debate.

Consider, for example, the currently popular issue of school choice: Should the public vote for and install a choice, or voucher, system? Should parents be given vouchers worth a designated amount, say $5,000, to apply toward tuition for their child in the school of their choice? This question certainly has its roots in the perennial questions of whether all children should receive the same education, whether parents should have some control over their children's education (how much?), and whether the right to control education should be restricted to those who can afford to pay for the kind of education they want.

We can see how philosophical analysis might be useful in identifying and clarifying basic issues. We might be able to decide by empirical test whether parents who avail themselves of such opportunities are better satisfied than they were without vouchers. We might even be able to judge whether schools with many satisfied voucher students do a better job on certain specified measures than they did before they became voucher schools. But how can we decide whether the possibly better outcomes for voucher students offset the likely deprivation of students who remain in schools deserted by peers from better informed and better endowed families? If vouchers lead to a form of cultural balkanization—each sect and subculture reigning in its own school community—is this result desirable or undesirable? Notice that the way I have worded my questions suggests strongly that I am not in favor of a voucher system. One of the tasks of philosophy of education is to analyze the language used in arguments and to offer alternative language that draws attention to other perspectives and possibilities. If you are in favor of a voucher system, you might try constructing questions that will reveal the one-sidedness of my questions.

These are the kinds of questions fascinating to philosophers of education. Some of them have been around since the time of Socrates; others are products of our own time and culture. All of them, however, require deep and careful thought, imagination, reflection, and a great capacity for patience in casting both questions and answers in a variety of ways designed to shed light on a problem of considerable importance. As we explore a few historical examples, you should ask yourselves how perennial questions change according to the context in which they are asked, how old questions die away leaving similar questions as their legacies, and how new questions are generated by the answers to old ones.

Socrates and Plato

What we know of Socrates (469–399 B.C.) comes to us entirely from the writing of his disciples—chief among them Plato. Socrates himself taught by engaging others in dialogue, not by writing, and most students of education immediately associate his name with the "Socratic method." This method of teaching, popular especially in law schools, begins with the teacher posing a deceptively simple question such as, What is truth? or, What does it mean to be just? When a student answers, the teacher responds with another question that prompts him or her to think more deeply and offer a new answer. The process—also called destructive cross-examination (elenchus)—continues until either teacher or student or both feel that the analysis has gone as far as they can take it at the moment.

In the following bit of dialogue taken from *Republic,* Book 1, Socrates convinces Polemarchus that his previous position on justice—that we ought to do good to the just and harm to the unjust—is faulty. Socrates starts the argument:

And instead of saying simply as we did at first, that it is just to do good to our friends and harm to our enemies, we should further say: It is just to do good to our friends when they are good and harm to our enemies when they are evil?

Yes, that appears to me to be the truth.

But ought the just to injure anyone at all?

Undoubtedly he ought to injure those who are both wicked and his enemies.

When horses are injured, are they improved or deteriorated?

The latter.

Deteriorated, that is to say, in the good qualities of horses, not of dogs?

Yes, of horses.

And dogs are deteriorated in the good qualities of dogs, and not of horses?

Of course.

And will not men who are injured be deteriorated in that which is the proper virtue of man?

Certainly.

And that human virtue is justice?

To be sure.

Then the men who are injured are of necessity made unjust?

That is the result.

But can the musician by his art make men unmusical?

Certainly not.

Or the horseman by his art make them bad horsemen?

Impossible.

And can the just by justice make men unjust, or, speaking generally, can the good by virtue make them bad?

Assuredly not.

Any more than heat can produce cold?

It cannot.

Or drought moisture?

Clearly not.

Nor can the good harm anyone?

Impossible.

And the just is the good?

Certainly.

Then to injure a friend or anyone else is not the act of a just man, but of the opposite, who is the unjust?

I think that what you say is quite true, Socrates.

This small piece of dialogue is quite characteristic of Socrates. He dominates the dialogue and leads the listener. Sometimes, as in a later part of the dialogue with Thrasymachus, he allows a partner to advance his own argument, and very rarely (as, again, with Thrasymachus), he fails to convince his partner entirely. In most of the dialogues, Socrates is a formidable teacher—leading, questioning, giving information (often in the form of a question), forcing his listeners gently and not so gently to see the errors in their thinking.

Many of you are no doubt familiar with an old television series (and a preceding film) called *The Paper Chase.* In it, the brilliant and irascible Professor Kingsfield terrorized his law students with his expert use of the Socratic method. Kingsfield and Socrates had much in common: great intelligence, penetrating wit, a willingness to use occasional sarcasm, and unfailing skill in choosing and pursuing questions of real importance. But Kingsfield had official power over his students. Their answers were evaluated, and failure to prepare for their professor's questions could lead to failure in law school and the need to consider another profession. Socrates, in contrast, met his students informally in various public places and private homes. Participants could come and go as they pleased, respond or not respond to Socrates' probing questions. Indeed, Socrates always insisted that he did not teach anyone anything, and certainly he was not a professional teacher, for he never charged his "pupils" anything.

As professional teachers—or as students about to become professional teachers—you should ask yourselves whether the Socratic method can be used in modern classrooms as Socrates used it. You might even want to consider whether Socrates himself always used it in ways you find appropriate. Did he show proper respect for the dignity of his students? Did he occasionally force opinions on them (or seem to)? Is it right (in what sense of "right"?) to cross-examine a student relentlessly in front of his peers? Can you think of ways to adapt the method so that it is acceptable to your own moral standards? Finally, if you aspire to become a Socratic teacher, what must you do to prepare yourself?[2]

We, like Socrates himself, might regard his method more as a method of learning or inquiry than a method of teaching. Socrates was a superlative thinker, and in Chapter 5, we will revisit his method of questioning as a method of critical thinking. It was not unusual for Socrates to start an investigation with one question and, after a brief exploration, switch to another, either because he had established that an answer to the second was necessary for analysis of the first or because the initial question was not well formulated for the investigation he hoped to complete.

Socrates did not employ his method on trivial questions. He was interested in the great questions of life: How can we find truth? What does it mean to know something? How should human beings live their lives? What is evil? What do we owe the state, and what does it owe us? What does it mean to be just? Here we should return for a moment to the content of Socrates' dialogue with Polemarchus. Notice that Socrates argues that a just person cannot, by acting justly, make others unjust and that, if we argue that harm or injury tends to "deteriorate a man" so that he becomes unjust, then a just person must not injure even those who are evil. This dialogue raises a host of questions that have been debated for centuries: Can retributive justice be defended? How should harm or injury be defined? (Is a guilty child harmed or injured by punishment?) Was Socrates right when he claimed that people cannot be made unjust by just acts?

As he explored these questions that fascinated him, Socrates was led to criticize those in both public and private life whose thinking and behavior revealed ignorance or apparently evil intentions. His message to students and politicians often ran something like this: Our analysis shows that *this* is what you are really doing or striving for. Consider well. For if you follow the analysis and understand, you will change your ways. Those who know the right, will do the right.

Socrates was concerned not only with social/political problems, but also with issues that demand self-knowledge. His dictum, "Know thyself," is still admired by most educators and intellectuals. As we will see in our later discussion of critical thinking, it is harder to turn the light of critical analysis on ourselves and our own ways of life than on others. Today some reject such Socratic reflection in schools as "therapy," but Socrates insisted (rightly, I think) that self-knowledge is basic to all knowledge. It accompanies and informs our critical examination of the larger society.

Socrates was permitted to engage in his criticism of the state and its prominent citizens for a long time, but eventually, in a time of great political unrest, he was charged with not believing in the state's gods and with corrupting the youth of Athens. As you all know, despite his elegant (and somewhat arrogant) defense, he was found guilty and sentenced to death.[3]

In philosophy of education, we could profitably spend weeks on the case of Socrates and what it implies for contemporary education. If you were to follow Socrates' example, you would certainly have to explore highly sensitive questions with your students. Would you be allowed to do so? Should the school district or state forbid you to discuss certain topics? Or consider the charge against Socrates that he did not believe in the state's gods. Do we hear similar charges hurled at various public figures today? Fortunately, in the United States, we do not condemn political candidates or other public figures to death for their errant religious beliefs, nor do we put teachers to death for discussing creation, evolution, sex, or communism. But people do still lose offices and jobs and, sometimes, even their good names in a battle Socrates fought long ago—in a cause he died for.

In later chapters on epistemology (theory of knowledge) and ethics, we will consider some of Socrates' ideas on these topics. Here we will briefly review the basic educational ideas of Socrates and Plato. Most of the ideas that follow are Plato's even though he had Socrates voice them. Even today scholars are not entirely sure which of the ideas spoken by Socrates in Plato's writing are those of Socrates himself and which are Plato's own. In what follows, I will refer to Plato.

Plato not only explored sensitive and complex questions about the relations of citizens to their state and all its functions, but in doing so, he created a Utopian state, the Republic, to illustrate his beliefs and principles. Much of *Republic* is concerned with problems of education.[4] Plato believed that students should be educated according to their capacities—that they should not all have exactly the same education. In this century, the great American philosopher John Dewey spoke with some admiration of Plato's astute observation that education should be tailored to the child. However, he faulted Plato for supposing that human beings necessarily fall into exactly three categories. Dewey wanted education to be fitted to each individual child. Further, Dewey rejected hierarchical categories of educational programs. Unlike Plato, he would not label one category better or higher than another.

Plato's plan provided for the special education of workers and artisans, of guardians (soldiers), and of rulers (the upper echelon of the guardian class). The first group was to be well trained in specific occupations so that, Plato says through Socrates, our shoes will be well made and our crops well tended. The second, identified by natural physical strength and spirit, was to receive an expert level of physical and moral training. Socrates described the noble auxiliary or guardian as well trained in philosophy, spirit, swiftness, and strength. Finally, potential rulers were to be educated with meticulous care in philosophy, mathematics, literature, and history, and their education would continue well beyond the usual school years.

Plato's model of education is "functionalist"—a model designed to produce competent adults to meet the needs of the state. Plato developed his thought on education in the context of describing the ideal state, and he could have argued—as Dewey did later—that there is no *inherent* conflict between the individual and the state. That is, educators could work to produce people who are both self-actualized and useful to the state. However, Plato had very definite ideas about the good life and what we today call "self-actualization." Only those who had the leisure to think long and deeply, to continue lifelong study, could participate in the truly good life. The contemplative life was closely identified with the good life. Because only a select few of the population were thought capable of real contemplation and because the manual work of the society had to be done, justice decreed that students be prepared for work consonant with their capacities.

Plato did not argue, as Dewey did later, that people in vastly different occupations could exemplify the truly human. That status was reserved for a few, but the few earned the right to their lofty position through their own merit. All children were to be given opportunities to show their abilities, and only gradually would they be sorted out. For Plato such an arrangement was thought to be just, and this line of thinking is still strong in today's educational policymaking. A particular way of life—one marked by high salary and prestige—is thought to be the best, and all children are to be given opportunities to learn the subjects that will prepare them for such a life. If they fail to succeed at these opportunities, their failure is not a violation of justice.

There are at least three ways to argue against Plato's conception of educational justice. One is to posit a wide range of exemplars of the good life—to deny Plato's single model or any other single ideal. Another is to insist that justice is not satisfied by equal opportunity; it must somehow produce equal outcomes. Still another, very popular today, is to deny that there are educationally significant differences among children—to insist that "all children can learn" whatever the school sets out for them to learn. We will revisit these possibilities in later chapters.

Jane Roland Martin raises another compelling argument against Plato when she accuses him of ignoring the reproductive tasks of his society.[5] For Martin, the "reproductive" processes are those in which women have traditionally engaged: raising children, homemaking, caring for the ill and aged, and the like. Plato says a great deal about the education of children but very little about their day-to-day care. He does say that members of the ruler class should be free of all such tasks—indeed they should not have families at all but communal marriages, which should produce fine offspring to be raised, also communally, by others. Without the attachment of family and personal property, guardians should be better able to devote their energy and wisdom to their state duties.

Martin's complaint is that although Plato (through Socrates as his spokesperson) proposed allowing females to be guardians (an astounding suggestion in his time), the women who are chosen for such roles become essentially sexless. They are to be educated in exactly the same way as males. Nothing in the education of either is derived from a consideration of home and family life; everything comes from a consideration of public life—a traditional male model. If education is to be the same for males and females, Martin argues, it should include the best and most significant features of both traditions. To develop such a model requires analysis and evaluation of both traditions and, most likely, a dramatic transformation of education. Plato deserves credit for insisting on the irrelevance of sex in choosing guardians, but his model of education assumes the superiority and desirability of male life.

The basic components of education described by Plato have remained at the heart of liberal education for more than 2,000 years. Literature, history, mathematics, and philosophy (which in Plato's time included natural science as a less lofty component) still form the backbone of the academic curriculum. Several contemporary philosophers of education question the wisdom of using the traditional disciplines as the core of the secondary school curriculum, and we will look at some of those arguments in the next several chapters.[6] For now, it may be enough to consider how philosophers of education might begin a critique of Plato's curriculum. First, we might challenge the appropriateness of his recommendations for current schooling. But second, we might question whether Plato's prescriptions were sound even for his own time. Much that he recommended was based on a glorification of war and warriors. If Athenians had not been so fond of war, if they had not been so parochial in their love for Athens, would their state have lasted longer? Which of his recommendations were directed specifically at the conduct of successful military campaigns and the production of warriors? Are there elements of our own curriculum designed for the same purpose? Is the aim explicit or implicit?

The purposes of this brief discussion of Plato and Socrates are several. We have seen that some questions in the philosophy of education have continued to intrigue philosophers and educators as they did Plato and Socrates. We have been reminded that fine teachers who persist in asking sensitive questions may be accused by authorities of corrupting youth. Plato and Socrates have led us to ask a host of questions about the state's role in education, the aims of education, the genderized nature of the traditional curriculum, the wisdom of the traditional curriculum for today's students, and the possibility of using (or adapting) a Socratic method. All of these questions are likely to remain with us at the end of a course in philosophy of education. Like Socrates, we will not claim to know, but we should be able to better identify and reject nonsense when we hear it and to make recommendations compatible with sound analysis.

Aristotle

We will look at Aristotle in much the way we looked at Plato and Socrates; that is, we will attempt neither a serious historical account nor full consideration of the body of Aristotle's work. Instead, we will look at an important legacy of Aristotle's thought that triggers rich debate even today.

Aristotle, in contrast to Plato, did not try to create an ideal state. His thought proceeded from things as they actually are to their critical analysis. Thus, in writing about moral life and ethics, Aristotle sought out and described those people and behaviors representing the best in Athenian society.[7] Of course, he had to have some criteria to separate the genuinely good from the only apparently so, but even these—the criteria—he sought in actual life.

Aristotle believed, as Plato did, that people should be educated or trained for their appropriate place in life. As they perform their tasks and fill their particular functions, they develop (or fail to develop) excellences peculiar to these tasks and functions. The best leaders, artisans, wives, and slaves all possess excellences or virtues, but these virtues differ. Those of a ruler differ from those of a slave; those of a husband are not the same as those of a wife.

Contemporary communitarians often refer admiringly to Aristotle.[8] They, too, believe that the community can and properly should make demands on its members and that universal individual rights can be carried too far—so far in fact that a society loses sight of its traditions and may suppose that any act of altruism requires ethical heroism from the agent and an explanation from philosophers. In contrast, Aristotle and today's communitarians insist that moral life grows out of the practices in our communities and the demands these practices make on us. A community's needs and welfare can, and *should,* from this perspective, sometimes override individual rights, and a good citizen expects to contribute to the state, not simply demand its protection of individual rights.

As we will see later, many philosophers argue that there have been only two serious challenges to Aristotle's model of moral life—the apparent nihilism of Nietzsche and the logical individualism of Kant. Whether we agree with this assessment or not, it is clear that the Aristotelian approach to moral thought is once again highly influential today.

Educators may take a special interest in Aristotle's moral thought because it established a model of moral education still widely popular. Aristotle recommended that children should be trained in morally appropriate modes of conduct. His model of moral education is largely compatible with one we find in much biblical writing: "Train up a child in the way he should go, and when he is old, he will not depart from it." Aristotle believed that the community should inculcate values in children and immerse them in supervised activities designed to develop relevant virtues.[9] He was not concerned with teaching them at an early age to reason about moral matters. Indeed, he believed that young people were not ready for such reasoning until sometime in their twenties. By then, he argued, they would be good (virtuous) people and could be trusted to analyze moral issues. Before that time, they should learn to respond ethically out of the habits of good character. In turn, this good character would furnish the ground upon which future reasoning might be safely conducted.

Many models of religious education have followed, and still follow, Aristotle in espousing character education. They, too, hold that children should first learn right conduct and later be allowed to question, analyze, and criticize. Many of you were no doubt brought up this way yourselves and may wonder on reading this: Is there another way? There are in fact several other ways, and we will explore them in the chapter on ethics and moral education. For the past four or five decades, other models of moral education have edged out the character education model, and in the past two decades, the cognitive-developmental model of Lawrence Kohlberg has been very influential.[10]

In the nineteenth century, however, and in the early part of the twentieth century, the character education model was widely accepted. An organization called the Character Development League issued *Character Lessons in American Biography for Public Schools and Home Instruction*.[11] The mode of presentation, if not the very virtues, would have been pleasing to Aristotle. The lessons were organized by "traits of character": obedience, honesty, unselfishness, consecration to duty, industry, courage, justice, patriotism, and many others. Further, they were organized in a linear hierarchy; each one was supposed to function as a foundation for the next. Obedience came first, and the list of thirty-one traits, according to *Character Lessons,* "leads to right living, and establishes character." For Aristotle, of course, simply reading about the virtues and their enactment in the lives of others would be insufficient. One learns to be honest by practicing honesty; one learns to be obedient by obeying. The league was aware of the need for practice, and *Character Lessons* suggests practical activities for children in addition to the readings and discussion.

Many philosophers of education worry about the indoctrination that seems inevitable in the character education approach, and this is another topic we will discuss in a later chapter. But there are contemporary philosophers of education who defend character education, and several thinkers today recommend a combination of cognitive and character approaches.[12] Alarmed by what seems to be a growing tendency in youth toward socially unacceptable or harmful practices, educators are taking a new, more appreciative look at Aristotle.

Another facet of Aristotle's thought is highly relevant for today's educators. Aristotle did not believe that people could, even with heroic effort, guarantee their own consistently moral behavior. Circumstances affect us. People of great virtue can withstand correspondingly great temptation and can be relied on to do the right thing in many extreme situations, but even heroes can be overwhelmed by conditions beyond their control. In this belief, Aristotle was closer to the Homeric Greeks than to later moral philosophers. He saw the awful dilemmas that lead otherwise good people into tragedy. This is a popular theme in contemporary philosophy,[13] and it has been welcomed by many who feel that moral philosophy had become too cerebral and disconnected from everyday life. It is especially interesting to educators because it encourages us to use biography and literature in an integral way in moral education. Of this development, too, Aristotle would no doubt approve.

Rousseau

If we were studying the history of education, it would be strange to skip over the early Christian era and all of the Middle Ages. But we are looking for questions and ideas that arose in philosophical thought and still intrigue or beset us today. Some of the educational ideas of Jean-Jacques Rousseau (1712–1778) certainly fall into this category.

Rousseau is often referred to as the philosopher of freedom because he seemed to extol the natural (or primitive) state of human beings over the civilized one, and in nature, human beings—like animals—are free of the pressures and corruptions of the political state. Indeed, Rousseau's views of nature and the natural played a central role in his philosophy. He believed that "man" was born free and good and could remain that way in some ideal state of nature. Having to live with other people and accommodate their needs begins a process of corruption in man that reaches its peak in the society characteristic of Rousseau's time. In social philosophy, Rousseau is credited with fundamental and impressive work on "social contract theory." On the negative side, he and all contractarians are criticized for promoting the myth of the presocial individual. Critics (e.g., contemporary communitarians, followers of Aristotle, Deweyans) say that it is ridiculous to suppose that genuine persons—individuals with the rational capacity for contract making—could exist before communities and a considerable core of culture. We will revisit this theme in some depth in Chapter 9.

However, Rousseau acknowledged that the search for an ideal state of nature could be little more than a thought experiment. He recognized that human beings cannot achieve their highest potentials as wild animals. He sought a civilized condition that would optimize self-reliance, compassion, civic duty, love of nature, and connection to God. His was an attempt to balance the needs of conjoint living with those of self-actualization.

With such a philosophical project in mind, Rousseau had to think about education. How should people be educated so as to preserve their natural goodness and also induce a positive sense of civic responsibility? As we consider Rousseau's program of education, we must stop using the gender-neutral language of "human being" and "people," for Rousseau recommended very different educations for boys and girls. Most of what we think of today as Rousseau's contributions to progressive education was directed at the education of boys. It is not too harsh to say that the "philosopher of freedom" believed in freedom for males but not for females.[14] In fairness, however, we should note that he believed both attitudes—freedom for males and sheltered coercion for females—were justified because both were "natural." Both attitudes, Rousseau thought, were compatible with the essential nature of the beings under discussion, and it is this dependence on a concept of the natural that saves his philosophy of education from inconsistency.

Rousseau described the education of free men in his *Emile*.[15] Because he believed that children are naturally good, Rousseau wanted Emile to be raised and educated with the least possible restraint. Emile did not have to be subjected to a rigid moral education; he was already good, and the task of his teachers would be to preserve that goodness while facilitating growth of the various competencies required for adult life. A rural setting was thought to be better than an urban one because the corruption of other people could be kept to a minimum. Emile was not to be pressured into abstract thought or early book learning. He was to learn according to his own interests and through hands-on experience. Senses and feeling were primary; thought and abstraction were to be at their service. Emile's education required exquisite sensitivity on the part of his teacher. The teacher was not to impose his own objectives for learning on Emile but rather was to facilitate Emile's inquiries. This meant that the teacher had to anticipate where Emile's interests might lead and be prepared to guide him in a healthy direction. We will see echoes of this view in the work of John Dewey.

If you have been a student of education for even a short time, these ideas may sound familiar to you. In the 1960s and 1970s, there was an educational movement called "open education."[16] It, too, recommended building education on the interests of children and giving them lots of hands-on experience. It emphasized doing, feeling, and observing, and it deemphasized formal lessons. Open education is still of enormous interest to educators, especially to educational philosophers and historians. Historians investigate the rise and fall of educational movements and "reforms." Why do certain ideas, such as Rousseau's, keep recurring? Do educational reforms occur in cycles? Must they occur in cycles, or is there a way to avoid ideological swings of the pendulum? Philosophers examine the underlying concepts, looking for similarities and differences between old and new manifestations of lasting ideas. As philosophers, we are interested in how educators and philosophers justify their ideas, and we are keen to locate logical flaws in their arguments.

Some of Rousseau's ideas are echoed in the writing of a twentieth-century psychologist and educator, A. S. Neill.[17] Neill, too, insisted that children are naturally good and that pressures to make them grow up too fast ruin them. In particular, Neill condemned formal lessons (unless children ask for them) and religious and moral education. In his school, Summerhill, children were free to play until they wanted to attend classes, and they had a say in how the school was to be run. Except in matters of safety, Neill himself had only one vote—just as each of his students did. Even if you differ with Neill on many matters (and I confess that I do), you may admire his commandment to teachers: Thou shalt be on the child's side!

When we study the work of John Dewey, we will see a few similarities between his educational ideas and Rousseau's, but we will also see some major differences. For example, Dewey did not believe that children are born good. Nor did he believe, as many religious educators do, that children are born sinful and in need of salvation. Rather, he believed that children are born with the potential for both good and evil and that transactions with an educational or miseducational environment would direct them toward one or the other. The main similarity between Rousseau's recommendations and Dewey's is their common emphasis on the child's own motivation and direct action. Periodically, educators renew the arguments of Rousseau and Dewey for hands-on activities, and when this happens, there is a flurry of interest in "manipulatives" in the classroom.

One other feature of Rousseau's educational thought should be mentioned before we turn to his treatment of girls and women. Rousseau believed that timing in education is crucial. Children are ready at certain times to learn certain things, and teachers need to observe their pupils carefully so that appropriate opportunities are made available. The ideas of readiness and timing are still important today. If you have studied developmental psychology, you know how important these ideas are to developmentalists.[18] Some prominent advocates of open education were developmentalists. As followers of Jean Piaget, they felt that learning should serve development. Therefore, teachers should know what their students are ready to learn and provide activities that will trigger development. Piagetians in particular believe that cognitive development proceeds in stages and that each stage is characterized by a distinctive cognitive structure. This fundamental structure acts as a mechanism to assimilate knowledge and build substructures. It is induced to change—to undergo accommodation—as the child (at an appropriate age) encounters problematic situations that will not yield to its direction. We will consider Piaget's work again in later chapters.

Contemporary followers of L. S. Vygotsky emphasize social interaction rather than the subject-object interaction so prominent in Piaget's work, but the concepts of timing and readiness are still crucial. Vygotsky said that every function in children's cultural development appears first at the social level; that is, children can perform certain tasks in social settings with the help of others. Later the same functions appear at the psychological level and can be activated by the individual children. Mathematics educators, particularly those who take the perspective of social constructivism (Chapter 6), are especially interested in the work of Vygotsky.

Another educational thinker took Rousseau's interest in timing even further. Maria Montessori taught that children go through "critical periods" in which certain capacities can and must be developed or lost.[19] Montessori was a physician and well versed in physiology. It is likely that her ideas on critical periods came from her studies of animal physiology; kittens, for example, will not develop sight if they are deprived of light during the critical period for ocular development. Building on this physiological example, Montessori suggested that children might lose the capacity for order if parents and teachers did not nurture it when its first signs appeared. Her insistence on the proper placement and use of all objects in the classroom arises from this belief. Today most educators either discount Montessori's view on critical periods or modify it considerably, but many do share Rousseau's, Montessori's, Piaget's, and Vygotsky's belief that timing is important in teaching and learning.

In summary, Rousseau's child starts out good. If he (and we must now use the masculine gender) is educated properly, he will grow into a free, loving, and responsible adult. He must, in an important sense, be allowed to guide his own education. His teacher should facilitate—provide appropriate objects and potential experiences, anticipate his needs and direction of growth, and abstain from the sort of coercion that spoils almost all children. Rousseau's is, in many ways, a lovely view of education.

How should Emile's female counterpart, Sophie, be educated? I am not going to reveal the whole story here; we will discuss it more fully in the chapter on feminism and education. But you should be aware—lest you leave this chapter with an uncritical glow of enthusiasm for Rousseau—that his recommendations for Sophie differed drastically from those for Emile. Whereas Emile was taught to think for himself, Sophie was taught to guard her reputation and do what convention prescribed. Whereas Emile was prepared for responsible, public life, Sophie was confined to the home. In the fifth book of *Emile,* Rousseau discussed the education of Sophie:

> The entire education of women must be relative to men. To please them, to be useful to them, to be loved and honored by them, to rear them when they are young, to care for them when they are grown up, to counsel and console, to make their lives pleasant and charming, these are the duties of women at all times, and they should be taught them in their childhood. To the extent that we refuse to go back to this principle, we will stray from our goal, and all the precepts women are given will not result in their happiness or our own.[20]

Some argue that Rousseau must be excused for his misogyny. After all, he—as is everyone—was a product of a particular time and place. But in answer to this, we may note that Rousseau was familiar with Plato and also with contemporary writing that considered women equal to men. Further, there is evidence that Rousseau himself was far more generous in his thinking about women in his younger days than when he wrote *Emile*. As students of education, you may be even more astonished and disconcerted to find that most older philosophy of education texts that treat Rousseau do not even mention Book 5 of *Emile*. The education of Sophie has been almost entirely ignored until recently.

Pestalozzi, Herbart, and Froebel

Rousseau has had great influence on philosophy of education. Among those deeply affected by his views were Johann Heinrich Pestalozzi (1746–1827), Johann Friedrich Herbart (1776–1841), and Friedrich Froebel (1782–1852). Many philosophers of education today entirely ignore the work of the three men we will consider briefly here, but there are several reasons for including them in our discussion. First, educators and even educational theorists too often neglect the history of education, and they fail to realize that many purportedly new ideas have been suggested earlier; other ideas have interesting antecedents, and it sometimes pays off to trace their development. Second, since we have discussed Rousseau's work, it makes sense to consider Rousseau's influence on work that followed. Finally, a brief discussion of this work will provide a bridge to our study of John Dewey's philosophy of education.

Pestalozzi followed Rousseau in recommending that children be educated through the senses. He refined Rousseau's ideas and, following John Locke, created an approach called the "object lesson."[21] An object lesson begins with the exhibition of an object and an invitation to students to describe it, tell how it works, and so on. For example, today we might present a table lamp (complete with cord, shade, and bulb) to a class of sixth graders and explore a host of questions with them. Is the cord safe? If not, how can we make it safe? How do electric lightbulbs work? Is this one bright enough for reading? In what room would you use such a lamp? Is it attractive? What material is used for shades? How is a lamp wired? After this last question, we might take the lamp apart and rewire it.

Pestalozzi's object lessons usually ended with a moral. He was much concerned with moral education and believed that all lessons should have a moral point as well as a cognitive one. Interestingly, most of us today associate an "object lesson" with only the moral part of a lesson; for example, we often comment on someone's failure at an ill-conceived or ill-intentioned task by saying, "I guess that was an object lesson for him." Many have never heard of the scientific-cognitive aspect of such lessons.

Besides his interesting work in refining and inventing specific implementations of Rousseau's ideas, Pestalozzi is also remembered for his devoted work with poor children. In his own school, he demonstrated that poor children, well cared for and skillfully taught, could learn as much as wealthier children. Two hundred years later, many people in our society still doubt that this is true, and today's reformers who agree with Pestalozzi decry the horrible inequalities found in poor schools.[22] Like Pestalozzi, many of these reformers are thought to be cranks and visionaries, and their work is often brushed aside for "more important goals." This also is a topic we will discuss more fully in a later chapter.

As a final comment on Pestalozzi's pedagogical methods, we might mention an especially interesting case. It is said that Albert Einstein had a very difficult time in regular schools and finally became both happy and successful when he was enrolled in a Swiss Pestalozzi-like school. There he encountered methods that appealed to his visual learning style—maps, tools, sophisticated equipment, and objects of all sorts.[23] As thoughtful educators, we may wonder how many budding Einsteins experience failure in today's schools because the prevailing methods do not meet their needs.

Herbart, too, built on Rousseau's ideas about the senses and their critical function in education. He described the mind's function in terms of presentations and something called an "apperceptive mass." The latter, Herbart thought, was a collection of previous experiences that could be called into play to understand a new percept or idea. As described by Herbart, the apperceptive mass is a forerunner of sorts for Piaget's "cognitive structure." A major difference between the two concepts is that Piaget's cognitive structures are operational mechanisms, whereas Herbart's apperceptive mass contains the actual content of experience. However, both function to assimilate new material.

An early advocate of scientific methods in education, Herbart believed that teaching methods should be designed to match the way minds work.

Teachers must prepare students for new material by bringing to consciousness relevant experiences students have stored in the apperceptive mass. Then teachers and students can go on to shape the new material so that it is deposited accurately and is accessible for future use. His method is highly cognitive and emphasizes the activity of the teacher more than that of the student.

Herbart, like Pestalozzi, tried to make his pedagogical method quite specific, and it was tailored, of course, to his philosophical thought on the mind and how it functions. Following his beliefs on how our minds work, Herbart suggested a four-step lesson that his followers made into five steps: preparation, presentation, comparison and abstraction, generalization, and application. You may notice with some surprise that these five steps have elements in common with today's "five-step lesson." It is doubtful, however, that Herbart intended the narrow and rigid implementation that many of his followers insisted upon.

John Dewey gave Herbart great credit for bringing "the work of teaching out of the region of routine and accident."[24] Herbart posed many questions that are still vital in the philosophy and science of teaching. But Dewey thought Herbart had made several mistakes. The greatest flaw in his theory, Dewey believed, was his neglect of the living organism and its purposes. Teaching, Dewey insisted, could not be described in so many steps for all students and all subjects. Teachers must begin with the purposes of their students, steer them into potentially rich experiences, and watch carefully for signs of growth. Dewey was vigorous in his criticism of Herbart:

> The philosophy is eloquent about the duty of the teacher in instructing pupils; it is almost silent regarding his privilege of learning. It emphasizes the influence of intellectual environment upon the mind; it slurs over the fact that the environment involves a personal sharing in common experiences. It exaggerates beyond reason the possibilities of consciously formulated and used methods, and underestimates the role of vital, unconscious attitudes. . . . It takes, in brief, everything educational into account save its essence—vital energy seeking opportunity for effective exercise.[25]

From our current position, we might use Dewey's ideas to analyze and criticize contemporary attempts to make pedagogy uniform and scientific.

Is the five-step lesson useful today? Is everything learned (or best learned) through direct instruction? Are Dewey's criticisms of Herbart thus applicable to today's pedagogical methods?

Froebel, a third thinker influenced by Rousseau, is best known today as the father of the kindergarten. In Froebel's metaphorical system, the kindergarten was a garden in which children, like flowers, unfold and grow. Rousseau's notion of the child's inherent goodness is reflected in Froebel's emphasis on nurturance and growth. From this perspective, the child is not wicked and in need of constant correction but is whole and beautiful. The kindergarten should preserve and nurture this goodness.

Froebel also wanted children to handle objects and observe shapes as part of their mathematical education, but he was not content simply to present shapes—circles, triangles, and the like—and have children learn their names and attributes. He attached a mystical symbolic meaning to each shape to give it importance in the spiritual and moral realm. John Dewey expressed considerable admiration for Froebel's loving attention to children and for many of his methods, but he thought the notion of unfolding was a mistake because it echoed Rousseau's contention that children are born with an essential goodness, and he ridiculed the idea that mathematical symbols must have a religious or moral connotation: "A single example may indicate [Froebel's] method. Everyone familiar with the kindergarten is acquainted with the circle in which the children gather. It is not enough [for Froebel] that the circle is a convenient way of grouping the children. It must be used 'because it is a symbol of the collective life of mankind' in general."[26]

This comment of Dewey's reveals something of the flavor of criticism philosophers of education sometimes direct at one another's work. We have seen that Dewey expressed admiration for something in the work of Rousseau, Pestalozzi, Herbart, and Froebel, but he also found difficulties—recommendations not fully grounded, inconsistencies, and ideas incompatible with Dewey's own underlying beliefs concerning the nature of the child, the meaning of education, the role of teaching, and the nature of lessons.

SUMMARY QUESTIONS

Because a major purpose for studying philosophy of education is to raise further questions and reflect more deeply on them, I will provide summaries in the form of questions.

1. Should the Socratic method be used in today's schools?
2. Should education prepare students for specific functions in society, or should it guide them toward self-actualization?
3. Should education put an emphasis on self-knowledge and reflection? What are some dangers in doing this?
4. Should the state control what teachers teach?
5. Should teachers criticize their government and leaders?
6. Should the traditional tasks and values of women be included in the curriculum?
7. Is the curriculum recommended by Plato—literature, history, mathematics, and philosophy—adequate for today's students?
8. Should the schools try to develop character? If so, what virtues should be taught?
9. Does character education necessarily involve indoctrination?
10. Are children born good?
11. Should teachers be guides and facilitators, or should they engage primarily in direct instruction?
12. Should moral lessons accompany academic lessons?
13. Why do certain ideas occur again and again in education?
14. Is religion bad for children?
15. Is timing important in teaching? In what ways?
16. Can poor children learn as much as rich children?
17. Does a society owe all its children an adequate education? Who should decide what is "adequate"?

INTRODUCTION TO THE LITERATURE

There is no substitute for reading some of the primary works: Plato, *Republic,* especially Books 2, 3, 5, and 7; Aristotle, *Nicomachean Ethics,* Book 10; and Rousseau, *Emile.* For more on Pestalozzi, Herbart, and Froebel, see Carroll Atkinson and Eugene Maleska, *The Story of Education.* See also notes for this chapter.

CHAPTER 2

The Philosophical and Educational Thought of John Dewey

In 1859, Charles Darwin published his *Origin of Species*. The same year marked the birth of John Dewey, whose work was greatly influenced by Darwin's ideas. Over a long lifetime (1859–1952), Dewey published so many books and articles that a bibliography of his writings takes 150 pages.[1] Many of them reveal his intense interest in evolutionary themes and his use of evolutionary metaphors. In discussing Dewey's work here, we will use the principle established in Chapter 1; that is, we will discuss those questions and issues raised by Dewey that still interest us today.

As students of education, you should read some of John Dewey's work. It is not easy. William James characterized Dewey's style as "damnable; you might even say God-damnable." But if you read enough of Dewey, you will begin to understand what he was getting at, and you will find a beautiful consistency in his lifelong beliefs and recommendations concerning students and their appropriate role in their own education. I often counsel my students to "believe" as they approach Dewey: Do not start out by objecting, challenging, or analyzing. Just believe and absorb. Later, when you know what Dewey was trying to accomplish, you will be ready to ask tough questions.

There is one other matter to discuss before we consider Dewey's thought on the meaning and aims of education. How influential has Dewey been? Opinions differ widely on this. There is no question that he was enormously influential in the domains of philosophical and educational thought, but we have no clear records to show how widely his thought actually influenced practice. He has been hailed as the savior of American education by those who welcome greater involvement of students in their own educational planning and activity. He has also been called "worse than Hitler" by some who felt that he infected the schools with epistemological and moral relativism and substituted socialization for true education. Dewey has been revered, castigated, admired, and ridiculed.[2] Interest in his work has waxed and waned. Just a few years ago, philosophy departments showed little interest in Dewey, but today interest is quite keen. Similarly, educators have vacillated between ignoring and adoring him. Students who study Dewey's work carefully usually agree that his contributions to educational thought are considerable; his work should not be ignored.

Dewey's Philosophical Orientation

Dewey was a "naturalistic" philosopher—he sought explanations in terms of natural phenomena, of objects and events accessible to our senses. He rejected explanations that involve supernatural sources, and he even defined *God* in terms of human ideals, plans, and action. He believed in what he called the method of science and advocated its use in every sphere of human activity. Given his naturalistic orientation, it is not surprising that his work contains so many evolutionary themes and metaphors.

In his philosophical education, Dewey was greatly influenced by the German philosopher Georg Wilhelm Friedrich Hegel. Hegel believed that only mind is real and that human thought, through participation in the universal spirit, progresses toward a preordained ideal by a dialectical process of resolving opposites through synthesis. Quite early in his career, Dewey abandoned the substantive claims of Hegel's philosophy (notions of preordained ideals and the like), but he retained the dialectical method. In his work, he often poses two extremes. In *Experience and Education*, for example, he contrasts the "old" education with the "new," but he does not unequivocally endorse the new. Rather, he points to good and bad features in each and holds forth a revised vision of education. Many observers think this revised vision is not really a synthesis but a new creation. Dewey used the dialectical method to clarify his thought and move on to a new level of planning and acting, but he did not claim that this new level was necessarily the final answer. It, too, was to be subjected to new rounds of scrutiny.

Dewey studied and wrote in almost all the branches of philosophy: logic, metaphysics, epistemology, philosophy of science, ontology, aesthetics, political and social philosophy, and ethics. In addition, he wrote on psychology and religion. But he insisted that philosophy of education is the most fundamental and important branch of philosophy because all others, in some sense, depend on it. Philosophy of education, for Dewey, was philosophy of life.

As a naturalistic philosopher, Dewey rejected not only the supernatural but also what some philosophers call the transcendent. An entity or concept is *transcendental* (in the sense Dewey rejected) if it is posited to explain observable events but cannot itself be observed or have effects clearly traced to it. Certain scientific entities were certainly acceptable to Dewey, even though they are invisible, because their effects are reliably observable. But concepts such as Piaget's cognitive structures might have aroused Dewey's skepticism. When you have read both Dewey and Piaget, you will surely see many commonalities in their recommendations on education and their descriptions of children's intellectual development. But Dewey never posited unobservable, underlying mechanisms of mind to explain what was accessible to observation. Were he alive today, he might be persuaded that the concept of cognitive structure is useful by analogy to the machine program of a computer, but we would have to show reliable effects from this program or Dewey's skepticism would rapidly return. Because of his rejection of both supernatural explanations and those that employ transcendental concepts, Dewey has often been labeled a behaviorist, but we will see that his beliefs differed from those of prominent behaviorists, too.

Dewey, along with Charles Sanders Peirce, William James, and George Herbert Mead, is often called a pragmatist, but Dewey himself had trouble with the word because it is often used pejoratively. Peirce intended pragmatism as a theory of meaning: "Consider what effects, that might conceivably have practical bearing, we conceive the object of our conception to have. Then, our conception of these effects is the whole of our conception of the object."[3] James carried the notion of effects into a theory of truth, much to Peirce's horror, and Peirce changed the name of his theory to pragmaticism to divorce his views from those of James. But Dewey preferred the term *naturalism.* Other sympathetic writers tried to substitute *instrumentalism* or *experimentalism* for pragmatism. Both *instrumentalism* and *experimentalism* evoked unfavorable connotations of their own, however, and some recent writers have recommended that we settle on *pragmatic naturalism.*[4] This term has the merit of conveying both the emphasis on naturalistic explanation and the focus on effects through a method of inquiry that involves hypothesis testing. As we discuss Dewey's views on education, we will occasionally refer to these terms again.

The Meaning and Aims of Education

Dewey often spoke of education as synonymous with growth, and growth was one of his most important biological metaphors.[5] Because so many people think of education as an enterprise that has a specific aim—an ideal person or way of life as its outcome—Dewey's positing of growth as education's aim did not satisfy most inquirers. Many asked, Growth toward what? Dewey insisted that growth is its own end; that is, to ask "growth toward what?" is inconsistent with the concept of growth. Growth tends toward more growth, he said, and we must not make the concept rigid by specifying its direction.

If we try to step into Dewey's organic-evolutionary frame of reference, we might think of growth as analogous to "life." What is the purpose of life? In much of philosophy, religion, and literature, writers have tried to answer this question, but in Darwin's biology, we would have to say the purpose of life is simply more life. Similarly, for Dewey, growth leads to further growth. Dewey was concerned that the lives of students were so often systematically sacrificed to some future good—that education was thought to have a purpose "out there," somewhere beyond the present interests and purposes of students. Determined to avoid this view of education, he insisted that experience is *educative* only if it produces growth—if, that is, students leave the experience more capable or interested in engaging in new experience.

Many philosophers of education have found difficulties in Dewey's concept of growth. He sometimes explained it in terms of opening doors or developing connections. Becoming more skillful as a burglar does not represent growth, Dewey wrote, because such activities close off connections and prevent further growth.[6] This seems right, but other cases are harder to evaluate. What about the young child whose interest in, say, mathematics is so all-consuming that he neglects other activities? Is his growth in mathematics true growth? Or what about the person who pursues monetary wealth to the exclusion of intellectual and spiritual matters? Surely, monetary wealth provides many opportunities and connections. Is such monetary accumulation growth?

I suspect Dewey did not intend that growth should serve as a fully operational definition of education. Consider again the metaphor of life. If the biological purpose of life is more life, surely that does not imply that the mere proliferation of life is always a good thing. If, for example, a community produces too many offspring, the quality of life may suffer to such an extent that future life is actually endangered. The purpose, to produce more life, is threatened. If the capacity to produce life is used as a criterion for the goodness or genuineness of life itself, we are led to ask a host of questions about the optimal production of life. For some communities at some times, the questions are very hard to answer, and reasonable inquirers may differ strongly.

This way of using the term *growth* may be what Dewey had in mind. Its use leads us to ask significant questions and to argue with one another about the pursuit of burglary, mathematics, or material wealth. The discussion leads us to think more deeply about the connection between present and future, and it steers us away from a notion of education as preparation for some predecided, specific future state.

I have attempted a defense of Dewey's use of growth staying entirely within his frame of reference, but we might challenge the frame itself. Just as many of us would be unhappy with the idea that the purpose of life is more life, we might be unhappy with a vague notion of growth leading merely to further growth. Socrates certainly wanted to say a great deal more about the purpose and meaning of life, and Dewey himself wrote movingly on the good life. Should we not, then, elaborate on the normative meaning of growth? Should we not describe in detail episodes that clearly deserve the label *growth?* I am not sure Dewey would object to such attempts. They could be part of the conversation he intended to initiate. But he would surely object strongly if our efforts culminated in a single ideal toward which all growth must move.

The aim of education, according to Dewey, is more education. Education thus functions as both end and means. He does not deny that particular aims are appropriate within education. Indeed, he insists that educative activities, by their very nature, must have aims. We (both students and teachers) are trying to accomplish something. But our aims are not fixed, and there is no grand, ultimate aim beyond continued education. As long as a particular aim functions adequately to guide our activity, we retain it. When it fails to give such guidance, we abandon it and substitute another, more relevant aim. Hence aims function in means-ends planning. If we are steadfast in our aim, as an end-in-view, and our chosen means do not seem likely to culminate in the desired end, then we must consider different means. In other cases, we reconsider the aim itself. Often a particular end-in-view serves as a means to further ends, and therefore we may treat it as we would any other means.

R. S. Peters, a British analytic philosopher, agreed with Dewey that the aims of education should not be conceived of as ends extrinsic to education, but he felt that Dewey was mistaken in using "purpose" and "aim" as synonyms. Peters's essays are models of linguistic analysis (which will be discussed more fully in Chapter 3), and his purpose was to show that "aim" and "purpose" suggest different emphases in educational discussion. *Purpose,* Peters said, is associated with reasons for an action. For example, we might ask someone who makes an odd motion, "What was your purpose in doing that?" *Aim,* in contrast, suggests a target, something at a distance, and "there must be concentration of effort and attention in order to hit it."[7] For Peters, once we have elucidated what we mean by *education,* there is little reason to talk at all about its aims, because its aims are built into the concept of education itself. Dewey and Peters do not disagree on this, but Dewey was interested in an analysis of education as a social phenomenon. His main interest was not linguistic or conceptual analysis.

An explanation of Dewey's views on aims leads quite naturally into the next topic—his views on the role students play in their own education. Dewey insisted that not only teachers must have aims for their chosen activities; students must be involved in setting objectives for their own learning. In the following, we see that Dewey does tend to use "purpose" in his discussion of aims and objectives:

Plato once defined a slave as the person who executes the purposes of another, and . . . a person is also a slave who is enslaved to his own blind desires. There is, I think, no point in the philosophy of progressive education which is sounder than its emphasis upon the participation of the learner in the formation of the purposes which direct his activities in the learning process, just as there is no defect in traditional education greater than its failure to secure the active cooperation of the pupil in construction of the purposes involved in his studying.[8]

Dewey's Psychology

Although Dewey sounded like a behaviorist when he rejected transcendental and supernatural explanations, he was very clear in his opposition to stimulus-response psychology. This psychology claimed that all of human behavior can be explained in terms of conditioned (or unconditioned) responses to stimuli in the environment. The environment controls us; we do not control it. The luckiest among us may indeed be able to manipulate the environment for the betterment of humankind, but our power to do this is itself a result of a chain of fortunate stimuli and responses. In one of his early essays on the subject,[9] Dewey demonstrated convincingly that the human organism does not merely respond to stimuli from without but actively selects stimuli and responds in ways consonant with its purposes or aims. His insistence that students, as active organisms, must be involved in the establishment of objectives for their own learning underscores his belief in the connection between purpose and activity.

In *How We Think,* Dewey explained that the well-known phenomenon of imitation in children is not as simple as it seems. Children do not *just* imitate. This can be inferred by observing that they do not imitate all adult actions. They select. When they imitate, they have adopted certain modes of behavior for their own purposes. The little boy who imitates his father's painting or hammering is trying to accomplish something. He watches and performs the same motions because the performance meets a current objective of his own. Therefore, imitation should not be mocked or considered merely "cute." Much of it is the real work of childhood.

Dewey was a fairly astute observer of children. Considering the fact that he often wandered about in a philosophical daze—and, it is said, even passed one of his own sons on the Columbia campus without recognizing him—his observations strike us as surprisingly accurate. In *The*

School and Society, he described the fourfold interests of children: making things (construction), finding out (inquiry), expressing themselves artistically, and communicating.[10] Many educators believe that these four interests can be used to create a rich elementary school curriculum and that there is no need to divide the day up artificially into disciplines such as English, history, and so on. In the course of pursuing their own interests, children can learn a great deal about the traditional disciplines if teachers arrange appropriate experiences for them.

A valid complaint can be raised against the claim that children can learn all they need to know within the framework of these four interests. What of sequential subjects such as arithmetic? If all instruction in arithmetic must be tied to the particular projects of children's inquiry, their mathematical knowledge may indeed exhibit great gaps. Is there a way around this shortcoming?

In addition to his discussion of educational aims, the psychology of elementary education, and the mistakes of stimulus-response theory, Dewey developed a model of thinking or problem solving that is still influential today. Thinking begins with a nagging sense that something is problematic, something is unsettled. Initial exploration yields a hypothesis that must be tested. Next, the thinker has to devise a plan—a set of means—by which the hypothesis can be tested. In each stage of exploration, the thinker considers alternatives. What are the competing hypotheses? What other means might be used? Then, of course, the plan must be enacted. The thinker undergoes the consequences of the previous decisions and evaluates the results. Careful thinkers reflect on the process. They consider whether other methods or explanations might be even better, and they also look into the future. How might what they have learned here be used in future situations? They make an attempt at generalization.

There are several crucial points to keep in mind about Dewey's model. First, he never claimed that one could or should move through it in exactly the sequence he described. One does, of course, have to form a hypothesis before testing it, but one can break off at any step and move backward or forward in the model. Second, some educational theorists have truncated Dewey's model by omitting the stage of undergoing consequences. For example, in the 1970s, a computerized mathematics program had students read a word problem (enter a problematic situation) and create an equation to solve it. If the equation was adequate, the computer excused the student from working it through to an answer and simply presented the next problem. The idea was to assure the student that the algorithmic work of solving equations could be done by the computer. The human thinker's job was to create the plan or equation. This procedure is obviously valuable for mature scientists and mathematicians, but learners may need to undergo the entire procedure in order to evaluate the worth of their plan. Whereas the scientist's problem lies well beyond the solution of an equation, the student's problem may consist of exactly this. As teachers, we have to remember that a textbook problem induces a myriad of different problems for different students. Dewey's problem-solving method, like Socrates' method of questioning, will be revisited in the chapter on critical thinking.

Besides analyzing the process of thinking and the nature of children's interests, Dewey is known for his analysis of experience and its centrality in education. Some philosophers have assessed his analysis of experience as one of Dewey's greatest contributions to philosophy. Others think the concept remains vague in Dewey's treatment. There are at least two important features of the concept for Dewey. One that he shares with existentialists is the emphasis on meaning and affect. An experience for Dewey is not a mere exposure or passive undergoing; it has to mean something to the one undergoing it. Second, experience for Dewey is social and cultural. Indeed, he once remarked that he should have called his major work on experience *Culture and Nature* rather than *Experience and Nature*. Thus, when Dewey talks about experience in the context of education, we expect to find an emphasis on personal meaning and social interaction.

He believed that to be educative, an experience has to be built on or connected to prior experience. Today we often translate this by saying that teachers must start where the students are. But teachers must also ask where a given experience may lead. There must be continuity in experience. Therefore, teachers must know something of their students' prior experience and design new learning experiences that grow out of it, but they must also observe their students' present experience and plan future experiences designed to move students toward a more sophisticated grasp of the subject. Subject matter must be prepared, that is, in light of both students' preparation and future needs. The logical structure of a subject as described by mature scholars is not pedagogically adequate.

Not only must there be continuity in educative experience, but the experience itself must have meaning for students here and now. There must be engagement—an interaction between students and the objects of their study. Dewey pointed out repeatedly that the absence of such interaction was a severe defect in the old education. When students are forced to plod through material with which they are not really engaged for some obscure future end, they lose interest in the material and confidence in themselves. They settle for giving answers and getting approval from their teachers. They give up the all-important belief that education has something to do with the construction of personal meaning.

Because of his consistent emphasis on the necessity of student engagement and activity, Dewey became associated with what has been called child-centered education. However, it is not strictly correct to label Dewey's position "child-centered." Dewey, you may remember, criticized Froebel's notion of unfolding as vigorously as he did passive forms of education that assumed material could be poured into students. He was a thoroughgoing interactionist who insisted on appropriate attention to both internal and external aspects of a learning experience, and he was not satisfied with "learning" activities that merely pleased or entertained children. In his later years, Dewey gently chided those of his followers who he thought had abandoned the responsibility to lead students to genuine learning.

Dewey's Theory of Knowledge

In a later chapter, we will look at theories of knowledge in some depth, especially as they affect pedagogy. Here we will lay a foundation for that examination by considering Dewey's theory of knowledge.

What does it mean to know something? Socrates wrestled with this problem and decided that, among other things, a claim to knowledge involves the truth of what is claimed. If A claims to know that p, where p is some proposition, then—for us to credit the claim—p must be true. We would not assent to "A knows that p" if we believe that p is false. The criterion of truth implies that the set of propositions we claim to know must be a subset of all those that are true, and this result in turn implies that propositions are true before inquiry begins. According to this traditional view, truth preexists human inquiry—in the sense that things and states of affairs to which propositions refer exist prior to inquiry—and successful inquiry discovers truth, thereby adding to the store of human knowledge.

Dewey, in his naturalistic approach, asserted that knowledge is bigger than truth. He argued that knowledge is properly construed as that body of information and skills we apply intelligently to inquiry. As we test our hypotheses, we may discard or revise some of the material with which we started. The end product of inquiry is something like truth; that is, it approximates the traditional notion of truth. Dewey called propositions that result from careful inquiry—propositions for which we can produce convincing evidence—"warranted assertions."[11] But all the propositions and skills that guide our inquiry still deserve the label *knowledge* until the results of inquiry bring us to discard them.

Dewey's position may sound strange to you, and indeed many philosophers have raised objections to it. We cannot answer those objections here; we cannot even identify all of the objections. But perhaps I can make Dewey's position a bit more plausible than it first appears. Remember that Dewey's philosophy is naturalistic. He wanted to avoid dependence on unobservable entities to which no clearly observable effects could be traced. He rejected capital-T Truth because it falls into this category. Similarly, he preferred "knowing" to "knowledge" because it clearly points to a process of inquiry. Material actually used to guide inquiry he was willing to call knowledge.

But, you may well ask, suppose some of that material turns out to be wrong. Would it still be knowledge? Dewey's answer would run something like this: When a proposition or routine seems wrong to us, we no longer use it to guide inquiry. We drop the faulty routine from our repertoire, and we delete the misleading proposition from our encyclopedia of information. Because such items no longer guide inquiry, there is no occasion to call them knowledge. We escape the difficulty encountered when we try to collect knowledge in some stable and static form. In fact, we move away from a noun-interpretation of knowledge toward a verb-form.

Consider an example. Suppose a math student uses the rule

$$\sqrt{x} + \sqrt{y} = \sqrt{x+y}, \ x, y > 0,$$

to guide her solution of a set of math problems. While she is using this faulty rule, believing it to be true, it qualifies as knowledge. (The teacher, of course, knows the rule is faulty because he or she has tested it and no longer uses it to solve problems.) When use of the rule consistently leads to unsatisfactory results, a careful inquirer will back up and question the rule itself. Our math student may actually test the rule. If it is true that

$$\sqrt{x} + \sqrt{y} = \sqrt{x+y}, \text{ then } \sqrt{4} + \sqrt{9} = \sqrt{4+9} = \sqrt{13}.$$

But we know (from previous successful inquiry) that

$$\sqrt{4} = 2 \text{ and } \sqrt{9} = 3. \text{ Therefore, } \sqrt{4} + \sqrt{9} = 5 \text{ and not } \sqrt{13}.$$

So the initial rule cannot reasonably be employed in further inquiry and, hence, will no longer be called "knowledge."

This example illustrates two points that are central to Dewey's theory of knowledge and pedagogy. First, human beings at every stage of maturity use material from prior experience to guide present inquiry. This is knowledge in the pragmatic sense because it has real effects. It explains what the inquirer is doing. Second, we are reminded that genuine problem solving involves undergoing the consequences of one's hypothesis making and testing. If we interrupt the student's inquiry at the outset by telling her, "That's wrong; here is the right rule," she may never understand why her own way is wrong. Worse, she will not learn how to inquire, how to test the procedures she chooses to employ in future situations. Math teachers who lean toward Dewey's views on knowledge are more concerned with their students' growth—their mastery of more powerful ways of testing their own procedures—than they are with correct answers on a particular exercise set. Correct answers may or may not signify increased opportunities for future success. Control over one's own procedural processes or heuristics, however, almost certainly represents growth.

As you study learning theories, you will see that some psychologists object to allowing students to use faulty rules. (This is a separate issue from what counts as knowledge, but it is important for teachers.) They argue that this will lead to students "practicing" their errors—that such practice will reinforce use of the faulty rule and make learning the correct rule even more difficult. Where the result is not easily tested for correctness or efficacy, as in some manual routines, these learning theorists have a strong point. Error-ridden practice in piano playing or typing or tennis playing may induce habits that are hard to correct. But these activities are not usually engaged in as inquiries, and often students have no clear sense of how to judge a satisfactory or exemplary outcome. Even when such a clear sense is present, students are likely to suppose that they just need more practice to achieve it. When students look at mathematics that way, the results are disastrous, but mere correction of the rule or routine does not avert the disaster. (I should note, before leaving this example, that some teachers of piano or tennis also construe learning as inquiry. Instead of simply correcting faulty routines, they emphasize the effects of using one routine versus another and help their students to judge the efficacy of their own procedures.)

In this very brief discussion of Dewey's theory of knowledge, I have emphasized aspects that are of current interest to educators. In a later chapter, I will say more about traditional epistemologies and also about a contemporary theory—constructivism—that is receiving a great deal of attention in educational theory. Constructivism has much in common with Dewey's position on knowledge. However, you should be aware that even at the conclusion of that discussion, we will have barely scratched the surface of epistemology. It is a huge and fascinating branch of philosophy.

Democracy and Education

In addition to his work on psychology and epistemology, Dewey also wrote extensively on social and political philosophy. He saw democracy as a form of "associated living" consonant with the methods of science, and he was particularly interested in the connections between democracy and education. In his most comprehensive book on education, *Democracy and Education,* he explored these connections in considerable depth.[12]

Dewey's discussion of democracy starts with a naturalistic description of human beings as social animals. People want to communicate, and this desire to communicate provides the impetus for the construction of common values. Note that Dewey does not begin with values preestablished in a prior world of forms. There are no eternal verities, no God-given guidelines for human conduct or development. Of course, Dewey acknowledges our common biological condition. We all need food and shelter, and most of us want to reproduce, protect our children, and enter into reciprocal relations with other human beings.

His naturalistic beginning leads swiftly to a position on education that differs greatly from most traditional views. Whereas Robert Maynard Hutchins (a well-known educator and longtime president of the University of Chicago) began his philosophy of education with a notion of universal culture, Dewey started with the impulse to communicate that precedes creation of culture. Hutchins insisted that people need common values and common knowledge in order to communicate, but Dewey wanted to qualify this. The values and knowledge to which Hutchins pointed are, for Dewey, products of inquiry and construction through social interaction. We do not begin with common values; we construct them. Therefore, the schools need not prepare students for eventual communication by pouring into them the culture's specific values and knowledge. Rather, children should be encouraged to communicate, inquire, and construct common values and knowledge.

Dewey did not deny that every culture has values it wishes to transmit, but "transmission," for Dewey, went well beyond telling and testing. A culture transmits its values by providing its young with the kinds of experiences that make their values real and significant for their own lives. For example, the school cannot prepare students for democratic life by simply giving them masses of information to be used at some later time. Instead, it prepares students for democratic life by involving them in forms of democratic living appropriate for their age.

Consideration of a current pedagogical method, the "whole language approach," may, by analogy, make Dewey's ideal clearer. In the whole language approach, we do not attempt to prepare children for future language activities by teaching them bits of sound, spelling, grammar, and the like. Instead, we immerse them in language experience. We encourage them to follow their own purposes in communication. From the first, children are helped to write their own stories and to read those of their classmates. They speak and listen, read and write for the purpose of communicating *now*.

Similarly, learning to participate in democratic life involves living democratically—students working together on common problems, establishing the rules by which their classrooms will be governed, testing and evaluating ideas for the improvement of classroom life and learning, and participating in the construction of objectives for their own learning.[13] From this perspective, student participation in democratic living serves as both an end in itself and as a means toward the achievement of adult democratic life. What is learned in such participation is not a batch of information to be applied at a future date but the skills and actual procedures, the very mode of life, of democracy.

Dewey did not look at democracy merely as a system of government in which everyone votes and the majority prevails. For Dewey, democracy was a mode of associated living, and decisions were to be made by a shared process of inquiry. Rules for the governance of community life were to be tried out and subjected to the usual empirical tests. They were not to be imposed arbitrarily and permanently on the whole population by a powerful majority. Clearly, Dewey expected citizens to be ruled by rationality and fellow feeling—not by a lust for power and selfish interest. If a society were to develop such a citizenry, it had to start with its schoolchildren. Democracy, in Dewey's description, is not a state; it is more a process, and its rules must be under continual scrutiny, revision, and creation.

Dewey developed his description of democracy from a two-part criterion. A democracy is characterized as follows: "There are many interests consciously communicated and shared; and there are varied and free points of contact with other modes of association."[14] A typical street gang, Dewey said, is not a democracy. Its members may indeed share interests, and those interests may even be consciously communicated, but the gang does not have free interaction with other gangs or groups in the society. For Dewey, the second part of the criterion provides a crucial test. Do people communicate freely across the lines of class, religion, race, and region? Whenever groups withdraw from connection, isolate themselves, and become exclusive, democracy is endangered. Notice that Dewey's conception of democracy is not that of the person in the street. An isolationist society has by its very isolation risked its status as a democracy because it has lost "free points of contact" and opportunities to inquire beyond its own borders.

You may find this second test useful in exploring the problems of pluralism in contemporary society. Many people have worried that "too much pluralism" threatens our democracy.[15] The fear is that society will break down into disconnected sets, all wary and distrustful of the others. Dewey was not so concerned with the number of subgroups as with the quality of their association. Do the groups maintain open communication with one another? Ecumenical movements in religion probably meet Dewey's tests: They identify shared interests and maintain interaction even across substantial ideological differences. A club of African American or Hispanic students on a college campus might or might not meet the tests. The racial identity of the group does not disqualify it; indeed, race may be regarded as an important shared interest. The crucial question is whether the group has open and healthy interaction with other groups. If it does, then it passes both tests. Incidentally, the word *healthy* here should be employed in much the way *growth* was used earlier. An interaction between groups is healthy if it leads to more (and not fewer) connections with the same and other groups.

Although these criteria are useful in sorting out some groups and explaining why they do not qualify as democratic groups, subtler cases seem to escape the criteria. Probably many groups in racist and classist societies could pass the tests (at some level) and still together form a highly effective network of oppression. An important objection to Dewey's work is that he paid little attention to forms of systematic oppression and cultural hegemony.

Just as he saw no necessary threat in the proliferation of subgroups in a society, Dewey saw no inherent conflict between the individual and the state. In contrast to Rousseau, who believed that individuals had to give up or drastically adapt their natural goodness in order to be useful citizens, Dewey insisted that state and individual are, ideally, in a relation of mutual support. A good society treasures its dissidents and mavericks because it needs the creative thinking that produces new hypotheses, expanded means, a larger set of alternatives, and, in general, the vigorous conversation induced by fresh ideas. The individual, similarly, needs a democratic state in which to flourish; it is therefore in his or her best interest to contribute generously to the maintenance of a democratic way of life.

Those of you who are interested in political philosophy may want to read more of Dewey. (Some suggestions appear at the end of this chapter.) You will see that he anticipated many of the current arguments between liberal individualism and communitarianism. Insisting that relations between the democratic state and the individual are balanced and naturally reciprocal, he maintained his thoroughly interactionist philosophy. Typically, he rejected both extremes that sometimes appear in individualism and communitarianism. For Dewey, the state does not exist primarily to protect the rights of individuals; neither do individuals exist merely as functional components of the state.

Translating this thinking to the democratic classroom, Dewey believed that schools ought not merely to promote fair competition among individuals, nor should students be treated all alike—as members of a faceless class. Rather, schools should be organized democratically—as places where the best forms of associated living are practiced. Schools are, then, minisocieties in which children learn through practice how to promote their own growth, that of others, and that of the whole society.

The Place of Subject Matter

Dewey defined subject matter in terms of the material used in resolving a problematic situation: "It consists of the facts observed, recalled, read, and talked about, and the ideas suggested, in course of or development of a situation having a purpose. This statement needs to be rendered more specific by connecting it with materials of school instruction, the studies which make up the curriculum."[16]

Dewey did not recommend abandoning the traditional subjects of the curriculum, but he wanted them to be taught in a way that makes them genuine subject matter. They should be presented so that students can use them in purposefully working through some problematic situation. Some philosophers of education today go well beyond Dewey in arguing that the traditional subjects are badly out-of-date (remember that they can be traced to Plato!) and that a new curriculum should be created.[17] Under Dewey's plan, the old subjects would still be treated, but they would be part of the curriculum only as they were actually used by students in their inquiries. Curriculum, for Dewey, is not a body of material established before instruction. Instead, it is the material gathered, used, and constructed during instruction and inquiry.

Geography and history both have significant roles in Dewey's account of education, but neither is to be presented as a body of unconnected facts to be learned by rote. Each should enter the curriculum as a way of explaining human activity, enlarging social connections, or solving social problems:

The classic definition of geography as an account of the earth as the home of man expresses the educational reality. But it is easier to give this definition than it is to present specific geographical subject matter in its vital human bearings. The residence, pursuits, successes and failures of man are the things that give the geographic data their reason for inclusion in the material of instruction. But to hold the two together requires an informed and cultivated imagination. When the ties are broken, geography presents itself as that hodge-podge of unrelated fragments too often found. It appears as a veritable rag-bag of intellectual odds and ends: the height of a mountain here, the course of a river there, the quantity of shingles produced in this town, the tonnage of shipping in that, the boundary of a country, the capital of a state.[18]

Dewey wanted students to puzzle over human events and activities. Why might these people have become traders? What might explain the growth of a great city at the confluence of three rivers? What else influenced the development of exactly this sort of city? What have ocean currents and winds to do with the activities of human beings? Why do we find thriving agriculture on one side of a mountain but not on the other?

Although Dewey did not advocate abandonment of the standard subjects, he hinted rather strongly that the lines between disciplines should be less rigid. He noted that the inclusion of nature study in geography seems, verbally at least, "forced." But in actuality, the two clearly go together. "Nature and the earth should be equivalent terms, and so should earth study and nature study."[19] Dewey wanted students to experience a personally unified curriculum—one that makes sense to them in terms of human experience and, particularly, in terms of their own experience.

Dewey Today: An Assessment

In several areas of thought, many of today's thinkers agree with Dewey. His description of students as active pursuers of their own purposes is widely accepted. His rejection of absolutes and the quest for certainty in epistemology is a dominant position in current thought. His discussion of the dilemmas involved in seeking community within a liberal society could have been written today. And his insistence on student participation in democratic forms from the earliest reasonable age still seems right to many educators.

However, even Dewey's strongest supporters admit that there are ambiguities in many of his basic concepts. Can we really talk meaningfully about growth without specifying its direction? What exactly is the "experience" that Dewey sometimes identifies with personal meaning and sometimes with culture? Is there any point in retaining the notion of God if there is no living entity behind the term?

Possibly the greatest objections to Dewey's work from the perspective of today's educators is that he gave so little attention to the problems of race, class, and gender and that he put such great emphasis on the power of scientific thought to solve our problems. What Dewey envisioned when he wrote of democracy was a community of thoughtful experimentalists—people working together, trying things out, evaluating and sorting through the possibilities. He did not give us much advice on handling race conflicts, pressure-group politics, growing gaps between rich and poor, and the unhappy possibility that science might aggravate rather than ameliorate our problems. Ardent followers of Dewey argue that solutions—or at least promising directions—for these problems can be found in Dewey's work. But the solutions seem to depend on an almost Utopian view of democracy. In an age complicated by power struggles and loss of faith at every level and in almost every arena, Dewey seems to many to be naive.

My own sense is that his view of democracy can be activated in schools and that if it were, the larger democracy might indeed be affected positively. My position is more modest than that of the social reconstructionists who challenged the schools "to build a new social order."[20] I do not think the schools, embedded as they are in a larger social structure, can do that. But, with Dewey, I think that schools can help the society to develop individuals who have a clearer, more responsible sense of what it means to live in a democratic community.

SUMMARY QUESTIONS

1. Must education tend toward some ideal, or is it sufficient that education lead to further education?
2. In the same spirit, is *growth* an adequate criterion of education? Is Dewey's treatment of growth adequate?
3. How should teachers formulate aims? Must students be involved in constructing objectives for their own learning? Having read Dewey's recommendations, how do you feel about teachers establishing learning objectives for every lesson?

4. Are all the steps of Dewey's problem-solving model necessary? Are there current models you find more accurate or helpful? How many of these models credit Dewey for some of their components?
5. Does Dewey's description of the fourfold interests of children ring true today?
6. Is it accurate to call Dewey's educational philosophy "child-centered"?
7. Should we call something "knowledge" if we are quite sure it is false? Why or why not?
8. Should teachers allow students to use faulty procedures? Under what circumstances?
9. Is there an inherent conflict between the individual and the state?
10. Does democracy depend on the transmission of common values? What should we mean by "transmission"?
11. What must children learn in order to participate intelligently in democracy? Does it matter how they learn?
12. How should "subject matter" be defined?
13. Is Dewey's two-part criterion for democratic groups adequate?
14. Is Dewey's defense of history and geography in the curriculum adequate?

INTRODUCTION TO THE LITERATURE

John Dewey, *The School and Society, The Child and the Curriculum, Experience and Education, Reconstruction in Philosophy, The Public and Its Problems, Democracy and Education;* and Robert Westbrook, *John Dewey and American Democracy.*

For students new to philosophy and philosophy of education, it is usually helpful to read Dewey's first important statements on education—*The School and Society* and *The Child and the Curriculum*—and his last such statement—*Experience and Education.* After that introduction, one should read *Democracy and Education,* Dewey's most comprehensive treatment of education. For biographical information, see Robert Westbrook, *John Dewey and American Democracy.*

CHAPTER 3

Analytic Philosophy

During the same period in which Dewey was developing his naturalistic pragmatism, Bertrand Russell (1872–1969) presented the philosophical world with his rigorous version of analytical philosophy. Analysis, of course, has always been a part of philosophy; that is, one task of philosophy is to take apart concepts, words, and sentences to figure out what each part means and what role it plays in the whole. Most intelligent people engage in this sort of task at least occasionally. In studying a paragraph, for example, we may analyze each sentence, sometimes each word, in our attempt to understand the paragraph. Russell, however, brought new meaning to the term. He believed that reality itself is analyzable—that it can be broken down into irreducible elements or relations. Most philosophers today do not engage in formal analysis as Russell described it. Instead, they try to elucidate or clarify concepts and words.

Analytic philosophy in all of its forms claims to analyze and clarify. In the form favored by Russell, it concentrates on the connection between language and reality. Syntactic analysis is an important part of this approach. Sentences are broken up into segments and a referent is sought for each segment. To what do these segments refer? What role does the order of words play in conveying meaning? Educational philosophers have more often been drawn to conceptual and ordinary language philosophy. An analytic philosopher might, for example, analyze the concept of teaching or of education. In doing so, he or she would try to separate the given concept from closely related ones, and considerable attention would be given to the various linguistic contexts in which the concept appears. In ordinary language analysis, the emphasis is on how language is used. It may, of course, be used to analyze concepts, and the terms *conceptual analysis* and *ordinary language philosophy* are often used synonymously. The important feature of all analytic philosophy is its claim to neutrality. Analytic philosophers try not to smuggle new meanings into the concepts they analyze. They try to clarify what is really there in a word, concept, or bit of writing. They insist on analysis, not interpretation. One of its earliest and most prestigious proponents, Ludwig Wittgenstein, claimed that philosophy "leaves everything as it is." That is, philosophy does not change the world; it just makes the world clearer.[1]

Many educational philosophers today consider themselves analytic philosophers. They are engaged in conceptual or contextual analysis, but usually they pay much more attention to the use of language and to the connections of various practices than to a search for irreducible elements or relations. Philosophers who reject the analytic approach often object to the lingering supposition that analysis can be performed neutrally; that is, they criticize analytic philosophers for supposing that their own presuppositions and preferred theories do not enter their analyses. In fact, these critics insist, analytic work and theory itself are both shot through with values. Philosophers cannot effectively set aside their values while they engage in analysis, and a better approach—from the perspective of critics—is to ferret out these values, confess them, and build one's case frankly on them. However, even when philosophers reject analytic philosophy in its purest forms, they engage in analysis. Plato, Aristotle, and Leibniz all engaged in analysis, but they did not—and most philosophers today do not—embrace Russell's extreme definition of analysis.

Philosophical Analysis in Education

Much of educational philosophy in the 1950s, 1960s, and 1970s was devoted to the analysis of educational language and concepts. A basic motivation for doing this work was the belief that ordinary language held a great treasure of meaning as yet unrealized because it had not yet been analyzed. A prominent philosopher of education, Jonas Soltis, put it this way:

Many of us ... would be hard pressed if asked to spell out in simple words the ideas which are contained in such ordinary concepts of education as teaching, learning, or subject matter. Yet these very concepts are basic to any thought or discussion about education. Furthermore, I believe that such an attempt to explicate these ideas would invariably result in the unveiling of nuances of meaning which we unconsciously assume in our actions as students or teachers. As a result, we would not only become more sophisticated and careful in their use, but would also gain a deeper insight into education as a human endeavor in which all men take some part sometime in their lives.[2]

Philosophers set about analyzing such concepts as teaching, indoctrination, learning, training, achievement, and many others.[3] In the last chapter, we mentioned R. S. Peters's analysis of the concept of "aims." A complaint often leveled at such analysis is that it doesn't get us anywhere. In keeping with its claim to "leave everything as it is," it fails to advance programs or assist in transforming the world. Sometimes, however, as in the case we will examine shortly, philosophers and empirical researchers work together to clarify concepts so that they can be appropriately operationalized for research. Sometimes, too, philosophical analysis contributes to the gradual abandonment of educational ideas. In the case of "discovery," for example, philosophers helped to show that the notion was too vague for credible research. Is "discovery" a way of learning, a method of teaching, or a form of teaching characterized by a certain outcome?[4]

While many philosophers of education turned to analysis as the proper task of philosophy, others continued to work in a way more closely connected to metaphysics. Metaphysics is the branch of philosophy that considers the ultimate nature of reality and being. It asks questions such as: Is the universe basically composed of mind/ideas, or of physical/material particles? These philosophers usually started with a metaphysical position, say, idealism, and then tried to show what this position meant for education. In mainstream philosophy, of course, there still were lots of arguments defending idealism against realism (or, more often, materialism), rationalism against empiricism, and monism against pluralism. But the arguments in philosophy of education were not usually sophisticated defenses of a basic position. More often, they were detailed descriptions of how education should be conducted by realists or idealists. In philosophy of education texts, chapters were often titled "The Realist Teacher," "The Idealist Teacher," and "The Pragmatist Teacher."[5]

Analytic philosophers thought that programs of this sort—trying to develop a realist or idealist program of education—were badly mistaken.[6] Suppose we watched two teachers on a given day and observed them using the same methods and interacting with students in roughly the same way. Both might be realists, both might be idealists, they might be of opposite persuasions, or they might hold some entirely different views. It is not possible, analysts said, to derive specific programs of action from basic philosophical positions, nor is it possible to trace particular methods unerringly to an underlying philosophical position. Most philosophers today would agree with the analysts on this, although they would admit that certain patterns of belief and action are more compatible with one position than another, and they do not deny that it is worthwhile to develop a philosophy of education that is coherent and consistent. We have to remember that you and I, starting with mostly different premises, may occasionally choose like positions, but we would defend those positions differently.

The argument between traditional philosophers of education and analytic philosophers sometimes became acrimonious. Analytic philosophers accused traditional philosophers of fuzzy thinking (as in the preceding discussion), and they were proudly affiliated with the mainstream of work in philosophy. Further, their work proved useful in the growing industry of educational research. But traditional philosophers may win our sympathy when we notice that they at least continued to ask some of the great questions handed down by Socrates, Plato, and Aristotle. Analytic philosophers often wrote and behaved as though the great questions about moral life, spirituality, and life's meaning were inaccessible to philosophy. Indeed, Bertrand Russell insisted that such topics, although interesting and vitally important to human life, are nonphilosophical. When he worked on them—and he did through a long life—he said he was *not* doing philosophy. From Russell's perspective, even intellectual life was analyzable; it could be broken down into a part susceptible to analysis and another part that could not be treated by analysis. Anything in the latter category was not philosophy. Although most analytical philosophers today do not follow Russell and the early Wittgenstein in this extreme view, they still claim a neutrality and detachment that traditional philosophers (and neo-Marxists and postmodernists, too) find both impossible and undesirable.

Some critics think that traditional ("systematic") philosophers made another error when they added Dewey's pragmatism to realism and idealism as starting points for educational thought. Dewey certainly challenged both realism and idealism, insisting upon starting with human beings as organic wholes acting in a world of which they are a part—neither as separated observers of something external nor as bits of some universal mind stuff. Dewey also challenged the epistemologies of rationalism and empiricism. But when he discussed education, he worked always from objects and events accessible to observation and reflection: the activities of children, the workings of intelligent action, the effects of interest on effort, the development of creative individuality in democratic settings, the observable (or at least easily inferable) motivational factors underlying imitation. Indeed, Dewey thought that the systematic positions connoted by the adjectives *realist, idealist,* and *pragmatist* got in the way of clear thinking about practical affairs. In his major works on education, he rarely used such terms, and when he did, it was usually to reveal the errors of such use. Dewey was neither a traditional nor an analytic philosopher.

Analytic philosophy has moved steadily away from Russell's vision. Further, educational philosophers could never have worked profitably in Russell's style. Their work is, by its very nature, concerned with value.[7] Any claim to neutrality either rings false—that is, we can find a value-laden position underlying the work—or it generates products relatively useless for educational theory and practice. Today, analytical philosophers of education use the powerful methods demonstrated in the work of Wittgenstein on ordinary language analysis.[8] Analysts in education try to uncover meaning and reveal conceptual errors by exploring how terms are actually used and by establishing limits on appropriate use. There are many fascinating examples of such analysis, and we turn next to an important example.

The Analysis of Teaching

What is teaching? On one level, teaching is an occupation, a way in which some people make a living. If, after you have secured a teaching position, you meet an old friend, Jake, whom you have not seen since high school days, Jake might ask what you are doing these days. Your answer would be "teaching."[9] This answer might well lead to elaboration on such matters as where you are teaching, at what level, what subjects, and so on. But the conversation would probably not get at the issues that concern philosophers. These issues begin with questions about teaching acts—exactly what teachers do when they teach and about how teaching can be differentiated from activities that have some of the same features.

One question that interests philosophers and might also occur to Jake is, How are your students doing? Are they learning? Your old friend might be interested in how your students are doing because he is thinking about teaching himself, or because he is concerned about how tax monies are used, or because he has heard horror stories about schools and wants to check them out firsthand. But the philosopher wonders about the conceptual connections between teaching and learning. John Dewey stimulated a whole program of analysis with these comments:

Teaching may be compared to selling commodities. No one can sell unless someone buys. We should ridicule a merchant who said that he had sold a great many goods although no one had bought any. But perhaps there are teachers who think they have done a good day's teaching irrespective of what people have learned. There is the same exact equation between teaching and learning that there is between selling and buying.[10]

Dewey published those words in 1933. In the 1960s, philosophers challenged the notion that "teaching implies learning." Most philosophers agreed that teachers *intend* to effect learning, but they pointed out that students often fail to learn even when teachers work hard to teach them. Some of these philosophers wanted to protect teachers from the unfair attacks that were directed at them in the 1960s. Teachers were under fire for allowing American students to fall behind their Soviet counterparts. After the 1957 Russian launching of *Sputnik,* the first human-made satellite, many Americans feared Soviet technological superiority and reacted by blaming schools and, especially, teachers for the nation's apparent shortcomings in technology. This story may seem ironic today because, as we well know, test scores have fallen steadily since that time; the troubled 1960s seem now an almost golden age of student achievement (although there are still those who identify the period as the "beginning of the end"). Further, given the breakup of the USSR, we now doubt that the great wave of post-*Sputnik* fear was at all well founded.

I have provided this bit of historical background to remind you that analysis is motivated by something. It may, as in Russell's work, be triggered by technical problems within an intellectual domain. Or it may be motivated by events in social life. In the latter case, even if the analyst strives for neutrality, the eventual analysis is likely to reflect the initial motivation.

The tone of Israel Scheffler's influential *Language of Education* suggests strongly that he wanted to defend teachers against the charges unfairly leveled at them.[11] Part of his analysis suggests also that he wanted to separate the work of human teachers from that of "teaching machines" and from that of technicians who merely follow scripts in the classroom. The thesis put forward by Scheffler and by B. Othanel Smith—that teaching does *not* imply learning—came to be known as the *standard thesis*. Scheffler argued that teaching is characterized by three criteria:

1. The teacher intends to bring about learning (intentionality criterion).
2. The strategies chosen by the teacher must be "not unreasonably thought to be likely to achieve the learning aimed at" (reasonableness criterion).
3. What the teacher does must fall under certain restrictions of manner (criterion of manner).[12]

Once such a characterization of teaching is available, it presents a host of intellectual challenges to philosophers. Look over the three criteria. Is there one you would like to challenge? Is there one you need to know more about?

As I said earlier, most philosophers and educators accept the first criterion: Teaching aims to bring about learning. But a few philosophers object even to this. Paul Komisar, for example, said, "It is not some kind of learning, but some form of awareness, which is the intended upshot in the teaching acts under discussion."[13] Komisar provided a long list of "intellectual acts" that could be considered teaching acts in the appropriate context—for example, introducing, demonstrating, hypothesizing, appraising, interpreting, and many others.[14] All of these, Komisar said, are used by teachers with the intention to make their students aware, not to produce particular bits of learning.

Dewey might have agreed with Komisar on this, at least in part. Right after passages in which he compared teaching to selling, Dewey wrote:

The only way to increase the learning of pupils is to augment the quantity and quality of real teaching. Since learning is something that the pupil has to do himself and for himself, the initiative lies with the learner. The teacher is a guide and director; he steers the boat, but the energy that propels it must come from those who are learning. The more a teacher is aware of the past experiences of students, of their hopes, desires, chief interests, the better will be understood the forces at work that need to be directed and utilized for the formation of reflective habits.[15]

Dewey insisted that teaching should induce learning, but he did not mean that it should cause every student to learn some piece of information or skill predetermined by the teacher. Dewey wanted students to be involved at the level of constructing their own learning objectives. Like Komisar, he believed that teachers should make students aware of various possibilities—possibilities in the domain of ends or learning objectives and possibilities among means for achieving their ends. Dewey used *learning* much more broadly than many psychologists and educators. By *learning*, he did not mean a particular response to a particular teaching act as stimulus. But he might still have insisted, against Komisar, that learning really is the end-in-view, that awareness is insufficient. From Dewey's perspective, teachers should not stop at awareness. They have a responsibility to follow up—to find out what students learn as a result of their initial awareness and consequent investigations.

Probably Komisar would not disagree. As Scheffler was trying to defend teachers against unrealistic expectations and a loss of autonomy, Komisar was trying to protect students from an overly narrow conception of learning. He did not want teaching to aim at learning if learning meant responding with a designated answer when the teacher asked a question.

This discussion challenges us to analyze the concept of learning.[16] We cannot do this here, but you should be aware that analyses have yielded several distinctions useful for educators. First, we might reserve the term for occasions on which pupils (or "subjects" of psychological research) give the appropriate response to a question or stimulus. Examples would be correct answers to stimuli such as the following:

1. Who was the ruler of England in 1492?
2. What is a transitive verb? Is "employ" a transitive verb?
3. Solve for x: $3x + 7 = 25$.
4. Define *erg*.

5. Name the major body parts of an insect.

If we describe learning as correct responses to questions of this sort, we might make a distinction between learning and "developmental learning" as Piaget did. The latter is thought to be the kind of learning that leads to or demonstrates structural changes in thinking. This way of talking prompts questions about the dividing line between "learning" and *real* learning or "developmental learning." For example, is giving an interpretation in literature learning in the first sense or second? How about solving a mathematical problem new to the student? And, if the distinction holds, is there a connection between the two senses of learning? Can a student give a literary interpretation without knowing certain vocabulary words, bits of grammar, and the like? Can a student solve a new problem without skills that can be described in the first sense of learning? Are there ways of teaching that make learning in the first sense more likely to lead to learning in the developmental sense? Are there ways that inhibit such movement/involvement?

A second way of using "learning" would reject the distinction we have just discussed and go on using it broadly to describe the acquisition of all kinds of information, skills, and tools of inquiry. Even awareness might then be described as a form of "learning that" something or other exists or is possible. In this sense, we could hardly deny that at least one aim of teaching is to produce learning.

It might not even have occurred to you to challenge the intentionality criterion. What about that of reasonableness? Scheffler says that teachers who intend to teach students to do something, say, solve linear equations, must choose methods that are deemed likely to produce the desired result. If a teacher spends all of class time telling stories about travel or exhorting students to political action, we would hardly expect his or her students to have learned how to solve linear equations. Such a person could not claim to be teaching because, logically, there is no reason to expect that the method chosen is likely to produce the outcome purportedly aimed at. Yet this does not rule out much. We still do not know how to judge when a relevant discussion is actually a reasonable method.

Some educational supervisors criticize teachers when they do not use methods currently thought to be those most likely to produce learning. Others are more cautious. Of these, some see that a great variety of methods meet the reasonableness criterion. Others withhold criticism not because they evaluate the teacher's methods highly but because they believe in teacher autonomy. For the latter, reasonableness is largely equated with professional judgment. Of course, you can see where this view might lead. We might now embark on an extended analysis of professional judgment.

There is another aspect of reasonableness as a criterion for teaching. In one of my early articles, I argued that if reasonableness were construed in a certain way, the end result would have to be the learning aimed at, and one would have to abandon the standard thesis and agree with Dewey that teaching does, after all, imply learning.[17]

The argument runs like this. Suppose a teacher, T, sets out to teach X to a student, S. Let's examine the course of a lesson in which S is supposed to learn X. T chooses a method at the outset that is acceptable to a set of professional observers. We (the professional observers) agree that it is not unreasonable to expect S to learn X through the method chosen. Now suppose the teacher just talks through the method without even looking at S, or T actually gives S practice exercises and the like and notes that S is not getting it. If, despite evidence that S is not learning, T persists in using the original method, is it still reasonable? Or must T keep revising and inventing methods in keeping with S's progress or lack of it? At what point does the use of an initially reasonable method become unreasonable? Next, suppose that at every checkpoint, the signs are favorable. The methods chosen were initially reasonable and remained reasonable throughout the lesson. How can learning not be the result?

This way of construing reasonableness puts great responsibility on the teacher. It does not seem too great a demand for T if there is only one student, S, and this may be one reason for the unusual effectiveness of home-schooling. Indeed, we would expect a responsible teacher to abandon X and try to teach something else if he or she had exhausted all the methods thought to be reasonable with still no success. But what happens when T faces a whole class of students? I would argue that the principle still applies. T's methods should be reasonable not only at the outset, t_0, but at every point throughout the lesson. The challenge is to find out how each student is doing at $t_1, t_2, \ldots, t_n$. Most of us would not fault a teacher if a few students had not learned X at the end of a lesson, but we might insist that T should at least know this and have some plan for these students.

Keep in mind as you assess my argument that I am *not* agreeing with those who insist that T should have a specific learning objective, X, for every lesson. On the contrary, I agree with Dewey that students should be involved in the construction of their own learning objectives. I would much prefer to guide students in an inquiry of their own choosing and ask at the end of it, What has the student learned? This is very different from setting out to teach X and asking at the end, Has the student learned X? But *if* we accept Scheffler's criterion of intentionality, that T must intend to teach something, X, and *if* we apply the reasonableness criterion as I have argued, then the learning of X follows so long as T's methods remain reasonable.

Some philosophers object to this line of reasoning on the grounds that a teacher, T, can, at one and the same time, be teaching and not teaching. How is such a result possible? Surely we should be able to judge a teaching performance as teaching or not teaching but not both! If one insists that teaching consists of intention plus a set of approved acts, this annoying anomaly is avoided. Further, this construal makes it possible for researchers to study teaching by watching teachers. Technically, there is no need to look at students at all. Smith even argued that a teacher presenting a lesson over television could "go on teaching" even if, unbeknownst to him, the power had failed![18] From the perspective I laid out, however, it is not at all discomforting to acknowledge that T may be teaching and not teaching at the same time. Indeed, many of us regard the ambiguity as salutary. It reminds us that teaching is a relation, one to which both teacher and student contribute.

Before considering Scheffler's third criterion of teaching, I should mention another important argument in favor of the standard thesis. Gilbert Ryle distinguished between "task" verbs and "achievement" or "success" verbs.[19] Words such as *race, seek,* and *reach* are task words; they describe activities, attempts to accomplish something. The corresponding achievement words are *win, find,* and *grasp.* Smith wrote that *teach* is a task word and *learn* the corresponding achievement word,[20] but this acknowledges, in possible contradiction of Smith's earlier comment about the television teacher, that we have to look at students and not just teachers if we are interested in successful teaching. Smith might escape the contradiction by arguing that we can still study *teaching* in isolation from learning but that we must look at students and learning when we are interested in *successful* teaching.

Notice that the *teach-learn* pair is different from the others *(race-win, seek-find,* and *reach-grasp)* in an important respect. In the others, the same person tries and succeeds; success does not reside in another's achievement. Aristotle also noted this peculiarity of teaching. Another pair of this sort is *treat-cure;* here, too, another person is the locus for application of the success word. Those who accept this analysis would, logically, have to give up their attempt to separate teaching and learning completely. Smith's hypothetical attempt to escape the contradiction cannot be effected.

Instead of counting *learn* as the success word paired with *teach* as a task word, some philosophers have preferred to say that we use *teach* in both senses, and this certainly describes common usage accurately. We do use the expression "I am teaching X to S" to convey both a sense of the task we are engaged in and a sense of what we are accomplishing. I would just add to this that when we know S is not learning, we usually soften our claim and say, "I am *trying* to teach X to S," and this acknowledges the connection that Dewey insisted on.

Finally, let's look at the criterion of manner. Scheffler said that teachers have to conduct their work in a certain manner if we are to credit them with teaching. He was trying to separate "real" teaching from the work of teaching machines and scripted programs. Teachers, unlike machines, are expected to acknowledge the rationality of their students. (That is why the criterion of manner is often called the "rationality" criterion.) If we want to know whether T is teaching, Scheffler said in a very nice line, we have to see whether what T is doing meets this criterion—"in particular, whether acknowledgement of the alleged pupil's judgment is made, whether, e.g., the pupil is not systematically precluded from asking 'How?' 'Why?' or 'On what grounds?'"[21]

Scheffler's rationality criterion can also be used as one test to separate teaching from indoctrination. A person's activity in indoctrination may very well meet the criteria of intentionality and reasonableness but would fail the final criterion of manner. But here we have to acknowledge that teaching may be described differently in different cultures. Many cultures might accept all three criteria but fill out the third very differently. It is also possible that even in a culture that prizes rational autonomy, we might choose to teach some subjects in a way that violates the rationality criterion. Notice, however, that Scheffler presents the criterion in a relatively weak form; he says that the student must not be "systematically precluded from asking" questions. He does not say that the student must be *invited* to ask, or *prompted* to ask, or *shown how* to ask (even though, I suspect, this might be his preference). Thus, a live teacher can meet the criterion more easily than can a machine of the 1960s. Such machines did systematically preclude students from asking the crucial question; a real live teacher could respond simply, "They *could* have asked, but they didn't."

As you consider your own teaching, you might want to ask what form of the criterion you prefer and why. Do teachers have an obligation to encourage "why" questions? Are there times when such questions should be discouraged? What might Socrates have said on this?

This is also a good point at which to review what you are learning about philosophical methods. Philosophers often do what we have done together in the last few pages. Starting with a scheme such as Scheffler's, they raise objections or reject certain points. They may argue for new or revised criteria, predict consequences that the original author failed to foresee, probe for suppressed premises, or reject the entire scheme as wrongheaded. Often a particular line of argumentation leads quite naturally into another domain for analysis. Analysis, as we have been discussing it, is central to philosophy. Analytic philosophers often try to separate their own values from their analyses, but even if they avow a particular social perspective, they use the methods of analysis to make their arguments.

In the discussion of Scheffler's rationality criterion, reference was made to indoctrination. Philosophers have given this concept considerable attention. In his analysis of teaching, Thomas Green constructed a topology of the teaching concept.[22] He noted that teaching is concerned with knowledge and beliefs on the one hand and with behavior and conduct on the other. In these two domains, it includes a range of activities closely or distantly related to the concept of teaching. For example, if we place knowledge and beliefs on the right side of a continuum, we might identify activities such as instructing, indoctrinating, propagandizing, and lying as ways of attempting to change people's beliefs and knowledge. (See Figure 3.1.) On the left, we might identify training, conditioning, intimidation, and physical threats as ways of attempting to change people's behavior.

With this continuum in place, Green invites us to consider a "region of intelligence." For him, propagandizing and lying (on the right end) and intimidation and physical threats (on the left end) fall outside the region of intelligence and, therefore, outside the family of teaching activities. Indoctrination (on the right) and conditioning (on the left) fall at the edge of the

56

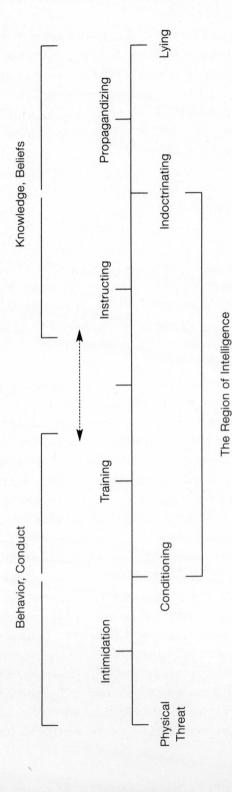

FIGURE 3.1   The Teaching Continuum Expanded
Source: Thomas F. Green, "A Topology of the Teaching Concept," in C.J.B. Macmillan and Thomas Nelson, eds., *Concepts of Teaching* (Chicago: Rand McNally, 1968), p. 36.

region of intelligence. At these border points, disagreement may arise, and indeed, educators continue to dispute the roles of conditioning and indoctrinating in teaching. Some say that teachers should never indoctrinate. Others insist that it is necessary to indoctrinate at certain ages or in certain matters, but that this should only be done with the understanding that at some later date (when students are more mature), questions concerning the grounds for belief will be encouraged. Of course, how one feels about indoctrination depends at least in part on the way it is defined, and this observation leads to another conceptual analysis.[23]

Current Analyses of Teaching

Philosophers of education are still engaged in analysis, and they continue to apply analytical methods to the concept of teaching. C. J. B. Macmillan and James Garrison have introduced an "erotetic" concept of teaching. They write: "To teach someone something is to answer that person's questions about some subject matter."[24] Their use of "erotetic" points to the logic of questions.[25]

Macmillan and Garrison do not mean to confine a teacher's work to answering the actual questions of particular students. Rather, they intend to open a huge and fascinating domain for analysis. They believe that in their teaching, teachers should answer the questions that students *ought* to ask, given their intellectual predicaments. This "ought," they write, is not a moral ought but an epistemological one. That is, given a problematic intellectual situation, people ought to seek knowledge that will clear up their confusion and allow them to move on to new problems. Hence, in planning, teachers need to know something about the intellectual predicaments of their students and the questions that logically arise in such predicaments. Teachers, then, create lesson plans that will answer these questions.

Macmillan and Garrison say that erotetic teaching can be powerful in motivating students to learn. Instead of promising rewards for good work or punishment for poor work, teachers can motivate students by addressing their intellectual predicaments and helping to extricate students from them by answering the questions students *should* ask. Here, it seems to me, there is some slippage from the domain of abstract knowers and the logic of questions to particular students in particular predicaments. A particular student may or may not be motivated by a teacher's attempt to answer the questions she or he *should* ask. The student may not even care about the alleged predicament, preferring to ignore rather than explore it.

This is a topic, Macmillan and Garrison might argue, that every teacher *should* think deeply about. But if you are not naturally motivated to reflect on it, your teachers may not be able to motivate you with purely intellectual acts. They may have to show that they care about *you* as a person and about *your* development as a teacher; they may even have to advise you about fields other than teaching that might be more satisfying for you. Macmillan and Garrison put all of these nonintellectual acts into the "periphery" of teaching, insisting that all such acts are aimed at preparing the ground for the central activities of teaching—intellectual acts, such as explaining, introducing, interpreting, summarizing, and the like.

Other philosophers of education think that the moral acts involved in teaching are central, not peripheral. Susan Laird, for example, takes the analytic tradition to task for its emphasis on rationality and intellectual acts.[26] Drawing on Ntozake Shange's historical novel *Betsey Brown,* Laird asks how analytic philosophy can help a teacher facing a seventh-grade English class described as follows:

Mrs. Mitchell was not happy even before Betsey entered the room in her sweat and anger at Butchy and Mr. Wichiten. [Betsey had been sexually harassed by Butchy and scolded by Mr. Wichiten for yelling at the offensive Butchy.] Plus, Liliana didn't say who Eugene was messin' with. There were so many things going on. Liliana sat with her legs wide open so Willis Ashington could look up her panties. Mavis was writing love notes to Seymour, who was staring at her breasts which weren't quite breasts, but pecans. Mrs. Mitchell's hands were already full when Betsey came in, dripping wet and late.[27]

Laird makes the point that teachers cannot always connect with students by analyzing intellectual predicaments that are themselves abstracted from fictional lessons and not from the real lives of students. Later in her article, she describes the genuine teaching of Carrie, a servant girl:

Carrie . . . teaches the Brown children (both boys and girls) how to clean house, collaborate with and care for each other, take pleasure in song and dance and work well done, forgive their runaway mother, comfort their lonely father, mind their manners, pray, and take pride in themselves and their families. . . . She teaches Betsey, the eldest girl, to honor her own emerging sexuality, to consider with care the pleasures, risks, and responsibilities that come with it. . . . [She] teaches Betsey how to raise and care for her younger siblings and to stand up against injustices to herself and her people.[28]

This, Laird suggests, is *real* teaching. Teachers must consider the *human* predicaments induced by school studies. Further, they must consider the interests and predicaments of particular, individual students, not just those of generalized students or "epistemological subjects." From this view, not only is the starting point of teaching not purely intellectual, but neither is the end point. To teach people self-respect, how to get along with others, and how to take pleasure in life's celebratory moments is not entirely an intellectual task, and it is not aimed at entirely intellectual outcomes.

If we use Bertrand Russell's conception of analysis, we would have to agree with Laird that the closer educational philosophy comes to Russell's form of analysis, the more certainly it will exclude matters involving individuals, concrete situations, love, and other emotions. One might agree that this is true and that although such matters need attention, they cannot be handled by philosophy. An alternative is to expand the domain of philosophy and find ways to analyze—or at least discuss with some rigor—the full range of human concerns. Most analytic philosophers today agree that such expansion is desirable. Laird goes further. Following Laird, we might expand our notion of rationality to include appropriate attention to emotional life. Is it rational, we might ask, to suppose that people value intellectual acts above all others or that they should do so? Is it rational for a teacher to approach teaching with such suppositions? But we should also consider ways in which we might promote intellectual activity directly through intellectual enticement. Can you think of such ways?

Today the debate continues between those who would hold to a narrower or stricter view of philosophical analysis and those who would expand the field to include analysis of literature and episodes taken from daily life. In the latter category, some philosophers now insist that teachers' voices and theorizing contribute much of the "data" for philosophical analysis. Lynda Stone, for example, writes that a philosopher's work is "personal theorizing—but . . . in a voice that reads differently than the voice of more experientially oriented researchers."[29] From this perspective, we should expect to see an interesting blend of empirical, literary, and philosophical analysis directed at the understanding of educational phenomena. Conceptual analysis, fascinating as it is, probably cannot meet all of the needs of actual teachers in actual schools. However, in later chapters, we will study further examples of analytic work as we discuss logic, critical thinking, and epistemology.

SUMMARY QUESTIONS

1. Can the language and concepts of education be broken down (analyzed) in a way that is value-neutral and meaningful?
2. Must we leave the domain of philosophy to talk about morality? About other values? About emotions?
3. Does teaching imply learning?
4. Must the criterion of manner be described in terms of rationality, as Scheffler described it?
5. Is awareness a form of learning?
6. Can teaching be separated from learning? Why might we want to do this?
7. Can a television teacher "go on teaching" if the power fails?
8. Can the concept of erotetic teaching be used to plan lessons? What questions *should* the students ask?
9. Do real live students ask the questions they should (epistemologically) ask?
10. Does teaching consist primarily of intellectual acts?
11. Can narrative and empirical studies be properly used in philosophical work? Are we still "doing philosophy" when we engage in such mixed methods?

INTRODUCTION TO THE LITERATURE

All of the following provide an excellent introduction to the analytic philosophy of education: C.J.B. Macmillan and Thomas Nelson, eds., *Concepts of Teaching;* R. S. Peters, ed., *The Philosophy of Education;* Denis Phillips and Jonas Soltis, *Perspectives on Learning;* Israel Scheffler, *The Language of Education;* B. Othanel Smith and Robert H. Ennis, eds., *Language and Concepts in Education;* and Jonas F. Soltis, *An Introduction to the Analysis of Educational Concepts.*

CHAPTER 4

Continental Philosophy

Besides Dewey's pragmatic naturalism and the analytic philosophy so well developed by British philosophers, American philosophers of education have been influenced by movements in Continental philosophy: existentialism, phenomenology, critical theory, hermeneutics, and, most recently, postmodernism. Again, it will not be possible to give a full account of any of these movements, but readers should know enough about them to appreciate what writers are trying to accomplish through each approach.

Existentialism

Existentialism cannot properly be called *a* philosophical school because it contains too many thinkers holding contradictory positions and because existentialists usually reject systematic philosophy, schools of thought, and the like. Existentialist ideas can be found as early as Greek philosophy and in both religious and atheistic thought. The basic themes of existentialism are "the individual and systems; intentionality; being and absurdity; the nature and significance of choice; the role of extreme experiences; and the nature of communication."[1] I will not discuss all of these themes here but only those of particular interest to philosophers of education. The theme of intentionality will be deferred until the discussion of phenomenology. But readers should be aware that the existentialist/phenomenological use of "intentionality" is very different from the one used in Chapter 2 to refer simply to a teacher's *intention* to get someone to learn something. It connotes, rather, a process of creating and referring to mental objects.

The most famous expression associated with existentialism is "existence precedes essence." Existentialists reject the idea of a preformed human nature that can be used to guide education, prescribe duties, predict fate, and describe the role of human beings in the universe. Clearly, the existentialist position flies in the face of most traditional religious philosophy. But there have been and are religious existentialists—Søren Kierkegaard, Martin Buber, and Paul Tillich, for example. All of them rejected and often mocked the traditional religious emphasis on ritual and hierarchy, an emphasis that elevates the system over the individual and rote obedience over choice. Each believed in the capacity of individuals to communicate with God directly (without priestly mediation), and each made human choice central in his philosophical writing.

Existentialists, both religious and nonreligious, emphasize the freedom of human beings. People are not thrown into the world with "a nature." By planning, reflecting, choosing, and acting, people make themselves. "Existence" is not mere brute life. It involves conscious awareness of our human condition—of our freedom, physical frailty, eventual death, and responsibility for the kind of person we become. In this sense, existence precedes essence. We make ourselves; we create our essence.[2]

Existentialists, in addition to rejecting the idea of an essential human nature, also reject what might be called the supremacy of systems. They do not study human beings as representatives of types or elements in orderly systems. Instead, they are concerned with individuals and how individuals exercise their freedom to define themselves. Kierkegaard, for example, expressed contempt for Christians who identified themselves merely as "Lutheran," obedient to the superficial and formal tenets of that faith. A Christian, for Kierkegaard, was an individual who consistently and continually renewed his or her choice to be connected to God through Christ. He had no patience with logical argumentation in religion, emphasizing again and again choice, faith, and commitment. There should be no rational quest for objective certainty in religion, Kierkegaard insisted. Rather, faith emerges as individuals recognize the awful tension between subjective certainty and objective uncertainty.[3]

Writing in a Jewish tradition, Martin Buber emphasized the responsibility of individuals to relate to one another and, through one another, to God.[4] Like Kierkegaard, he wanted people to depend less on ritual and formality and more on individual relations. God was not to be made an object of study, Buber said. God is, rather, a partner in dialogue, someone with whom individuals communicate in an I-Thou relation. This is not to say that the study of religion was unimportant to Buber. On the contrary, such study occupied his life. But Buber found God through the study of concrete stories—stories of human encounter and reflection. Like Kierkegaard, he rejected the notion that religion starts with a God whose nature and commandments are known a priori. An individual must connect with a God who is revealed little by little—and only occasionally with clarity—through human encounter.

Paul Tillich in his approach was more abstract than Kierkegaard and Buber, but his emphasis was still on the individual's freedom to choose and the responsibility that accompanies that freedom. For Tillich, God was closely associated with "ultimate concern."[5] Each human being needs an ultimate concern to guide his or her life and to give it integrity. Without an ultimate concern, Tillich said, life could have no meaning. It would deteriorate into an incoherent set of brute concerns.

I have spent a few paragraphs discussing religious existentialism because students unacquainted with existentialism often identify it with atheism and pessimism. Some readers thus may be more receptive to existentialism upon learning that there are existentialists who study and write about faith, encounter, courage, hope, and joy. Indeed, there are many beautiful and moving passages in the work of Kierkegaard, Buber, and Tillich that could be used with high school classes. I myself have been deeply influenced by Buber in developing my philosophy of education, and I will say more about his views on education a bit later.[6]

The existentialism that captured (or repelled) the popular imagination in the 1940s and 1950s was for the most part atheistic, and it was portrayed by those who had not studied it as inordinately gloomy, preoccupied with nausea, despair, and death. The work of the novelist, playwright, and philosopher Jean-Paul Sartre did much to convey this picture of gloom and despair to the public. Some years ago, a cartoon appeared (in the New Yorker, I think) showing a well-to-do middle-aged man staring morosely at the city below from the window of his fashionable apartment. His wife, standing beside him, asks, "What possessed you to read a book with a title like Being and Nothingness anyway?"[7]

But Sartre himself eloquently defended existentialism against such charges. Existentialism should not be charged with pessimism, Sartre insisted, but with "optimistic toughness." If we want things to be better, we must work to bring about better conditions. If we want to claim a talent for ourselves, we must do something or produce something that manifests that talent. For Sartre, there is no use talking about "what ifs" and "could have beens." There is only what is, and we are responsible for that. Here is what Sartre said:

> Man is nothing else but what he makes of himself. Such is the first principle of existentialism. It is also what is called subjectivity. . . . But what do we mean by this, if not that man has a greater dignity than a stone or table? For we mean that man first exists, that is, that man first of all is the being who hurls himself toward a future and who is conscious of imagining himself as being in the future. Man is at the start a plan which is aware of itself, rather than a patch of moss, a piece of garbage, or a cauliflower; nothing exists prior to this plan; there is nothing in heaven; man will be what he planned to be. Not what he will want to be. . . . Thus, existentialism's first move is to make every man aware of what he is and to make the full responsibility of his existence rest on him. And when we say that a man is responsible for himself, we do not only mean that he is responsible for his own individuality, but that he is responsible for all men.[8]

By this last sentence, Sartre means not only that we have a responsibility to improve human conditions so that all people can live with greater awareness and thus themselves accept their own full responsibility, but also that we have the responsibility of defining what it means to be a human being ("a man"). Because we are entirely free, we can accept or reject the first "responsibility," although Sartre had contempt for those who reject it. The second responsibility is inescapable. "There is no human nature, since there is no God to conceive it."[9] Therefore, what you and I do defines what it means to be human. What will it mean to be human? To be cruel or compassionate? Involved or detached? Energetic or lazy? Heroic or cowardly? Intelligent or stupid? It depends on what we choose, and what we choose is revealed in our action, what we do.

Atheistic existentialists like Sartre often refer, usually through characters in their novels or plays, to "absurdity." Those looking for a rational plan of life handed down to human beings from God will be disappointed.

There is no such plan. Life and human *being* are absurd, without a priori meaning. What meaning there is in life, we must create. If we find ourselves bored and discouraged, asking daily "Is this all there is?" it is up to us either to accept the emptiness of life or to fill it with meaning through our choices and action.

Recognition of our freedom induces anguish; we must decide. Realization that there is no God brings forlornness. "Forlornness and anguish go together," Sartre said.[10] We create value through our choices. If we are courageous, we acknowledge our choices, the values created, and the effects of our choices on the world.

These themes appear repeatedly in the literature of Sartre, Camus, Dostoevsky, and the other existentialist writers. In the agony of extreme conditions (plague, war, impending death) or the ennui of everyday life, characters look for meaning. They struggle to find meaning in suffering and deprivation, in repetition and ordinary events. Either they find none and conclude that life is indeed absurd, or they come to realize that meaning resides in exactly what they are doing: treating the sick, although many will die; suffering torture rather than betraying one's comrades; returning to home and family instead of seeking adventure; or forsaking family to seek adventure.

Existentialism, with its great emphasis on human subjectivity, has roots in Cartesian rationalism, the philosophy of René Descartes. Sartre takes his beginning explicitly in the Cartesian cogito: I think; therefore, I exist. "There," writes Sartre, "we have the absolute truth of consciousness becoming aware of itself."[11] The capacity to reflect, to plan, to choose, and to become is the fundamental work of human existence.

Existentialists, however, resist some later developments of rationalism. They usually reject abstractions like Piaget's epistemological subject or other attempts to characterize mental life in terms of fixed categories and operations. Such moves once again subordinate individuals to a system. Existentialists are interested in *subjects*—living, aware human beings—not abstractions of which they are assumed to be manifestations.

Before we look at existentialism in education, we should discuss one last existentialist theme to which we have already alluded. Existentialists often choose stories rather than argumentation as their mode of communication. They do this because they believe that life is not the unfolding of a logical plan; one cannot argue from trustworthy premises what a life should be like or how it should be lived. Rather, meaning is created as we live our lives reflectively. Stories give us accounts of the human struggle for meaning. They inspire and frighten us. They tell us how we might be—for better or worse—if we choose to act this way or that.

The great bulk of Buber's scholarship centered on stories. Kierkegaard told oppositional stories, speaking now with one voice, now with another. Sartre communicated his philosophy as effectively (some would say more effectively) through his novels and plays as he did through his expository philosophical writing. The present emphasis on narrative in educational research and teacher education is, in an important sense, an existentialist trend, although it is rarely based on explicit existentialist thought. We have already seen how effective stories can be in Susan Laird's use of *Betsey Brown* to criticize the analytic approach to teaching.

The foremost philosopher of education to draw regularly and powerfully on existentialism is Maxine Greene. In essays and books spanning several decades, Greene has discussed themes such as alienation (a state of unresolved or unrecognized forlornness), the centrality of human connection and relation, the need for awareness or "wide-awakeness," and freedom.[12]

In her analysis of freedom, Greene explores the variety of ways in which human beings have construed freedom. She clearly locates herself in an existentialist tradition (if we dare refer to such a thing) as she rejects the notion of a system conferring freedom on its elements or members: "I believe it unthinkable any longer for Americans to assert themselves to be 'free' because they belong to a 'free' country. Not only do we need to be continually empowered to choose ourselves, to create our identities within a plurality; we need continually to make new promises and to act in our freedom to fulfill them, something we can never do alone."[13] Notice the explicit connection that Greene makes between freedom and choice, particularly the choice of the selves we will be. But notice also that she does not portray the individual as permanently alone, isolated in an agony of personal freedom. She consistently and powerfully shows us a way to resolve (not overcome forever) the problem of forlornness. We connect with one another, we define our freedom in relation with others, and we achieve the relatedness we long for as we make and keep promises to living others and future generations.

This kind of thinking can provide a stimulating starting point for a discussion of pluralism and identity. In this view, people must use their inner freedom to create their own identities. We are free to identify ourselves by our blackness or whiteness, maleness or femaleness, Americanness or Frenchness. But we should realize that a thorough awareness of our freedom can carry us beyond these systemlike identifications. I am not just a white, female, American academic, although I am all of these. I am what I do, what I make of myself.

This is an especially important theme for today's educators. People in this country have, for the most part, claimed their freedom to identify themselves by their racial and ethnic origins. Now the question arises whether we have used our full freedom if we are unwilling or unable to go beyond this identification to an even more reflective personal identification. Such a quest for freedom could lead either to greater individualism or to a move beyond race and gender and even beyond humanism to identification with all living (and nonliving?) things.[14] From the perspective of various ideologies, we *ought* to choose one orientation or the other; from the perspective of existentialism, we must choose and accept responsibility for the choice we make. There is no assurance that we are "right" in making one choice or another; we can only pledge ourselves to stand responsible for the choice and its consequences.

It is worth pointing out here that there are existential themes in Socrates (how should we live our lives?) and in Dewey. For Dewey also, there is no fixed human nature. We participate in our own creation. But Dewey gives greater emphasis to the role of environment in shaping us. For Dewey, freedom is not a basic condition that is either recognized in anguish or denied in cowardice. Rather, it is an achievement, one that is attained primarily through adequate information and thorough reflection. Where Dewey and Sartre part company is in Dewey's faith that scientific method will ensure progress. Sartre would not argue against the clear thinking that Dewey espoused, but he would counsel against assuming that human beings will continue to use this method (or any other) or that the method itself guarantees progress. Each human being must make a choice; that challenge will never disappear, and one cannot substitute scientific method or Marxism (although Sartre embraced it for its contemporary usefulness) or anything else for the eternal stability once grounded in God. Sartre regretted the nonexistence of God, but he was unwilling to substitute another entity or immutable method in God's place.

Another existential theme that interests contemporary philosophers of education is the individual-in-relation. As we have seen, all existentialists reject any view that subordinates individual human beings to a system. But some existentialists, Buber for example, also reject the notion of stark and lonely individualism found in the writing of their colleagues. Buber noted of his inaugural course at Hebrew University: "This course shows, in the unfolding of the question about the essence of man, that it is by beginning neither with the individual nor with the collectivity, but only with the reality of the mutual relation between man and man, that this essence can be grasped."[15] The use of "essence" here may be confusing. Not all existentialists reject the notion of essence; rather, they insist that existence precedes essence. Essence, then, is something constructed in the struggle for meaning and self-creation. Still, the way Buber uses the word, one feels that a person who fails to live in positive relations with other human beings also inevitably fails to satisfy Buber's "essence." We are left to ponder whether this essence is a construction, a discovery, or a preestablished ideal.

Buber was deeply concerned about education, and two of his essays on the subject appear in the collection *Between Man and Man*. He believed that teaching accomplishes whatever it does through relation: First, something of the teacher's own character and intellectual interest flow into the student, setting an implicit example; second, the teacher, by practicing inclusion, sees what the student is trying to do and to become and, if the projects are worthy, gives energetic support and guidance.

"The relation in education is one of pure dialogue."[16] Buber elaborates this principle with a storylike introduction:

I have referred to the child, lying with half-closed eyes waiting for his mother to speak to him. But many children do not need to wait, for they know that they are unceasingly addressed in a dialogue which never breaks off. In face of the lonely night which threatens to invade, they lie preserved and guarded, invulnerable, clad in the silver mail of trust.[17]

Notice how Buber uses familiar existential themes of loneliness, darkness, and threat but then points the way to consolation and connection through dialogue, which for Buber is not only a way of speaking and listening but also a way of receiving one another in silence. Children need this kind of relation in which to grow. Buber continues:

Trust, trust in the world, because this human being exists—that is the most inward achievement of the relation in education. Because this human being exists, meaninglessness, however hard pressed you are by it, cannot be the real truth. Because this human being exists, in the darkness the light lies hidden, in fear salvation, and in the callousness of one's fellow-men the great Love.[18]

Some current work in philosophy of education also emphasizes the importance of relation.[19] This work sometimes draws on existentialist literature; at other times, it draws on empirical studies that give dramatic evidence of how important relations are to students in the everyday events of schooling.[20]

Again, Buber refers to basic existential themes—existence, meaninglessness, fear, love. But his references are embedded in a way of looking at education. Education is relation. Buber does not expect isolated individuals to educate themselves, nor does he recommend systematic reform. Probably he would not have objected to systematic attempts to improve facilities and resources, but he would certainly have objected to the movements we now call "school reform." Insisting that all children study the same subjects, that all meet preset standards, that all teachers use a particular lesson form, or that all schools follow a national curriculum—all of these would be, for Buber, starting with the collectivity. Buber wanted us to start instead with the "reality of mutual relation."

Much of my work follows Buber in this (although I do not classify myself as an existentialist).[21] Other philosophers of education are giving close attention to the concept and practice of dialogue, but in most cases they do not use Buber's work and are not existentialists.[22] The theme, however, is an existential theme. Similarly, the current popularity of narrative in research, teacher education, and moral education may be thought of as an existentialist trend.[23] In Philip Jackson's essays, we hear the existentialist voice very clearly, even though Jackson mentions neither Buber nor existentialism. Here is a sample from the preface of his 1992 book of essays:

This book is about the influence teachers have on their students, though not the kind of influence that shows up on tests of achievement or other conventional measures of educational outcomes. It treats instead what we learn from our teachers about ourselves and others, and about life in general. Some of these "lessons," most of them "untaught" in the sense of not being part of the teacher's explicit agenda or lesson plan, take the form of things we remember about our teachers long after we have bid them adieu.[24]

Phenomenology

Phenomenology in philosophy is a highly technical method, but the word is also used to point to a variety of descriptive methods in psychology and social research. When philosophical phenomenologists use the word *phenomenological,* they, too, are talking about description but not in the ordinary sense of scientific or casual observation. If you take a walk and later describe the things you saw and heard on your way, you are not doing phenomenology. Similarly, if you study classroom life through the lens of a theory of culture, you are not doing phenomenology. Phenomenology is a descriptive science concerned primarily with the objects and structures of consciousness.

Contemporary technical phenomenology started with the work of Edmund Husserl,[25] but it has roots in Descartes's attempts to found knowledge on what is indubitable to human consciousness. Descartes's famous dictum "I think; therefore, I am" suggests a constituting subject, a consciousness that shares in the construction of reality. Sartre, who was a phenomenologist as well as an existentialist, referred repeatedly to Descartes's "method of doubt" as the basic method of phenomenology.[26]

Husserl said that phenomenology is not an empirical science but an a priori science, one that uses empirical facts only as illustrations. By a series of adjustments—bracketings and reductions—phenomenologists try to identify the features of subjectivity that "persist in and through all imaginable modifications."[27]

In the section on existentialism, I mentioned that phenomenologists use the term *intentionality* in a technical way. *Intentionality* is a basic characteristic of consciousness. Consciousness, for phenomenologists, is always consciousness of something. The constituting subject creates the objects (intentional objects) of its own contemplation. Phenomenologists study these objects, their nature, and the structures of consciousness in which they are revealed.

Educational philosophers have little reason to engage in technical phenomenology as it was established by Husserl, but many of us use methods familiar to scholars in psychological phenomenology. We set out to study something like *hope* or *trust* or *faith* and systematically vary the situations in which such terms are used so that we may capture the essence or basic characteristics of the thing we are studying and of the subject experiencing it. Most of us do not use the word *essence* to describe what we find, because we either reject the absolutist claims of technical phenomenology or we recognize and admit that our methods are not exhaustive.

Perhaps an example will help here. In my work, I have attempted a phenomenology of *caring*. The basic questions are directed at a description of caring as a relation between two people—a carer and a cared-for. To simplify the discussion, I will concentrate here on just a caring encounter (as contrasted with caring over considerable intervals of time) and confine the exploration to one question: What characterizes the consciousness of a carer in a caring encounter? In everyday language, how *are* we, what is our mental state when we care? You can try an exploration of this sort yourself.

Think of a time when you encountered another individual in a way you would call *caring*. You may recall many features of the particular situation—the physical setting, particular remarks made, feelings of alarm or grief. Set these aside. (They are interesting and important, but we are after characteristics that are invariant, that are not attached to one particular encounter.) Now change the scene a bit. If your original recollection involved someone very close to you, make the next case one with an acquaintance or professional colleague. Then consider an instance when the cared-for was a stranger. Vary the ages of the cared-fors; vary their predicaments; vary the observable affects—fear, happiness, sadness, and the like.

What I found in my own analysis are two characteristics that seem to describe the consciousness of carers in all caring encounters: First, the carer attends to the cared-for in a special way that I have called *engrossment*.[28] Other writers—Simone Weil and Iris Murdoch, for example[29]—use the word *attention*. This attention or engrossment is thoroughly receptive; that is, when we really care, we receive what the other person conveys nonselectively. We do not lay on our own structures, nor do we assimilate what the other says as a mere bit of information. We feel what the other is going through. Indeed, Simone Weil said that the implicit question we ask as we attend in this way is, "What are you going through?"[30]

Second, as we receive what is there in the other, we feel our energy flowing toward the other's predicament or project. We want to relieve a burden, activate a dream, share a joy, or clear up a confusion. Temporarily, our own projects are put aside; we are caught up by an internal "I must" that pushes us to respond to the other.

Of course, this is a mere sketch of the phenomenology of caring. We also have to explore the consciousness of the cared-for. In addition, we have to move beyond encounters to the forms of caring that endure over time. In educational research, we are also led to move from explorations of consciousness to scientific study of the empirical conditions in which caring occurs or fails to occur. But perhaps this brief example is sufficient to give you some sense of the ways in which a modified phenomenology can contribute to social and educational research.

Critical Theory

Nancy Fraser begins her discussion of critical theory with Marx's definition of the enterprise as "the self-clarification of the struggles and wishes of the age."[31] "What is so appealing about this definition," Fraser writes, "is its straightforwardly political character."[32] From the perspective of critical theorists, philosophy must be engaged with the great struggles and social movements of its times. The contrast between the analytic philosophy discussed in Chapter 3 and critical theory is dramatic. Whereas analytic philosophy prizes detachment and the search for a neutral form of truth embedded permanently in language or the real world, critical theory insists that such detachment is both intellectually and morally irresponsible. According to critical theorists, even if thinkers strive for neutrality—a sort of positionless position—they cannot bring it off. We are all, inevitably, immersed in the tasks and values of our historical situation.

Philosophers of education have been greatly influenced by critical theory, and many articles in this vein appear every year. Articles on racism, sexism, and classism (three of the great struggles of the age) often draw directly on the work of critical theorists—sometimes on Marx but more often today on Antonio Gramsci, Max Horkheimer, Herbert Marcuse, Theodor Adorno, Michel Foucault, and Jürgen Habermas. All of these writers are part of a project to "extend universal freedom by criticizing the partial, limited forms of human autonomy."[33] That is, they are concerned with political freedom and dignity, and their focus is real, historically situated human beings, not so much the supremely free consciousness of Sartre's existentialism. Sartre himself, it should be said, accepted Marxism because the freedom of existentialism could not be fully exercised under oppressive political conditions.

Starting with Marx, critical theorists have insisted on analyzing the social conditions that underlie, accompany, and result from forms of domination. Marx was, of course, interested in the economic domination of one class over another. He saw workers alienated from their products, work itself reduced to labor for a wage, and the great prosperity of a few gained at the cost of enormous suffering for many. For Marx, the plight of workers represented the great struggle of his age.

Other critical theorists, as deeply concerned as Marx about economic conditions, concentrated their attention on different facets of the struggle. Antonio Gramsci, for example, analyzed the ways in which dominant groups exercise cultural hegemony over subordinate groups. Literacy, on the one hand, can be regarded as a tool of social improvement. It enables people to hold better jobs, obtain better services, and perform their civic tasks more intelligently. Withholding literacy can be a powerful (and obvious) means of complete domination. On the other hand, extending literacy can be seen as a method of ensuring hegemony. People who can read and write can be appealed to as consumers and dupes of the more powerful. First, they can be convinced to accept political and social structures that are really not in their best interests; second, they can be persuaded to spend their hard-earned wages on products they do not really need. Because a few lower-class children will succeed in climbing the ladder of economic prosperity, the message of upward mobility will have cogency. But the knowledge that counts—privileged knowledge—will remain the property of a few.

Paulo Freire is one of the educational theorists who have emphasized the necessity of raising consciousness in the newly literate.[34] Oppressed populations need to know something about the forms of oppression and the ways in which the dominant group will try to exploit their literacy. As they learn to read and write, oppressed groups also need to generate themes describing their own problems and possible solutions.

Among contemporary theorists, Henry Giroux has carried Freire's arguments into an analysis of American educational practices.[35] He advocates *critical literacy,* a form of literacy that is directed to the analysis of individual and collective problems. Without the capacity and power to criticize, literate people may simply accept the messages given by the dominant culture. They become accomplices in their own exploitation. Critical literacy requires a mode of critical thinking (to be discussed in Chapter 5). People need to know not only how to read but also how to question, analyze, and solve problems.

Feminist theorists, too, have analyzed the ways in which women, as an oppressed group, have been denied the power to give names to important phenomena in every domain of life and, in general, to create language. Mary Daly, for example, sees the power of *naming* as central to human liberation: "Women have had the power of *naming* stolen from us. We have not been free to use our own power to name ourselves, the world, or God."[36] From this perspective, literacy alone—without the power of creating language and criticism—allows one only to share in a language designed for the purposes and profit of others.

What role does the school play in enhancing freedom or ensuring domination? In the 1970s, critical theorists in education wrote about something called "correspondence theory."[37] They believed that the structures of schooling and classroom discourse correspond directly to the class structures of society and that this correspondence explains how the school "reproduces" the society's class structure. Even in the early days of correspondence theory, however, sensitive writers noted that the correspondence is not perfect and that students and teachers are not mere pawns in a giant game over which they have no control. Correspondence theory was modified by discussions of resistance. Interestingly, it soon became clear that resistance itself sometimes serves to maintain the control of the ruling class, as when working-class boys resist the efforts of formal schooling and thus—through their very resistance—ensure their assignment to the working class.[38]

As we have learned more about the complexity of issues surrounding the notions of race and class, some thinkers have suggested that despite students' resistance, liberal education should be the standard form of education for all students. It has long been argued that liberal education "frees" minds and builds a citizenry capable of autonomous action. It has also been recognized that restricting access to liberal education is a powerful means of maintaining the privilege of the controlling class. Many theorists today insist that all children should have access to what we usually call the "college preparatory" curriculum. Mortimer Adler, for example, says that everyone should have exactly the same course of study through at least twelfth grade.[39] This is necessary, he believes, to maintain our democracy. In a later chapter, we will find much to criticize in this view.

Many critical theorists also believe that providing all students with "privileged" knowledge will help to break down the barriers of race and class.[40] But critics of the critical theorists—among them many feminists— argue that the standard liberal arts curriculum is merely the *manifestation* of privileged knowledge. Forcing all children to take algebra, physics, and foreign language will not in itself give them a share of privileged knowledge. Indeed, such a move may very well extend the hegemony of the dominant class.[41] Not only will students be deprived of the choices Dewey thought so important to participation in democratic processes, but they may come to believe that there is only one ideal or model of educated persons. In a society that needs a vast array of excellences, this could be debilitating. For children whose talents are ignored or undervalued, it could be tragic.[42]

Another criticism directed at critical theory is that it is supposed to be aimed at action yet is cast in highly abstract intellectual language that itself tends to privilege the class of intellectuals. Why, if its object is to "change the world" (as Marx insisted), should it describe itself in language inaccessible to all but a few? And why does it assume that the material labeled "privileged knowledge" is somehow educationally valuable? Why, that is, does it tend to valorize the class of educational elites and suppose that something generous and democratic is accomplished when everyone is given a chance to emulate the elite model?

One might try to describe what is going on in inner-city schools from the perspective of critical theorists or their critics. From the view of some critical theorists, the remedy for inner-city schooling is to recognize the capacity of poor children and racial minority children to learn the standard school subjects. Many conscientious parents in our inner cities have adopted this position. They believe that success at a standard education will give their children a chance at the material goods of this society. Critics of this approach fear that such parents may be victims of false consciousness. Perhaps it would be better, they suggest, to insist on forms of education designed for the varied and particular needs of students. At the theoretical level, educators might question the educational value of the present curriculum instead of accepting it as a given and trying to give all children access to it.[43] The debate over the curriculum and privileged knowledge may be one of the most important in which today's educators engage.

Hermeneutics

Hermeneutics has long been associated with the interpretation of biblical texts. Today the label is more often attached to a philosophical search for meaning that rejects both the quest for certainty characteristic of foundationalism and the nihilism often associated with Nietzsche and sometimes with existentialism. Philosophers who engage in hermeneutics accept contingency and historicity. They seek meaning in both texts and life itself as it unfolds historically.

One can do hermeneutics from a variety of perspectives. For example, many critical theorists engage in hermeneutics; naturalistic philosophers like Dewey and W.V.O. Quine employ hermeneutic methods. Hermeneutics involves a careful search for meaning without an expectation that exactly one meaning will be found or that it will be anchored in an unassailable foundation.

Richard Rorty describes hermeneutics as an approach that "sees the relations between various discourses as those of strands in a possible conversation, a conversation which presupposes no disciplinary matrix which unites the speakers, but where the hope of agreement is never lost so long as the conversation lasts."[44] Hermeneutical work enlarges the scope of our vision, suggests new meanings, and encourages further conversation. It pushes us into a holistic practice of sorts, one in which we can rarely attach separate meaning to the atomistic parts. As Rorty says:

> This holistic line of argument says that we shall never be able to avoid the "hermeneutic circle"—the fact that we cannot understand the parts of a strange culture, practice, theory, language, or whatever, unless we know something about how the whole thing works, whereas we cannot get a grasp on how the whole thing works until we have some understanding of its parts. This notion of interpretation suggests that coming

to understand is more like getting acquainted with a person than like following a demonstration.[45]

Notice that this approach is very different from that of analytic philosophy. It does not claim that we can get an understanding of a whole concept by taking it apart and examining the pieces, but it also rejects the idea that a holistic view is sufficient in itself.[46]

Hermeneutics has a practical bent. It tries to make sense out of history and contemporary contexts without tying either to rigid theoretical foundations. In telling the story of current philosophy's turn to narrative and conversation, Richard Bernstein points out the contrasts in Plato's work: One part represents the metaphysical Plato, a Plato who led Western philosophy on its fruitless search for certainty; the other is the ever-questing, conversational Plato. Bernstein quotes Dewey on this contrast:

> Nothing would be more helpful to present philosophizing than a "Back to Plato" movement; but it would have to be a back to the dramatic, restless, cooperatively inquiring Plato of the *Dialogues*, trying one mode of attack after another to see what it might yield; back to the Plato where the highest flight of metaphysics always terminated with a social and practical turn, and not to the artificial Plato constructed by unimaginative commentators who treat him as the original university professor.[47]

Although we will not often use the word *hermeneutics* in the rest of this text, we will encounter the hermeneutical spirit again and again. Whenever philosophers reject ultimate purposes and fixed meanings, whenever they urge a diversity of views and a continuing conversation, whenever they recognize pluralism and reject monistic tendencies, when they use both analysis and interpretation, they are working in the hermeneutic spirit.

Postmodernism

Postmodernism is more a mood than a movement. Various writers elaborate on different aspects of a mood or view that raises profound doubts about the projects of modernity and, particularly, the Enlightenment. Most postmodern thinkers have abandoned the Enlightenment quest for absolute truth; in this, postmodernists agree with Dewey. They accept what might be called "local truth"—facts of the sort that we might agree upon either through common observations or through methodological conventions. For example, we might all agree that much of what is reported in daily newspapers—scores of sporting events, reports of accidents, announcements of deaths and marriages—is true. Similarly, postmodernists accept as true the basic rules of mathematics and certain postulates of science. Even these may be regarded as local or limited in the sense that they apply to entities and events with which we are so familiar that we no longer think about the locus of their application. They may in fact be local, but their locality is so extensive that they seem almost universal.

Many philosophers today share with postmodernists some skepticism about ultimate or foundational truths, but the postmodern rejection is accompanied by a challenge to the traditional field of epistemology. Postmodernists believe that the search for one all-encompassing description of knowledge is hopeless. Instead, they emphasize the sociology of knowledge—how knowledge and power are connected, how domains of expertise evolve, who profits from and who is hurt by various claims to knowledge, and what sort of language develops in communities of knowers. In one sense, postmodernism implies postepistemology; in another, it suggests a drastic revision of traditional epistemology. When we look more deeply into epistemology, we will see that contemporary educators are caught up in something called "constructivism," which is thought by some to be an epistemological position and by others to be a *post*epistemological position.[48]

Postmodernists also attack the long-standing belief in objectivity. Because it is impossible to build an argument or interpret an event or even gather data without a purpose and perspective, objectivity in the traditional sense becomes a myth. Something like objectivity may be attained, however, through intersubjectivity; that is, an aggregation of interpretations from various perspectives may yield as nearly an unbiased picture as we can obtain. Probably you, like all people who have undergone higher education in Western institutions, have been encouraged throughout your school career to "try to be objective." With this exhortation, your teachers have been urging you to put aside your personal opinions and prejudices—to avoid "subjectivity"—and give an account backed by impartial evidence. Not only do postmodernists deny that this can be done, but they also claim that the very attempt to do so has already biased any investigation. An investigation or argument so launched is riddled with the assumptions of standard modernist thought.[49]

Perhaps we can make clear what is at stake here by referring to a critical theorist, Jürgen Habermas, who retains faith in the Enlightenment project—that is, the project to improve the condition of humanity through the proper understanding and application of reason. Habermas claims that a form of rational communication free of distortion should place us in a position to base decisions on "the force of the better argument." Commenting on this claim, Richard Bernstein writes:

> Abstractly there is something enormously attractive about Habermas' appeal to the "force of the better argument" until we ask ourselves what this means and presupposes. Even under "ideal" conditions where participants are committed to discursive argumentation, there is rarely agreement about what constitutes "the force of the better argument." We philosophers, for example, cannot even agree what are the arguments advanced in any of our canonical texts, whether Plato, Aristotle, Kant or Hegel, etc.—and there is certainly no consensus about who has advanced the better argument.

Bernstein goes on to remark that philosophers do not even agree on the role that argumentation should play in philosophy. Agreeing with the postmodernists on this, he notes that

> appeals to argumentation become ideological weapons for dismissing or excluding philosophical alternatives—for example, when analytic philosophers complain that Continental philosophers (including Habermas) do not argue, or indulge in "sloppy" argumentation. Who decides what is and what is not an argument, by what criteria, and what constitutes the force of the better argument?[50]

Bernstein does not suggest abandoning argumentation. Certainly, good thinkers can separate configurations of words that reveal logical flaws and gaps from those that are "better" in this sense. But at bottom we simply cannot depend on being able to identify the best argument. Many issues stubbornly remain issues despite the great efforts of philosophers to settle them by argumentation.

One great flaw in the "argument for arguments" is that argumentation, governed as it is by rules and criteria laid down by authorities in a particular domain, tends to exclude voices, words, and pleas from those who do not use the standard forms. Worse, the criteria are claimed to be universal so that the excluded voices appear to exclude themselves through ignorance or perversity. Jacques Derrida has been particularly eloquent in pleading for the inclusion of outsiders, Others, who use a different language and see from a different perspective. He asks us "to let Others be"—to respect their otherness and stop trying to assimilate them into our own language and stories.[51] In this plea, we hear an echo of existentialist thought—essence is an achievement and not an a priori ideal.

Derrida's plea to let others be is a call to abandon grand narratives. We can no longer assume that people can all be described by some overarching theory, that they all long for exactly the same goods, respect exactly the same virtues, or mean the same things when they use similar words. To make such assumptions is to be guilty of "totalizing," of summing up unique parts of human experience in one grand description that emphasizes similarity and covers up difference.

You can see that the educational problem alluded to earlier—that of deciding whether to provide the same curriculum for all children—may be approached very differently if we follow the thought of a critical theorist like Habermas or that of a postmodernist like Derrida. In the chapter on social philosophy, we will look at this problem and several others in considerably more depth. At this point, it should be clear that an effort to force all children into the same course of study—however well-intended the attempt—is, from the perspective of postmodernism, a totalizing move. It improperly (and unethically, Derrida would probably say) assimilates all children to the model of an elite established by criteria constructed by an exclusive few.

We should discuss one more topic of postmodern thought before turning to the description and analysis of educational problems. Many postmodern thinkers have expressed doubts about the constituting subject—both the abstract and the particular human knower/agent that have been at the center of modern philosophy. Recognizing the multiple ways in which people are shaped by their histories and cultures, by their personal experiences, and by their interactions with others, postmodern writers have described a *constituted* subject and multiple identities. Such a view challenges not only the rational subject of Cartesian epistemology but also the existential subject described by Sartre. In this view, we do not make supremely free choices, nor can we be held fully responsible for the persons we become.

Unfortunately, the "death of the subject" not only sweeps away the somewhat haughty knower of Descartes and Sartre and the lofty moral commander of Kant; it also threatens the autonomy and agency of ordinary actors. Feminists, even those who lean toward postmodernism, worry about this.[52] If the death of the subject were a metaphysical claim, we would have to accept or reject it as a claim to truth; there either is or is not such an entity. But postmodernists do not make metaphysical claims (at least not deliberately); they urge us to abandon metaphysics. Therefore, the claim has political import and should be approached from a political perspective. Hence, feminists must ask whether this claim aids or hinders the feminist program. Women today are just beginning to feel like agents, like persons who can exercise autonomy. Is this the time, then, to write the obituary of the subject? It is rather like losing one's driver's license immediately after buying a car and learning to drive. We will revisit this problem in the chapter on feminism.

In sum, postmodernism is a mood that shakes the whole structure of modern thought. It challenges cherished assumptions, methods, attitudes, modes of thought, and values. Thoughtful educators should be aware of ways in which its proponents help us to think better about educational problems, but they should also be wary of accounts that merely use postmodern buzzwords or that lure readers into accepting potentially harmful moves along with helpful ones. One does not have to accept every pronouncement of postmodernists to be postmodern. Indeed, it might be better, especially from the postmodern view, to reject such labels entirely.

Before leaving this chapter, we should consider why some of the movements discussed here have had so little effect on education. It seems odd that analytic philosophy with its avowal of neutrality and detachment has had far more impact on education than has existentialism with its powerful exploration of the human condition. One reason for this apparent oddity is that we live in a society dominated by technology and a long-standing faith in scientific progress and control. Even the philosophy of John Dewey, cogent as it is in its plea for the participation of students in democratic processes, echoed the great American faith in science. Because analytic philosophers could contribute clarity and consistency to educational research, their work has often been cited in research articles. Existentialism, with its talk of human freedom and its rejection of systems, just does not fit the culture of a nation bent on systemic reform.

Many philosophers, including philosophers of education, use modified phenomenological methods, but few identify themselves as phenomenologists. In part this is because phenomenology is highly technical and difficult to learn. But largely it is because phenomenology made claims to suprascience, a foundational science lying below and beyond science, and all such claims have fallen into disrepute.

Finally, although critical theorists have had great influence on a wide range of educational thought, they are scolded for using a highly intellectualized language that seems incompatible with their stated desire to change the world.

In the chapters that follow, we will revisit some of the positions discussed here as we explore the specific topics that most interest philosophers of education today.

SUMMARY QUESTIONS

1. Existentialists put great emphasis on the individual as free agent—one who chooses, creates a self, and takes responsibility. Do you think this stance is compatible with religion? With social service?
2. In what ways might you personally be responsible for what it means to be human?
3. What interests might serve as "ultimate concerns"?
4. Are the concepts of anguish and forlornness useful in analyzing problems of schooling?
5. Should we attempt to describe a new humanism, or should we promote views that encourage people to identify themselves by race, class, ethnicity, gender, or some other category?
6. If you were a phenomenologist, would you be more likely to study the life cycles of insects or the human tendency to worship? Why?
7. What are the struggles and wishes of this age in which you live? What do you think are the struggles and wishes of high school students today?
8. Should philosophy be political? Must it be?
9. Is literacy liberating?

10. Is the power of naming important?
11. How does one become part of the working class? Does the school play a role?
12. Should all students, say through grade ten or twelve, have exactly the same curriculum?
13. Is there anything you regard as an absolute truth? How might someone argue from a different perspective that your absolute truth is better described as a "local truth"?
14. In what sense can a conscientious investigation be objective?
15. How does one judge the force of an argument?
16. What might it mean to follow Derrida's plea to "let Others be"?
17. Are there educational policies today that tend to "totalize"? Is this good or bad?
18. Should we celebrate or mourn the death of the subject?

INTRODUCTION TO THE LITERATURE

For an existentialist view of education, see Maxine Greene, *The Dialectic of Freedom*. A liberatory view is beautifully expressed in Paulo Freire, *Pedagogy of the Oppressed*. For a Marxist view of education, see Paul Willis, *Learning to Labour*. For a lucid and lively introduction to postmodernism, see Richard J. Bernstein, *The New Constellation*. For an introduction to feminism from the perspective of critical theory, see Nancy Fraser, *Unruly Practices: Power, Discourse and Gender in Contemporary Social Theory*. See also Mordechai Gordon, ed., *Hannah Arendt and Education*.

CHAPTER 5

Logic and Critical Thinking

Each of the introductory chapters included a mention of critical thinking in some context: Socratic questioning as a critical thinking strategy, Scheffler's criterion of manner as an obligation of teachers to recognize their students' rationality or capacity for critical thinking, Dewey's analysis of problem solving, and Giroux's emphasis on critical literacy. Philosophers and educators have long agreed on the importance of critical thinking, but they have not agreed entirely on what it is, and they have agreed even less on how to teach it. In this chapter we will consider the thoughts of philosophers of education on three main approaches to the teaching of critical thinking and close with the possibility that a fourth—as yet not fully developed—might be even more useful. The first three approaches have been dominated by analytic philosophy; the last comes from a different angle.

Formal Logic

Philosophers and educators have occasionally recommended the teaching of logic as a means to critical thinking. We will consider some of the arguments given for doing this in a bit, but first let me give an example of the sort of use that has attracted educators. Do not assume from my use of this example that I recommend formal logic as a pedagogical basis for critical thinking. This discussion will lead to a critique and then to a consideration of alternatives.

When mathematics educators were excited about the "new math" in the 1960s, they put emphasis on set theory and logic. Many texts, especially

p	~p	p∨~p
T	F	T
F	T	T

Excluded Middle

p	~p	p∧~p	~(p∧~p)
T	F	F	T
F	T	F	T

Law of Contradiction

p	q	p∧q
T	T	T
T	F	F
F	T	F
F	F	F

Conjunction

p	q	p∨q
T	T	T
T	F	T
F	T	T
F	F	F

Disjunction

p	q	p→q
T	T	T
T	F	F
F	T	T
F	F	T

Implication

p	q	p→q	~p	~q	~q→~p	(p→q) ⇄ (~q→~p)
T	T	T	F	F	T	T
T	F	F	F	T	F	T
F	T	T	T	F	T	T
F	F	T	T	T	T	T

Equivalence of p→q and Contrapositive

FIGURE 5.1   Basic Truth Tables

geometry books, began with a chapter on basic propositional logic. Such introductions worked from the fundamental assumptions of Aristotelian logic without comment on alternatives and often without discussion of the nature of the expressions to be treated. The statements to be treated, symbolized by letters such as p and q, were only those that can be judged unequivocally true or false; the law of excluded middle that says a statement p must be either true or false (symbolized p∨~p) was accepted without comment, and so was the law of contradiction [~(p∧~p)]—not both p and ~p. Students were introduced to the basic truth tables (Figure 5.1) and asked to work through sets of exercises requiring the use of truth tables, the translation of verbal sentences into symbolic form, and the proof of various theorems of logic.

Starting with p→q, students learned how to form the inverse (~p→~q), converse (q→p), and contrapositive (~q→~p). They also learned something about syllogisms and the law of detachment (modus ponens): p→q and p, ∴q. This background in logic was supposed to give students a preliminary understanding of proof so that work with geometrical theorems would not seem so new and strange.

Consider an example. Suppose students were asked to prove the following: If two sides of a triangle are congruent, the angles opposite those sides are congruent. Students might be advised to begin by symbolizing the statements:

p: Two sides of a triangle are congruent.
q: The angles opposite those sides are congruent.
p→q: If two sides of a triangle are congruent, the angles opposite those sides are congruent.

Next students might examine the truth table for implication. They would see that when p is true, p→q is true only when q is true. Hence, if they can show that q is true as a consequence of p's being true, the theorem is proved. Now, the pedagogical argument goes, students will know what they are doing when they launch into the traditional proof.

Following conventional method, students draw a figure (Figure 5.2). They draw an auxiliary line from B to the midpoint of AC; call the midpoint D. Next students establish that AB≅CB, BD≅BD, and AD≅CD. They give reasons for each of these statements. They then draw on a statement that has already been accepted: If two triangles have three sides of one congruent respectively to three sides of the other, the triangles are congruent. Therefore △ABD≅△CBD. Again the basic rule of syllogism is emphasized. Finally, they use the rule again in this syllogism:

1. Corresponding parts of congruent triangles are congruent.
2. ∠A and ∠C are corresponding parts of △ABD and △CBD.
3. ∴∠A≅∠C

Now the teacher returns to the symbolic form with which the class started and points out to the students exactly what has been accomplished. Starting with the truth of p, they have established the truth of q

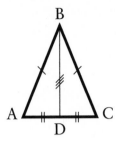

FIGURE 5.2   Triangle ABC

and hence of p→q. The theorem has now been demonstrated and can be used as a reason in future proofs.

As a math teacher in the 1960s, I found this way of beginning geometry both intriguing and useful. Many of the students I taught (honors students) liked the work on logic and seemed to profit from it. They found the method traditionally labeled "indirect proof" so easy that it was often their first strategy. Understanding that a statement and its contrapositive are equivalent gave them two ways of approaching the theorems they had to prove, and they were not in the least mystified by labels such as "indirect proof" or "reductio ad absurdum." As a result of such positive personal experience, I would certainly present a unit on logic if I were teaching math today to highly talented and motivated students.

Personal experience, however, provides very thin empirical evidence. We would have to hear from many teachers and gather evidence under a variety of conditions. Apparently, most teachers and students did not share the experience I have described. Further, personal experience is not a substitute for philosophical argumentation. If we can muster a persuasive philosophical argument, we might convince mathematics educators that despite a poor or ambiguous showing in the first empirical tests, teaching logic in mathematics is worth another try.

One argument (now largely discredited) for the teaching of logic rested on the notion that logic is actually a description of the rules by which a competent mind works. From this perspective, the rules previously discussed represent the way our minds work whether or not we are actually aware of the rules. Noam Chomsky's analysis of transformational or generative grammar as a description of the way in which the mind produces linguistic products is another example of such theorizing. These theories are often called *competence theories* because they describe the operation of an ideal (or competent) thinker or speaker.[1]

Discussion of competence theories and their current epistemological status would take us far beyond the scope of our present purposes. What we need to ask here is this: Even if, especially if, logic describes the natural workings of a competent mind, is that a reason for teaching its explicit rules? Why teach that which, under normal conditions, functions naturally? Oddly, in the comparable case—that of transformational grammar—some educators actually devised an elementary school language arts curriculum based on transformational grammar. The argument given was that if our minds actually perform transformations on language from deep structure into surface structure, they will do it even better with an understanding of the explicit rules of operation. Many educators found this unpersuasive. After all, human beings had been producing linguistically beautiful and grammatically perfect forms for centuries without the slightest knowledge of transformational grammar. Indeed, if we were to reflect continually on what our minds are doing as we produce language, we might well become tongue-tied rather than more competent. Most philosophers and educators concluded that competence theories open a vast domain of fascinating investigation, but the theories cannot profitably be translated into specific curricula. They can, however, be used to help us predict student readiness for certain learning tasks.

Putting aside questions of how the mind (in an ideal sense) works, we may still posit that a study of logic will contribute to critical thinking; that is, we may argue that students will think better as a result of studying logic. Some logicians have made this argument. Patrick Suppes, for example, wrote in the introduction to his logic text: "Our everyday use of language is vague, and our everyday level of thinking is often muddled. One of the main purposes of this book is to introduce you to a way of thinking that encourages carefulness and precision."[2]

It is clear from what Suppes said next that he believes the study of formal logic has relevance for thinking in all fields: "A correct piece of reasoning, whether in mathematics, physics or casual conversation, is valid by virtue of its logical form. . . . Fortunately, this logical structure may be laid bare by isolating a small number of key words and phrases like 'and,' 'not,' 'every,' and 'some.'"[3] Many philosophers of education (including this one) doubt this. Michael Scriven, for example, points out that by the time a complex argument in everyday language is reduced to symbolic or structural form, the hard work has actually been done.[4] Nothing further is accomplished by the formal encoding itself. Here I will give another personal anecdote, but remember that such a story can only trigger further speculation; it cannot settle the question of whether the formal study of logic contributes to critical thinking.

I had taught a unit of the sort described earlier in a geometry class. I had emphasized the point that if the major and minor premises of a syllogism are true, the conclusion must also be true; that is, if p→q is true and p is true, then q is true. We had studied a few common fallacies (affirming the consequent or reasoning from the converse and some other frequent errors), and I reminded the students repeatedly of the basic rule. On a test, this exercise appeared:

1. All fish can swim. (Alternatively, if x is a fish, x can swim.)
2. I can swim.
3. ?

Students were asked to draw a conclusion or state why one cannot be drawn. A surprising number drew the conclusion "I am a fish."

Such a result dismays even the most patient, optimistic teachers. Most of these students remembered that odd and counterintuitive things are accepted in logic; it is, after all, somewhat odd that p→q is true if both p and q are false. But I had also emphasized that if 1 and 2 are true, then 3 must also be true, if one uses valid reasoning. No student believed that he or she was actually a fish, and yet many drew this conclusion.

If such results occur widely, we might speculate that the formal study of logic actually impedes logical and/or critical thinking. Surely, before studying p's, q's, and truth tables, these students would not have announced to the world that they were fish! Thus, it not only appears foolish to teach logic on the grounds that it describes how the mind actually works; it also seems at least questionable to suppose that the formal study of logic will improve ordinary logical thinking.

Would I, then, still teach logic in a mathematics class? Yes, if proofs were part of the curriculum, I would do so for two reasons: First, the formal application of logic *is* mathematics or a substantial part of it.[5] If proof is to be emphasized, the rules of deductive inference must be understood.

(Note here that we might choose to teach mathematics without emphasizing proof, and I have not argued that we should emphasize it.) Second, work on logic can add interest to our lessons and provide considerable fun.

I regularly used *Alice in Wonderland*—Martin Gardner's *Annotated Alice*—in geometry classes.[6] This work is loaded with both valid and invalid reasoning, and my students enjoyed analyzing some of the passages. You may recall the scene in which the Pigeon accuses Alice of being a serpent. The Pigeon says, "I suppose you'll be telling me next that you never tasted an egg!"

> "I *have* tasted eggs, certainly," said Alice, who was a very truthful child; "but little girls eat eggs quite as much as serpents do, you know."
>
> "I don't believe it," said the Pigeon; "but if they do, why then they're a kind of serpent: that's all I can say."[7]

Whether the Pigeon is guilty of reasoning from the converse depends on how we formulate her first statement. If her first statement is number 1 of the following two choices, then she is guilty of affirming the consequent or reasoning from the converse. If, however, her first statement is 2, then her reasoning is valid.

> 1. If x is a serpent, then x eats eggs. (or, All serpents eat eggs.)
> 2. Only serpents eat eggs. (or, If x eats eggs, then x is a serpent.)

Notice that although the Pigeon's reasoning is valid when she starts with 2, her conclusion (that little girls are a kind of serpent) is false because the major premise is now false. Students typically have great difficulty in distinguishing between truth and validity. Notice, also, that Scriven's point is well illustrated here. By the time we have uncovered the likely structure of the Pigeon's argument, nothing further is gained by symbolic encoding.

"Lewis Carroll" is, of course, the pseudonym for Charles Dodgson, and Dodgson was a professor and logician. *Alice* is filled with bizarre and tortured reasoning, but sometimes the mad characters correct Alice's faulty thinking, as in this passage:

> [Alice has said in response to an expression she takes to be a riddle, "I believe I can guess that."]

"Do you mean that you think you can find out the answer to it?" said the March Hare.

"Exactly so," said Alice.

"Then you should say what you mean," the March Hare went on.

"I do," Alice hastily replied; "at least—at least I mean what I say— that's the same thing, you know."

"Not the same thing a bit!" said the Hatter. "Why, you might just as well say that 'I see what I eat' is the same thing as 'I eat what I see'!"

"You might just as well say," added the March Hare, "that 'I like what I get' is the same thing as 'I get what I like'!"[8]

Of course, Alice's statement is somewhat different from the others and may trigger an interesting debate in philosophy of language. Could she be right, after all, to say "I mean what I say" is the same thing as "I say what I mean"?[9] I will leave that debate for possible class discussion.

One philosopher of education who has promoted the connection between formal logic and critical thinking is Robert Ennis. In a very influential paper, Ennis defined critical thinking as "the correct assessing of statements."[10] Even though his work, in both its early and later stages, goes well beyond the study and use of formal logic, his early definition certainly implies a concentration on formal logic. *Statements* are expressions that can be labeled unambiguously true or false; by confining his definition to statements, Ennis deliberately left out value judgments. Further, one may suppose that "correct" means valid. Hence, his definition is certainly compatible with the view that logic and critical thinking are, if not synonymous, at least closely related. However, because his work really is not confined to the applications of formal logic, we will consider it in the next section.

Informal Logic

How does informal logic differ from formal logic? Writers differ in their answers to this, and so far as I can determine, there is no consensus forthcoming on a definition of informal logic. It seems reasonable, however, to demarcate formal logic as we did previously; it involves the valid manipulation of symbolic forms. In formal logic, as Suppes wrote, we are concerned with the *form,* not the content, of expressions, and we deal with statements (symbolically represented) that can be judged true or false. All other approaches to logic are "informal." By this standard, Ennis's work after 1962 certainly falls into the informal category.

In his 1979 address to the Philosophy of Education Society, Ennis described his conception of a rational thinker.[11] Rational thinkers, according to Ennis, exhibit certain proficiencies, tendencies, and good habits. Each of these categories is elaborated in some depth. Under proficiencies, Ennis listed observing, inferring, generalizing, conceiving and stating assumptions and alternatives, offering a well-organized or well-formulated line of reasoning, evaluating statements and chains of reasoning, and detecting standard problems. He explicitly rejected formal logic as a method of teaching rational thinking as "too elaborate"; further, he objected that it largely ignores "the most difficult part of applying deductive logic . . . translating in and out of the system."[12]

Although he separated himself from formal logic as the method for teaching critical or rational thinking, his approach is still heavily oriented toward form and process. He believes that students can learn something about thinking in general that will serve them well across domains. He points to mathematics as an analogy. The mathematics learned in math class may indeed be useful in science classes. On the face of it, this seems true, but there are two areas of concern: First, one can only use math in science class if one knows the science well enough to decide when certain mathematical procedures should be applied. Without such knowledge, the mathematics is useless. Similarly, one may have the proficiencies and tendencies described by Ennis and be at a total loss to use them in a foreign domain. Ennis acknowledges this and requires that rational thinkers exercise their skills in familiar fields of experience. This complaint against informal logic strikes me as relatively unimportant because it applies equally to all of our basic skills. For example, no matter how generally articulate we are, we may not be able to express ourselves persuasively or even sensibly in a field entirely alien to us. But second, and more serious, it may not be possible to learn critical thinking effectively outside a particular domain of knowledge. This is the complaint brought against informal logic by John McPeck.[13] We will examine this objection shortly.

Informal logic is, at this time, a powerful aspect of the critical thinking movement, and Ennis is not its only spokesperson. Richard Paul advocates a method similar to Ennis's in several ways: It concentrates on process, it directs students' thought to their own thinking, and it claims to be transferable.[14] Paul contrasts the products of critical thinking to faulty thinking in a list of dichotomies: clear versus unclear, precise versus imprecise, specific versus vague, accurate versus inaccurate, fair versus biased. As critics have pointed out, however, no one of these is necessarily an attribute of critical thinking. A product may be accurate, for example, and still be the product of rote learning. On the other side, a powerful example of critical thinking (so judged by experts) may contain inaccuracies. Further, not all critical thinking is characterized by precision, specificity, or even plausibility. And judgments such as relevance and significance might depend more on the field of application than on the reasoning itself.

Neither Ennis nor Paul claims that critical thinking can be taught in a totally context-free manner. Both recognize that critical thinking must be *about* something. But the context may vary with the bit of informal logic to be taught. For example, if we want to teach students to recognize certain fallacies, we can present cases that contain such fallacies, and it is not necessary that the cases be drawn from the same content field.

The informal logic movement is not the only effort in curriculum and instruction to emphasize skills over content. The elementary science program Science—A Process Approach (SAPA) was also organized in this way.[15] Its designers supposed that such skills as observing, classifying, inferring, and measuring could be taught in isolation from stable content. Children might be asked to classify leaves by shape on one day, blocks or buttons by color on another, pieces of cardboard by shape or size on still another. This approach assumes that there is a cognitive proficiency called "classifying" that is somehow separable from the objects to be classified. In what sense might such a claim be true?

Consider the following. Most of us know what a taxonomy is. We can create outlines, categories, and hierarchies, and we can interpret such devices when other people have created them—sometimes. But no matter how familiar we are with the form of taxonomies, we may be almost helpless faced with Bailey's *Manual of Cultivated Plants*. Unless we understand the vocabulary, are familiar with the parts of plants, and have actually observed at least some of the plants in the field, we may find Bailey's taxonomy indecipherable. Cast this way, the objection sounds like the first one—namely an objection against the transferability claim. But I brushed that one aside, noting that responsible thinkers like Ennis recognize it and take it into account. The complaint here is really more serious; it questions whether there actually are skills that can be plausibly described or learned outside a concrete domain. Does it make sense at all to say "Jimmy knows how to classify"? Can Jimmy display increasing competence in something called "classifying"? My own experience as an amateur gardener struggling with Bailey's *Manual* has increased my skepticism.

An important contribution of Paul's approach to critical thinking is his separation of "weak" sense critical thinking from "strong" sense. People capable of critical thinking in the weak sense exhibit many of the attributes identified by Paul but only in opposition to arguments directed against their own positions. People capable of critical thinking in the strong sense can challenge their own assumptions and arguments. Strong critical thinking is obviously much rarer than weak critical thinking, but it is the form educators profess to prefer and work toward. Closely related to this strong sense of critical thinking are the notions of worldview and habits or attitudes internal to the thinker. A "strong" critical thinker has to see beyond isolated arguments and atomistic bits of those arguments to networks of thought and the worldviews of both opponents and self. In his emphasis on self-knowledge, Paul's position reminds us of that of Socrates.

Paul's introduction of "strong" and "weak" sense critical thinking has been praised for its practical and pedagogical usefulness. Nevertheless, philosophers have raised objections. Harvey Siegel objects to Paul's emphasis on worldviews and concerns internal to thinkers. Siegel launches his objection by summarizing Paul's position:

> First there is the rejection of "atomism" in favor of argument networks or "world views"; relatedly, there is the conception of argument exchange as being a clash of opposing perspectives in which the critical thinker seeks to transcend atomic bits of argument in order to achieve a sympathetic grasp of the underlying world view of her opponent. Second, there is a focus on self-deception, and a concomitant disposition for the critical thinker to "know herself" and understand the psychology of her "rational" commitments. Third, there is a sensitivity to egocentric and sociocentric components of one's own world views, and a commitment to overcome these components and secularize or depersonalize one's world view. Critical exchange thus appears more a matter of dialogue between opposing perspectives than a series of atomistic criticisms

and deflections. It is "global," rather than atomistic, in that it brings to bear a whole host of considerations absent from the atomistic approach. And it is Socratic in its dictate that the critical thinker should "know herself"; that is, should actively seek out and question her deepest beliefs and commitments, and challenge them with all the energy she devotes to the challenging of beliefs and commitments she does not hold.[16]

Siegel does not reject Paul's "strong" sense of critical thinking; rather, he wants to plant it in firmer ground. Tying it to worldviews risks a descent into relativism. After all, a particular worldview may reject critical thinking itself, and in such a case, proponents of critical thinking would use their best arguments futilely. Apparently, Paul and Siegel do not disagree fundamentally on this. Paul sees "relativism" in the application of criteria for critical thinking, not in the criteria themselves; Siegel prefers to eliminate "worldviews" because they introduce the difficulty concerning relativism that Paul then has to explain.[17] A question that should remain for us, as critical and interested listeners, is whether the epistemological relativism implied in Paul's account can be defended without recourse to the usual conception of critical thinking. We will explore that possibility briefly in the last section of this chapter.

Siegel worries, too, about the lack of a public test in "knowing myself" and avoiding egocentric and sociocentric stances. He notes, rightly I think, that observers cannot always tell when an argument or conclusion is defended objectively or egocentrically. Similarly, knowing oneself is an achievement not easily evaluated by others. Siegel wants criteria that apply unambiguously to products (acts and utterances) publicly available. What we need, Siegel says, are *reasons* that can be examined by all. Notice that we may agree with him (as I did) on the difficulties an observer might encounter in assessing whether people know themselves or have avoided egocentric and sociocentric stances and yet *not* agree that this is something to worry about. We might instead accept the indefinite quality of such attributions and yet leave them as guides or ideals for individual, internal inspection. Someone interacting with people who profess such an achievement would have to judge—if judging becomes necessary—not on the basis of an assessment of reasons but on a whole constellation of exchanges, attitudes conveyed through body language, and acts. Commitment to intellectual integrity—even if others fail to credit us for it—is nevertheless something to maintain and cherish. That was the message of Socrates, and it is one way to answer Siegel.

We might note here that Paul is working very much in a Socratic tradition—a tradition that represents the second Plato (not the metaphysical one), a Plato constantly seeking and inviting dialogue. Socrates, like Paul, was not worried about what third-person observers would think. He argued that one has to know oneself in order to exercise virtue. Further, if we abandon the quest for ultimate criteria and certainty, we need not worry so much about relativism as long as we keep the dialogue going. An end to conversation and investigation is more to be feared than divergence of views.

Paul's emphasis on dialogue has been criticized by several philosophers. Siegel, as we have seen, fears the loss of objective criteria by which a worldview itself may be criticized. Mark Weinstein notes that dialectic exchange does not necessarily produce accuracy.[18] Anchoring critical thinking in natural language rather than formal symbolic language will not solve Paul's problem, Weinstein writes, because dialogue in natural language can be used for weak critical thinking as well as strong. Both Siegel and Weinstein admire Paul's stress on intellectual virtues such as intellectual courage and humility, but both see that there may be no foolproof way of detecting their exercise and, more important, of judging their products.

Weinstein briefly explores an alternative to Siegel's quest for epistemological objectivity—a clearly stated public test for all elements of an argument. He notes that Paul's view (in contrast to McPeck's, which we will look at next) reflects "the optimistic liberalism of progressive education; the belief in a unitary political and social discourse, without which democracy loses it rational core."[19] Paul's critical thinking, he notes, is open and available to all. It stands above the specialized discourses of disciplines and allows all well-trained speakers/thinkers to join in social debate. But Paul's view—if he recognizes the way criteria apply differently in different domains (and he does acknowledge this)—seems to lead to McPeck's position that critical thinking is discipline-specific. If Paul denies this, Weinstein speculates, it may lead to something far more radical: "How do 'arguments' made in rap videos fare when subjected to critiques such as Paul's? What is his response to Peter McLaren's insight that 'youth resist the dominant culture at the *level of their bodies*,' thus rendering suspect the sufficiency of discursive thought as the central vehicle for a critical pedagogy?"[20]

We will revisit the possibility of more radical positions later.

McPeck's View of Critical Thinking

McPeck has been best known for his sustained attack on the notion that critical thinking can be taught in some "general" as opposed to domain-specific way. Many philosophers have brushed aside his complaint, arguing that although any specific act of thinking is, of course, an instance of thinking about something, all such acts—thinking itself—might easily be the object of thought.[21] From this perspective, we do indeed need some knowledge about the domain of application, but it also helps to know something about the rules of valid thought, fallacies that are frequently made, and the like. Further, this latter knowledge is useful in getting a quicker grasp of arguments in new domains, and it is essential in tackling everyday problems.

McPeck agrees that it is a laudable educational goal to help students think critically on everyday problems, but he insists that all such thinking, beyond the trivial, manifests itself as an application of one or more of the disciplines.[22] The disciplines, McPeck says, are the fruits of critical thinking in all the problem-domains of human experience; further, they embody what it means to think critically. There is no such thing as thinking critically in general.

If we were to accept McPeck's claims, we would concentrate our educational effort on teaching the disciplines well, and this means teaching not only their accumulated content, but also their epistemology. Students must learn what it means to make a valid mathematical, scientific, or historical argument, and they must learn how to apply such arguments to everyday problems. Students must learn to adopt an attitude of reflective skepticism toward claims in a given field; they also must learn the technical language of the field and the accepted criteria for its use in argumentation.

Critics of McPeck's position often label it "exclusionary." If we accept it, we must logically exclude from any debate all those who have not had adequate training in the discipline needed to discuss and solve a given problem. In contrast, the far more liberal perspectives of Paul, Ennis, and Siegel allow all parties to participate if they accept and meet the generally established criteria of critical thinking. However, McPeck can try to avoid the charge of elitism and exclusion by making the disciplines accessible to all students. This is a move we encountered earlier in a brief mention of Mortimer Adler's *Paideia Proposal*.[23] The charge is not so easily met, however. As we saw in the previous discussion, *requiring* all students to master studies once offered selectively to a relative few can itself be seen as a form of elitism. It may also be judged exclusionary because it excludes studies and pursuits that might be congenial and profitable for many students and forces them to compete in domains of little interest to them.

Another difficulty in McPeck's position is his assumption that everyday problems will yield, if they yield at all, to disciplinary approaches. Many thinkers today believe that there are crucial human problems not easily situated within one discipline. Even if McPeck acknowledges this and calls for multiple perspectives, the difficulty may remain. It is at least conceivable that disciplinary approaches may obstruct the solution of everyday problems, and as several feminists have argued, there are domains of human (largely female) experience that either have been distorted within the disciplines or entirely omitted.[24]

Finally, McPeck claims that "the public schools have been engaged in the business of trying to provide students with the knowledge and understanding contained in their disciplinary networks, concepts, and procedures" because of the power and relevance of the disciplines.[25] This reason certainly has been given for organizing the curriculum around the traditional disciplines. But how good is it as a reason? Is it an example of weak or strong critical thinking?

An Alternative Approach

Although debate over the generalizability of critical thinking skills continues, definitions of critical thinking have tended to converge toward an emphasis on reasonableness, reflection, skepticism, and commitment to use one's capacities for reason and reflection.[26] This is not to say that there are not important philosophical arguments about the definitions, but the important figures in the debate have—as critical thinkers should—listened to one another and modified their views accordingly. Ennis, for example, now defines critical thinking as "reasonable reflective thinking focused on deciding what to believe or do."[27] Within this broader definition, Ennis includes his earlier notion of critical thinking as "the correct assessing of statements." Most writers in the field seem to agree that critical thinking should be useful in the problems of everyday life, that it includes propensities or virtues, and that it is reflective—it is thinking that looks at itself.

Teachers are likely to be eclectic in their choice of strategies. Because their working conditions press them to teach subject matter with conventional disciplinary labels, they may find McPeck's approach practical. Critical thinking, if it can be taught at all, must be taught within each subject. At least two difficulties arise here. First, teachers often do not have the sophistication to teach as McPeck has suggested; they are not often familiar with the epistemic features of the subjects they teach. Thus, what goes on in mathematics or history classes by way of critical thinking may not meet McPeck's standards. Further, even if teachers were to understand the epistemology and standards of thought in a particular discipline, is it reasonable to expect that students could achieve such sophistication in the full range of school studies?

Second, if it were possible for teachers and students to learn the various and distinctively different ways of critical thinking in each of the disciplines, would this carry over in any significant way to critical thinking in everyday life? McPeck says that everyday life is what school subjects are about, and we will revisit that claim in a bit, but most philosophers and educators doubt that this is so. If it is not so, then an approach that addresses the problems of everyday life should be more reasonable.

Approaches that claim a degree of generalizability for critical thinking offer more hope pedagogically. In criticizing McPeck's view, Harvey Siegel says: "McPeck writes that 'knowing what an assumption *is,* and knowing what a valid argument *is* are far from sufficient for enabling people to engage in effective critical thinking.' I agree. *But it helps.* How much it helps is an empirical issue."[28] McPeck has stated more than once that such knowledge may indeed help but not much. Siegel believes that it may help quite a lot. Thus the difference on this issue is one of degree, and teachers might reasonably adopt the position that "it can't hurt" to teach something about assumptions and valid arguments.

A much more important issue for teachers centers on the purposes of critical thinking. Why do we want our students to become critical thinkers? Why should we want them to be "appropriately moved by reasons," as Siegel suggests, or to overcome their egocentric and sociocentric thinking, as Paul suggests?

Jane Roland Martin raises the question whether critical thinking is "an unalloyed good."[29] Confessing that she once thought it was, she now has grave doubts. Too often, she writes, critical thinkers become spectators rather than participants. They allow injustice and pain to continue while they pick apart arguments and make "higher" points out of the tragedies of real people. Martin's reservations raise moral issues and draw our attention to a point I made in my introduction to this text: Dividing philosophical problems into epistemological, ethical, metaphysical, and the like is not always satisfactory. As we have seen, there are clearly conceptual and epistemological components of the debate on critical thinking, but the most basic problems may be moral.

Martin titled the chapter in which she raised moral questions about critical thinking "Critical Thinking for a Humane World." She wants educators and philosophers to think seriously about the point of critical thinking:

> One does not have to attend esoteric lectures or conferences to encounter critical thinking gone awry. One need only look at public policy discussions on nuclear war where hawks and doves alike transform a problem of the fate of life on earth into questions of military technology and strategy about which they exercise their considerable powers of critical thinking. It is to be found also in discussions of medical ethics where expert physicians and philosophers turn real cases of birth and death that bring catastrophe into the lives of family members into abstract questions of "the patient's best interest."[30]

Faced with an objection of this kind, proponents of critical thinking could respond by criticizing the examples Martin has labeled as critical thinking. One might be able to show that the "hawks and doves" referred to are not, by some definition, really engaging in critical thinking. Or one might try to show that a particular argument stands up to the criteria of critical thinking while others do not. But remember Richard Bernstein's comments (quoted in Chapter 4) on the perpetual disagreements among philosophers over what constitutes the best argument. Martin now adds to our uncertainty. Not only can we not tell which argument is "best" by some logical or conceptual standards; neither can we assume that a bit of thinking is morally acceptable simply because it is adequate "critically."

A related problem arises in the application of critical theory to critical literacy. If oppressed people learn to read and listen critically, they may shed their false consciousness and see their true condition. When that happens, they may act to overthrow their oppressors or, at least, to press somehow for a change in their conditions. But often—and this has caused a great sadness for Paulo Freire and others working to overcome oppression—the newly liberated turn right around and behave like the former oppressors. Critical thinking serves a morally admirable purpose in the first stage and an ignoble one in a later stage, or, as advocates of critical thinking might argue, it is simply abandoned in the later stage.

Paul's distinction between weak and strong critical thinking is useful here. We would expect weak critical thinking to produce the oppressed-becomes-oppressor result. Strong critical thinking, in contrast, should turn on itself and condemn behavior that violates its own precepts. But why should one engage in strong critical thinking? We could answer, To be consistent! but real people are rarely motivated by the desire to be consistent outside of domains that require consistency for participation. I could not, for example, work as a mathematician if I reject consistency in my mathematical products. But I certainly could remain a mathematician and behave (and argue) inconsistently in a wide range of situations where mathematics is applied. Logically, we do not need a moral reason for adopting strong critical thinking, but practically most of us do, and without a moral purpose, even the strongest critical thinking may be rudderless.

These observations lead us to a further exploration of Paul's emphasis on dialogue in critical thinking. Recall that Paul claims it is dialogue that helps to move us from our egocentric and sociocentric positions. In dialogue we learn something about worldviews and values different from our own. We are moved out of our own frame of reference into a different one or, perhaps, a larger one of which ours is now just a part. But is such a move always good? Suppose I once believed that arguing from a single case is a mistake (a lapse in critical thinking), but now, as a result of dialogue with people who regularly use this strategy, I think, "Well, maybe it is okay after all."[31] As Siegel pointed out in his criticism of Paul's position, critical thinking is itself now at risk. It has no epistemological anchor.

Paul's best strategy here might be to accept this result. Perhaps what we need is not an epistemological anchor but, as Martin suggests, a moral one. From this perspective, the purpose of strong critical thinking is not only or always to produce the best argument but to connect with others in a way that would make the world demonstrably better—less violent, less cruel, and less insensitive to the pain around us. This does not mean that we should wash out all the epistemological glue that holds our arguments together but, rather, that we should learn to converse in a variety of modes, not all of which are subject to the criteria of argumentation. Looked at this way, critical thinking is bigger than argumentation and different even from argumentation supplemented with intellectual and moral virtues. It becomes the kind of thinking that can "let the Other be," as Derrida puts it, in all his or her otherness.

We can now see the powerful challenge launched by Weinstein's earlier comments: "How do 'arguments' made in rap videos fare when subjected to critiques such as Paul's?" and how do we respond to McClaren's youth who "resist the dominant culture at the level of their bodies"? It may be that Paul can answer those questions if he is willing to move critical thinking beyond argumentation.

McPeck will have a harder time answering such a challenge because he believes that the disciplines now taught in schools are actually relevant to everyday life. The conversation beyond argument that I believe is hinted at in Weinstein's remarks and required by Martin's thinking might be impossible to entertain within the traditional disciplines. McPeck claims (in the same volume that contains Martin's chapter): "School-subject knowledge is not isolated from, nor distinct from, nor irrelevant to everyday life. Rather, that is precisely *what it is about*. . . . The whole point of school-subject knowledge is to enlighten people about their everyday life."[32]

Perhaps McPeck means that school knowledge *should be* as he has described it, but hosts of youth tell us "with their bodies" that it *is* isolated from and irrelevant to everyday life. Further, many feminist, postmodern, and pragmatist philosophers insist that the problem is not one of implementation. There may be something fundamentally wrong with a system that claims sufficiency in a particular constellation of subjects, and something equally wrong with subjects that claim universality when they have been constructed largely out of the experience of a small set of humankind. We will explore these claims more deeply in the following chapters. Here we should simply note that if the critics just mentioned are right, the conversations into which McPeck and others[33] would initiate the young are not the only possible and potentially valuable conversations. They might indeed be part of a sociocentric position that some critical thinking advocates urge us to surpass.

If we were to take seriously an approach to critical thinking aimed at moral purposes, how might we teach? One strategy we might employ is *pedagogical neutrality.* The term as it has been used by Donald Vandenberg refers primarily to the teacher's obligation to respect the rationality of his or her students.[34] Matters that qualify as issues, Vandenberg writes, necessarily have more than one side; otherwise, they would not be issues. Teachers have a special obligation to present all sides and submit the various arguments to the judgment of their students. Most advocates of critical thinking would agree with this, but they would add that teachers should also inform their students about the canons of evaluation accepted in either general or domain-specific critical thinking. In other words, we are to do more than lay out all sides; we must also help students to apply the appropriate criteria.

Insisting on the application of particular criteria may, however, violate pedagogical neutrality. Suppose, for example, that a science teacher presents as fully as possible all those views on creation that are extant in her community and, additionally, some that are historically interesting—perhaps several from cultures not represented in the immediate community. If she follows this presentation with a requirement that all views be judged by particular scientific criteria, is she really respecting the rationality of her students? Is she respecting them fully as individuals? As members of various religious and ethnic groups? There should be no objection to the teaching of criteria appropriate to each view; that is, teachers should, under the requirement of pedagogical neutrality, be encouraged to describe the criteria by which each of the creation stories is defended, but pedagogical neutrality is violated when teachers insist that only one set of criteria may be used for the final evaluation. This insistence, it might well be argued, induces weak critical thinking.

In my view (I have no reason to believe Vandenberg would agree with this), an important purpose of pedagogical neutrality is to contribute to critical thinking in the moral sense. Our aim is not just to present arguments and help students to select the best. Rather, our aim is to help students to understand that flesh-and-blood human beings hold these views—some of which are repulsive—and to give them a sense of both the possibility and tragedy of human encounters. Through critical thinking aimed at human connection, we hope to make it unthinkable for educated human beings to destroy one another or treat one another cruelly in the name of some great principle. Note, however, that even this should be open to discussion. I believe critical thinking should be directed by this sort of moral purpose, but others may disagree with me, and by my own principles, their views should be heard.

Pedagogical neutrality is not the same as moral or intellectual neutrality. I may believe strongly that a particular act is wrong in the moral sense or that a set of statements or an explanation is wrong intellectually, and I may even share my beliefs and reasons with my students and hope they will accept them. But I still have the special moral and intellectual obligation that goes with teaching. I must present views in opposition to my own. There is no final resting place or foundation for my insistence on pedagogical neutrality. I can demonstrate my commitment in the way that I teach. I can argue for pedagogical neutrality. If I believe that I have got the argument right (and that is certainly *one* aim of critical thinking), I will persist in trying to persuade. But more important, as a result of critical thinking morally directed, there are strategies that I will simply never use in my encounters with others, and there are conversations I will enter that bear little resemblance to the arguments currently described as critical thinking.

SUMMARY QUESTIONS

1. What arguments might be advanced for teaching formal logic as an aid to critical thinking? Why else might we teach formal logic?
2. How might formal logic help in teaching and learning mathematics?
3. Why might a normally intelligent student draw the conclusion exhibited in the following invalid syllogism?

   1. If x is a fish, x can swim.
   2. I can swim.
   3. I am a fish.

4. How might a high school math teacher use *Alice in Wonderland?*
5. What are the strengths and weaknesses of Ennis's early definition of critical thinking as "the correct assessing of statements"?
6. Why are certain propensities and intellectual virtues essential to critical thinking?
7. What is the distinction (made by Richard Paul) between weak and strong critical thinking?
8. Are there such things as general thinking skills?

9. In what ways might knowing oneself be important to critical thinking?
10. Is critical thinking necessary for democracy?
11. Is critical thinking in mathematics different from critical thinking in history? How?
12. "How do 'arguments' made in rap videos fare when subjected to critiques such as Paul's?"
13. Are the school subjects directly relevant to everyday life?
14. Why is McPeck's view criticized as elitist and exclusionary?
15. Ennis now defines critical thinking as "reasonable reflective thinking focused on deciding what to believe or do." What might this allow that was precluded by his earlier definition?
16. How much and in what ways is a critical thinker helped by knowing what an assumption is and what a valid argument is?
17. How does critical thinking go awry and serve inhumane purposes? Is such thinking really critical thinking?
18. What does Martin mean when she refers to many critical thinkers as "spectators"?
19. How does pedagogical neutrality differ from moral and intellectual neutrality?

INTRODUCTION TO THE LITERATURE

For a comprehensive introduction to the field and its major debates, see J. B. Baron and Robert J. Sternberg, eds., *Teaching Thinking Skills: Theory and Practice;* Robert Ennis, "Critical Thinking and Subject Specificity: Verification and Needed Research," *Educational Researcher* 18, no. 3 (1989):4–10; John McPeck, *Critical Thinking and Education;* Stephen R. Norris, *The Generalizability of Critical Thinking;* Richard Paul, "Teaching Critical Thinking in the Strong Sense: A Focus on Self-Deception, World Views, and a Dialectical Mode of Analysis," *Informal Logic Newsletter* 4, no. 2 (1982):2–7; Harvey Siegel, *Educating Reason: Rationality, Critical Thinking, and Education.* For recent work on the topic, see Nel Noddings, *Critical Lessons: What Our Schools Should Teach.*

CHAPTER 6

Epistemology and Education

Epistemology is the large and important branch of philosophy that treats questions in the theory of knowledge. There are far too many theories, subtheories, and issues for one brief discussion, but educators need to know something about the traditional problems of epistemology in order to evaluate the material they teach, the methods recommended to them by researchers, and the connection between knowledge and power. Sample questions of interest to educators include these: Should we insist that the material we teach be true, and if so, what do we mean by "true"? How strong are the various (and competing) claims about the methods and results of a particular teaching strategy, say, small-group learning? If it can be shown that certain bodies of knowledge have been presented to an exclusive group of students with the effect that social and cultural power has remained in the hands of a favored few, should we now make this knowledge accessible to all students? Can an *epistemological* argument be made for such a move? Educators also need to know something about epistemology in order to understand the current debate over a view called *constructivism*.

Further, all teachers, qua teacher, are interested in the question, What does it mean to know? When should we credit a student with knowing—when, for example, he or she gives the right answer? (Suppose he or she overheard someone else whisper the answer and, without the slightest notion why the answer is true or even whether it is, gives the "right" answer. Or suppose that after solving a mathematics problem, a student explains what she has done but includes a reason that is incompatible with the others in her explanation.)

We will begin this chapter with a view that has dominated epistemology for centuries, explore its roots in the investigations of Socrates and Plato, and then consider some of the significant ways in which it has developed. As we do so, it will be important to keep in mind that although the basic questions have ancient roots, the great age of epistemology started with Descartes. From his time until now, epistemology has been dominated by the notion of a universal "subject" who variously recalls, receives, or creates knowledge. Much contemporary debate centers on objections to the separation of subject and object and to the nature of this subject as it has been described since the time of Descartes. A second, closely related objection—one raised by both naturalistic philosophers and postmodernists—concerns philosophy's role in the theory of knowledge. From Descartes to Husserl, many philosophers have claimed epistemology as a special, nonempirical domain created and maintained by philosophy. Others, as we shall see, find this claim untenable at best and pernicious at worst.

After the basic background discussion, we will consider the relevance of epistemology for education, and we will conclude the chapter with a critique of constructivism and its influence on contemporary pedagogy and educational research.

Justified True Belief

Socrates begins the discussion of knowledge with his brilliant pupil Theaetetus (in the dialogue of that name)[1] by exploring the possibility that knowledge is perception. The temptation to define knowledge as perception is strong because we do often claim knowledge on the basis of perception. To say "I see it," "I hear it," or "I feel it" is tantamount in many circumstances to saying "I know it." But Socrates and Theaetetus note that we also claim to know things that are not perceived. All of the following are things we might claim to know, but we would not claim to perceive them: If an object is red all over, it cannot be blue all over; a statement (of fact) cannot be true and false at the same time; if p is true and q is true, then p∧q (p and q) is true. Noting that there are truths that the mind knows without the necessary participation of the senses, Socrates and Theaetetus conclude that knowledge cannot be equated with perception. (This Socratic conclusion did not prevent some later philosophers from arguing that observation statements—statements based on perception—are the basic foundation blocks of knowledge.)

Next, Socrates explores the possibility that knowledge is opinion. But surely, Socrates says, we would not credit a person, S, with knowledge if his opinion or belief is false. If S says "I believe 3 + 2 = 6," we would not say S *knows* that 3 + 2 = 6. So false opinion or belief is ruled out. (Again, we will see that some contemporary philosophers are not so sure about this. Some argue that it depends on what S does with the bit of so-called knowledge.)

But even true opinion does not satisfy Socrates. S may believe rightly that the world is round but be entirely unable to give a convincing reason for this belief. Or consider an example that teachers see frequently: S gets the right answer to a math problem but cannot explain or show how he did it. Most teachers refuse credit in such cases. "You must show your work!" is a commandment that all students have heard from their math teachers. We, like Socrates, believe that people must have justification for their claims to knowledge.

It is an interesting question whether Socrates, in this dialogue, represents the Platonic search for certainty or the second Plato extolled by Bernstein and Dewey. Later philosophers certainly picked up the quest for certainty and tried to elaborate an airtight view of knowledge as justified true belief, but Socrates seems to have been warning us that this quest is doomed to failure. Nevertheless, you should hear something about this fascinating project. In summarizing the view that has guided epistemology for centuries, we may write:

S can be said to know that p if and only if
1. S believes that p.
2. p is true.
3. S is justified in (has good reasons for) believing that p.

Even these criteria did not satisfy Socrates, because he saw that to have good reasons or an adequate explanation involves knowledge—the very thing he was trying to define. Nevertheless, this definition of knowledge has been widely accepted, with many variations, as the nearest we can come to saying what it means to "know." As you read more about episte-mology, you will learn that philosophers have argued extensively over all three of Socrates' criteria but especially over the last. What should we de-mand of a "good" reason?

Foundationalism

So far, we have asked what it means for a person, S, to know something, p. But philosophers are not so much interested in individual knowers as they are in the status of knowledge claims. Thus we have to ask under what conditions a claim to knowledge, p, should be granted status as knowledge. Much debate has centered on the reasons offered in claiming p as a bit of knowledge. What does it mean to have a good explanation or good reasons for believing something? Socrates saw that as we offer rea-sons for believing p, we present, in effect, claims to know other proposi-tions—q, r, and s. To defend these claims, we must offer still more reasons until, eventually, we are left with a proposition, say t, for which we can give no further reason. Thus our definition of knowing does not entirely satisfy our initial quest; we cannot justify our belief that t.

To meet the stringent requirements laid down by Socrates, we would have to anchor our chain of beliefs in initial beliefs that are indubitable or self-justified. Such beliefs could be used as a foundation for all knowledge. Philosophers concerned with providing a firm foundation for knowledge *(foundationalists)* have explored two basic ways of doing this. Rational-ists have held that we are justified in halting the chain of reasons when we reach a statement that is self-evident. Such statements include the "truths of reason" that Socrates pointed to in refuting the claim that knowledge can be equated with perception.

Consider an example. Suppose you bump into a friend from your old hometown that you have not visited for years. You talk about neighbors, friends, and old school acquaintances. Your friend tells you that old Mr. Johnson, who always yelled at you for crossing his lawn, is still alive and well. Not only that, but so is Mrs. Warren, your old kindergarten teacher. Now suppose we write:

1. p: Mr. Johnson is alive.
2. q: Mrs. Warren is alive.

You might well demand proof for either or both of these statements, but if a satisfactory demonstration of the truth of each is available, you would not hesitate to conclude:

3. p∧q: Mr. Johnson is alive and Mrs. Warren is alive.

For this statement, no further reason need be given. If p is true and q is true, then (p and q) is true. Similarly, if we have established that p is true, then, in Aristotelian logic, ~p cannot also be true. Many philosophers have also included the basic statements of arithmetic as well as those of logic in the set of self-evident truths, but there has been lively controversy over the nature of mathematical truth—especially when we get beyond arithmetic.

If we proceed this way in trying to establish a foundation of certainty for knowledge, we may have a hard time in saying anything about the world outside our minds. You may yourself have objected that p∧q tells us nothing we did not already know when we were convinced of the truth of p and q separately. What amazed you, in the conversation with your old friend, was p itself (or q). "What?" you might have said, "Mr. Johnson is still alive? Why, he looked about one hundred, when I was five! I don't believe it." What could your friend do to convince you?

Empiricist foundationalism seeks certainty through our senses. Your friend might say, "I kid you not. I saw him myself just yesterday." That might be enough for you, but perhaps not. You might reasonably say, "You must be mistaken. I will have to see for myself." And so you drop everything and go off to see the alleged Mr. Johnson yourself. Upon encountering the old man, you might conclude: I see Mr. Johnson.

This kind of statement—a report of observation in the present tense—is so basic that hardly any of us would ask for further evidence. But clearly we cannot establish absolute certainty this way either. First, when you turn away from Mr. Johnson, you have to give a past-tense report: I *saw* Mr. Johnson. This is still quite powerful (especially to you, the one reporting), but it is neither unassailable nor incorrigible. Others may doubt your report as you did that of your friend. They would be justified in expressing doubt; we now have considerable evidence that eyewitness reports are notoriously unreliable.

Second, you might doubt your own observation. Indeed, we sometimes say, "I couldn't believe my eyes!" Perhaps this old man who looks like Mr.

Johnson and apparently lives in his house is not, after all, Mr. Johnson. Maybe it is his younger brother or an impostor. This is exactly the sort of challenge that a rationalist might fling at the empiricist. You cannot, ultimately, depend on your senses. You have to find something absolutely reliable, something that cannot possibly be doubted.

It was this kind of quest that led Descartes to his famous cogito: I think; therefore, I exist. One thing Descartes could not doubt was that he was thinking; the very act of doubting proved the presence of thought. But Descartes had to rely on the existence of God (for which he offered two proofs) and the assumption that God is not a deceiver to justify the content of his thought. You might try the Cartesian exercise on the case of Mr. Johnson. What could you do to be absolutely sure that the old man you see is Mr. Johnson? How could you be sure that you are not the victim of an elaborate hoax? How, for that matter, could you be sure that you are not dreaming?

Many philosophers today have given up the search for absolute truth or certainty, but thinkers in all fields still rely heavily on a combination of observation statements and self-evident truths of reason to back their claims to knowledge.[2] To answer the objection raised against one-person observation reports, scientists demand replicability; that is, they insist that all experimenters or observers should be able to "see the same thing" under the same conditions. In law, when we have pushed things back to undisputed matters of fact and valid logic, we say that we have proved our case. And in everyday life, we support our arguments in a similar way; "I saw it myself" and "I heard it myself" are still often taken to be conclusive *if* we judge the speaker to be reliable (but this caveat raises another interesting set of questions to which we will return).

Some philosophers also argue for a form of "fallible foundationalism." They admit that the search for absolutely certain initial beliefs is hopeless, but they use probability theory to argue for a degree of certainty.[3] This approach to the theory of knowledge is compatible with other, nonfoundational approaches. It is worth pointing out that mathematical systems also start with foundations that are chosen but not claimed as certainties; the foundations serve as carefully identified starting points. Before looking more closely at nonfoundational views, however, we need to consider what is meant by *truth*. If an adequate account of knowledge deals with true statements, what are the criteria of truth?

Truth

Intuitively, most of us have no difficulty agreeing with Socrates that we would not credit someone, S, with knowing that p, if p is false, and we discard items from our various knowledge bases when they are shown to be false. But what does it mean for p to be true, and how is its truth established? Here we may worry that knowledge—the very thing we are trying to define—is again implicated, for if p is true, does not that imply that someone knows that it is? Many philosophers and theologians have accepted a view that construes every statement or belief about objects and events—past, present, and future—as prerecorded in the mind of God. Hence, there are truths independent of the human mind, and people must discover them. When people do discover these truths and can justify their beliefs, they may properly lay claim to knowledge. Knowledge is that subset of truth that has been acquired by human investigators.

You may recall from Chapter 2 Dewey's view that knowledge is bigger than truth. For Dewey, all statements or beliefs that guide inquiry are to be regarded as knowledge. Not all such statements will survive the tests of inquiry, but those that do we may call "true." (Dewey preferred to say of such statements that they have "warranted assertability.") We will return to Dewey's views and also consider others that reject the notion of fixed and absolute truth in a bit, but for the moment I draw it to your attention for contrast.

Philosophers do not have to regard truth (the set of all true statements and beliefs) as existing in the mind of God in order to adopt a view of truth as "out there," outside the minds of human beings. However, without an omniscient mind to contain truths, philosophers must refer to states of affairs—configurations of objects and events. These, we can argue, are as they are, and true statements correspond to them; this is the basic contention of *correspondence* theories of truth. A true sentence, in this view, "corresponds with the facts." (This intuitively simple claim has led to an enormous body of philosophical thought involving, among other things, the meaning of "fact." Is a fact to be identified with a "state of affairs," with a belief, with a sentence itself, or with something entirely different?)

Let's just explore the intuitively plausible claim made by the correspondence theory of truth. Surely, this is what most of us have in mind when we use the words *true* and *truth* in everyday talk. When we say "The Giants won yesterday," or "It is raining," our statements are true if the Giants *did* win yesterday and it is actually raining. In practice, everyone accepts this view of truth at what might be called the "local" level.

But can we describe all truth this way? Suppose someone says, "The battle of Actium was fought in 31 B.C." Theoretically, this is either true or false, and, a correspondence theorist would argue, it is true or false according to whether or not the alleged event actually took place in the year 31 B.C. Practically, however, there is no way to check the statement against an actual state of affairs. In our example of the Giants winning yesterday, we have many living eyewitnesses and fresh records to justify our belief. Events farther away in time and space have to be confirmed in a similar way; however, the correspondence may be difficult to establish. Historians may produce a chain of documents that purport to do this, but often it is impossible. Then historians must see how the statement fits with others that have been firmly established. Indeed, many historical "facts" have been revised because, in their initial form, they contradicted a body of accepted beliefs. Theories that evaluate truth (or knowledge) in this way are called *coherence* theories.

Notice, however, that a correspondence theorist need not be greatly troubled by this example. She could respond by asking how the set of accepted beliefs was established. Surely the most secure beliefs in the set were established by correspondence with the facts. Thus, she would argue, the use of coherence as a test for the acceptance of one statement is just a method that depends ultimately on the correspondence of statements with actual objects and events that are independent of human minds.

But consider a statement of this sort: p: 2 + 3 = 5. Mathematical signs—numerals, for example—do not correspond to anything in the world of objects and events, and when they do, as in 2 cups of water + 3 cups of sugar, p is not always true. If 2 and 3 point to objects in the real world (objects accessible to our senses), p requires an interpretation. In mathematics, numerals signify numbers, and numbers are not elements or components in states of affairs. Platonism handles this problem by positing a real world of forms to which our minds have access through intuition. Numbers, lines, triangles, and other geometric figures exist as pure forms in this special world. But a theorist who insists on matching sentences and parts of sentences to objects in the observable world has a difficult task.

First, as we have seen, observation statements lose much of their power when they must be cast in the past tense; second, much of our most powerful language points not to states of affairs but to other language; and third, what we observe—what we take to be objects and states of affairs—seems to depend heavily on the theories and language we use.

For the reasons just discussed, mathematicians usually rely on coherence as the test of truth. In the strongest possible sense, every statement in a mathematical system is implied by some irreducible set of initial statements or axioms. Each statement is true if it can be derived validly from the axioms and if the axioms are accepted as true. But coherence cannot give us general criteria for truth because a different axiom system will yield different "truths." Thus, mathematicians usually speak of consistency and confine their claims to a particular axiom system.

In everyday life, as I have noted, we regularly use informal notions of correspondence and coherence to justify our claims to knowledge. But philosophers have sought a foundation for *all* knowledge, and the establishment of a theory of truth has been fundamental in this quest. If one theory of truth cannot cover all cases, then the hope for a theory of knowledge that describes all cases of knowing is considerably weakened.

Some philosophers today have suggested that we abandon the traditional questions of epistemology. For them, truth is described "locally" or as a function of power or as an artifact of language having no meaningful reference to anything outside language. In all of these radical views, however, it is still possible to speak of truth-telling and lying. One can honestly report a local happening or deliberately deceive listeners. One can convey information that will be useful to others or deliberately misinform or underinform to keep them helpless and dependent. One can use language that conforms to local conventions or language that defies such conventions and makes it more difficult for listeners to construct meaning. The virtue of truth-telling does not disappear when the concept of truth is confined to "local" truth.

It is important to recognize, however, that there is now a strong trend away from the rejection of truth and of talking about "local" truth. As we saw in Chapter 4, some philosophers have rejected the notion of what they refer to as "capital-T" truth along with all attempts to universalize or create "grand narratives." Although those who reject universal truths should be credited with positive social/ethical motives, rejection of the traditional notion of truth may be too heavy a price to pay, and it certainly leads to philosophical difficulties.[4]

Nonfoundational Theories of Knowledge

Some philosophers have retained an interest in epistemology even though they have given up the quest for absolute truth or even for one theory that will adequately describe truth in all domains of knowledge. As we have seen, Dewey preferred to speak of warranted assertions rather than truth. Karl Popper refers to truth as a "regulative ideal"—something unattainable toward which we nevertheless strive.[5] From this perspective, we can never establish the absolute certainty of scientific statements, but we can show that some are false. As we advance various conjectures and they are falsified, we discard or revise them and, thus, get closer to the "truth." Because he believes that continuous conjecture, test, and refutation are the best we can do (a hypothesis is never totally confirmed, although it may resist falsification on any given try), Popper insists that all scientific hypotheses and theories be formulated in a way that makes it clear how they might, in principle, be falsified.

Another alternative to foundationalism is naturalism, of which Dewey is a prominent representative, and one branch of naturalism is called *externalism,* a doctrine that substitutes a historical account of how knowledge claims develop in place of the traditional demand for justification. If we follow this line of thinking, we are concerned with what causes or brings about a particular belief, and if the right relation exists between a belief and its cause, we acknowledge the move from belief to knowledge. Again, as in empiricism, perception plays a powerful role. If I believe that President Bush was on the Stanford campus yesterday because I saw him there, I *know* he was there. The difference may seem subtle, but actually it is substantial. In supporting my claim, I do not give a chain of reasons culminating in a basic statement that is considered infallible or incorrigible. I simply tell how my claim developed. In everyday pedagogical language, I tell "how I got it." The view of science that emerges from an externalist position is rich in social interaction, political maneuvering, failed attempts to make criticisms stick, and energetic defenses of degenerating paradigms.

The advantage of this naturalistic approach is obvious. My account (even if I cannot give it myself) will be convincing if it satisfies hearers in a particular domain, and the entire process can be held up for public scrutiny. We do not posit a narrow class of self-evident beginnings to which all claims must be referred. I may even be credited with knowledge if I claim *that p* on the basis of having heard it from an authority, say A. Here, of course, we are depending on the belief that A can give a convincing account of how *she* arrived at p.

The shift from justification to a historical or generative account directs our attention away from knowledge claims themselves to knowers. We now want to ask how knowers have arrived at their claims to knowledge. We examine a history of conjecture, test, challenge, revision, and acceptance as we consider the strength of a claim. The line between epistemology and psychology becomes blurred, and we can no longer study knowledge without studying the knower.[6]

Here you may wonder if the shift is as dramatic as I suggest. After all, Socrates was interested in knowers in the sense that he wanted to evaluate their claims to knowledge. But notice that Socrates was concerned with an abstract knower, not a particular person or set of persons, and he was not interested in the process so much as the underlying reasons for accepting or rejecting a claim. Similarly, modern epistemology from the time of Descartes has posited a unitary, universal, and faceless knower whose claims to knowledge are to be evaluated by standard criteria. The actual human process of knowing—both individual and collective—has been largely ignored. Thus the shift we are discussing has huge political and social ramifications.

Let's return for a moment to the case in which I claim to know something because A told me so. A reasonable listener will want to know something about A. If I am making a geological claim, you are more likely to accept what I say if (1) A is a geologist and (2) you consider me to be trustworthy than if (1) A is a lawyer and (2) you know that my imagination tends to run away at times. Both conditions—A's status and my reputation—involve the trustworthiness of the people involved. A's status as a geologist gives him or her prima facie trustworthiness when A speaks on matters of geology. My trustworthiness must be established through some history of reliable interaction.

You may be thinking now that this naturalistic description fits most of what goes on in schools. Students make claims to knowledge on the basis of what they have learned from reliable sources. In the case of mathematical knowledge, they are more often asked "how they got it" than why their answers are true, and if they can give an account using legitimate operations, we credit them with knowledge.

A foundationalist might agree that ordinary people in everyday circumstances do indeed establish their claims to knowledge in just the way naturalistic philosophers describe. But they might insist that, ultimately, the authority, A, must give an account that meets the criteria of justification. A, being the final court of appeal so to speak, cannot simply give a historical account. We cannot settle that basic argument here, but some externalists attempt to reconcile the two positions by arguing that a causal account of belief may in fact be considered as justification.[7]

Dewey's naturalism is different. As a form of naturalism, it (like externalism) refuses to go beyond human experience in seeking and formulating its explanations. But Dewey was concerned with the consequences of our beliefs, not their causes or genesis. In his framework, a statement p may appropriately be called knowledge if it is useful in inquiry. This view, too, fits our commonsense attitudes toward both science and everyday investigations. We are quite sure, for example, that much of what scientists "know" today will some day be overturned, but we still refer to what is currently used as *knowledge*. The more p has been tested and used successfully, Dewey said, the greater is our warrant for asserting it. Notice that Dewey's is a forward-looking epistemology; it emphasizes verification in use rather than justification through reasons referring to antecedent conditions.[8]

Another form of nonfoundational epistemology with which educators should be familiar comes to us through Jean Piaget. He, too, insisted that we cannot study knowledge without studying knowers. Piaget's *genetic epistemology* combines features of both rationalism and empiricism. In agreement with rationalists, Piaget posited mechanisms of mind that make knowledge possible; in agreement with empiricists, he insisted that organisms must test their knowing in the world of sensory experience and that epistemologists must test theirs similarly. This requirement sets Piaget apart from traditional epistemologists, most of whom accept a sharp separation of epistemology from psychology. In his assumption that epistemology must concentrate on accounts of knowing, Piaget's is a naturalistic epistemology. However, some naturalists, D. C. Phillips among them, are disturbed by Piaget's reliance on abstract and nonobservable mechanisms of mind—the cognitive structures posited to account for his developmental stages.[9] Why not, they argue, concentrate on observable behavior and its products? Why insist on nonobservable structures of mind like those associated with Piaget's sensorimotor, preoperational, concrete operational, and formal operational stages?

An important answer to objections of this kind is that theoretical structures can be powerful in directing empirical research. Piaget's developmental theory has produced a host of hypotheses and a prominent school of thought in psychology. Even so, critics argue, his cognitive structures are not just invisible to the naked eye (as electrons are, for example) but in principle nonobservable. Piaget used a biological metaphor for "organic" structures that cannot be located in the human organism.[10] Piaget's defenders claim, however, that the *workings* of these structures can be observed in behavior and that explanation is greatly facilitated by positing their existence.

Piaget's epistemology is one form of constructivism—a position enormously popular in education today. Piaget himself traced his constructivist roots to Immanuel Kant, who, Piaget said, first emphasized the interaction of cognitive mechanisms with the world in constructing knowledge. Kant's position was a rejection of two important earlier positions—the innate ideas characteristic of rationalism and a form of passive reception of sensory material from the external world characteristic of early empiricism. Kant claimed instead that the innate structures of mind interact with the world; both the world and mind itself limit the forms of human experience. We can never know the world-in-itself, only the world as it is constructed in our experience. Piaget, too, believed that the structures of mind are instrumental in knowing, but he claimed that Kant made a mistake by describing the structures of mind as static and entirely given at the outset:

> The construction characteristic of the epistemological subject, however rich it is in the Kantian perspective, is still too poor, since it is completely given at the start. On the other hand, a dialectical construction, as seen in the history of science and in the experimental facts brought to light by studies on mental development, seems to show the living reality. It enables us to attribute to the epistemological subject a much richer constructivity, although ending with the same characteristics of rational

necessity and the structuring of experience, as those which Kant called for to guarantee his concept of the *a priori*.[11]

Piaget was interested in both the historical development of knowledge and the developmental growth of individuals. His epistemology is *genetic* in the sense that it claims a parallel between the development of knowledge in the human race and the development exhibited in individuals. It is *constructivist* in the sense that it claims that all knowledge (and perception itself) is constructed, neither merely received nor innate. We will return to Piaget's constructivism in our later discussion of constructivism in education.

It may be useful now to review the differences among the epistemological views we have looked at so far. When Socrates asked about the conditions under which we would credit a person with knowledge, he was not particularly interested in how a person comes to knowledge; that is, he was concerned not with the knower so much as knowledge itself. The tradition of justified true belief sought criteria by which statements could be sorted into those accepted into the body of human knowledge and those to be rejected or set aside for further investigation. Even some philosophers leaning toward naturalism have preferred to separate the logic of discovery (how we come to knowledge) from the logic of justification or verification. Most of these would also separate psychology (how we learn, how we know) from epistemology (the nonempirical study of knowledge and how it is constituted).

The study of justified true belief is fascinating in itself. Some philosophers sought ultimate justification in self-evident truths of reason; others sought it in basic observation statements. Some defined truth as correspondence with the facts; some defined it as coherence with a body of accepted beliefs. Some rejected the notion of truth as a criterion of knowledge, declaring it to be, at best, an ideal—something unattainable. Others attacked the notion of justification, suggesting that a historical or developmental account is the best we can do, and still others recommended that we look forward to the usefulness of our conjectures rather than backward to their roots. In the last two cases, philosophical interest shifted from knowledge as a set of statements and theories to knowers and the process of knowing.

The move to emphasize knowing and knowers is associated with the "naturalization" of epistemology. After giving up the quest for certainty, some epistemologists join psychologists, historians, sociologists, and anthropologists in studying the actual growth of knowledge in individuals, disciplinary domains, and the human race generally.

Having mentioned knowledge in "the human race generally," I must now discuss a set of views even more radical than those that recommend collapsing the line between epistemology and psychology. Postmodernists suggest that we cannot study "knowledge in general" in any meaningful way. Knowledge is so thoroughly contaminated with social and political power that we simply must concentrate on the sociology of knowledge. From this perspective, it is chasing a will-o'-the-wisp to seek foundations for knowledge, and even accounts of where knowledge came from or where it leads are incomplete if the ideological context is not described. Knowledge is established by power, not by justification in the neutral sense that Socrates envisioned.[12] However, as noted earlier, this claim probably goes too far. How is social power involved in claiming that 2 + 3 = 5, or that Mumbai received 37 inches of rain on one day in 2005, or that human beings cannot leap over tall buildings in a single bound?

Feminists, too, have launched strong critiques of traditional epistemology. Some, working from the perspective of critical theory, argue that women and other oppressed groups are in a privileged position with respect to their own oppression. Feminist "standpoint epistemologists" claim that knowledge of women's condition constructed from the standpoint of women has an authenticity that so-called objective knowledge can never achieve. These theorists reject claims to universal knowledge and objectivity, especially in the domain of social knowledge, and argue that since bias itself is unavoidable, the only way to avoid *pernicious* bias is to include the views of all interested parties in our accounts and arguments. In all matters involving oppressed groups, the views of the oppressed groups themselves have special weight.[13] Notice, however, that such claims suggest that we should describe knowledge and truth differently as we move from one domain to another. Social knowledge may rightly be subject to different criteria than mathematical knowledge.

Feminist theorists, whose work we will examine again in a later chapter, reject traditional epistemology (in both rationalist and empiricist forms) not only because they believe it is intellectually inadequate but, even more strongly, because it has destructive political effects. Even when it has been cast in liberatory language—that of the free individual and the constituting subject—it has been used, they say, to maintain the privilege of white men. Naomi Scheman writes: "Ironically, by the very moves that were meant to ensure universal enfranchisement, the epistemology that has grounded modern science and liberal politics not only has provided the means for excluding, for most of its history, most of the human race but also has constructed, for those it authorizes, a normative paranoia."[14]

Scheman argues that an epistemological orientation that seeks one right view through one right method induces a form of madness, the key characteristic of which is the delusion that one's own views and conclusions must necessarily be those of every other rational thinker. Those who do not conform to the standard view and/or have not learned the right method are excluded. It seems, of course, that they have excluded themselves by choice, ignorance, or recalcitrance. But in reality, Scheman says, their authentic and possibly liberatory views are excluded by the very epistemology that advertises itself as rational and universal. Other feminist philosophers argue, in partial disagreement with Scheman, that each version of traditional epistemology must be examined for its own intellectual adequacy and that it is, in any case, a mistake to condemn the whole tradition for the political and social uses to which it has been put.[15]

The future of epistemology is not at all clear. Sophisticated work continues along traditional lines, but the "naturalized" approach seems to have many adherents. Some feminists and postmodernists have acknowledged considerable sympathy for the naturalistic orientation, but others want to move beyond epistemology entirely. Many critical theorists, feminists, postmodernists, and naturalists would prefer to give up epistemology completely and engage in hermeneutics. From this perspective we can continue the search for meaning, employ local truth, and claim local knowledge, but we reject the basic project of epistemology.

Epistemology and Education

Teachers do not usually share the epistemologists' concerns about the foundations of knowledge, but there are several reasons why teachers should be concerned with epistemology. First, teachers need to make decisions about the status of material they teach: Is it true? Does it matter whether it is true? Second, teachers need to evaluate the "knowledge" that comes to them from educational research. Third, teachers must decide whether the knowledge long reserved for a few students should or can be made accessible to all. These problems are, once again, huge, and we cannot do more than sample them here. I will give an example in each category, and readers can follow up with further reading and discussion.

We generally assume that the material we teach, if not actually verified as true, is at least accepted by a scholarly community as not false. We recognize that today's scientific knowledge may be falsified or revised in the future, but we do not intentionally transmit to our students material that is false or misleading. Of course, textbooks and teachers often fail to inform students about the tentative nature of much that appears in the curriculum, and both are guilty of omissions and various biases in their presentations. For example, in recent years, we have become aware of earlier dogmatic claims about Columbus's "discovery" of America, the cruel treatment of indigenous peoples by the European "discoverers," and the general neglect of historical contributions made by subordinated groups. But for all our bias and insensitivity, we do not defend the practice of teaching what we know to be false.

Educators rarely make explicit statements that reject the importance of truth. More often, doubtful or biased material is defended as true, and quite frequently the form or source of proposed material is considered more important than its likely usefulness in capturing students' interest. Some social studies educators, for example, recommend that we identify and utilize only substantial knowledge in constructing a curriculum.[16] By this, they mean that we should use material already gathered under the rubric of a discipline—material authoritatively endorsed as knowledge. But here, the objections of feminists and critical theorists are important. Power does play a role in establishing the content of a discipline and, although we may avoid outright falsehoods by clinging to widely accepted material, we may also fail to tell the whole truth. Perspectives are often lost. As Stephen Thornton points out, an alternative is to build the curriculum around significant problems that require students to formulate questions, gather information, discuss alternatives, and make decisions.[17] Differences in educators' beliefs about knowledge are clearly illustrated in these choices.

The debate between those who insist that knowledge is best described and transmitted through the disciplines and those (like Dewey) who claim that knowledge must be described in terms of its effects or usefulness reached its heights in the 1960s and 1970s. Philosophers and curricular-ists made strong arguments for arranging subject matter according to the "structure of the disciplines," and many now-classic pieces of analytical philosophy were produced. A host of issues arose: Is there a structure of every discipline? What is a discipline? If there is a structure (or several structures) of a discipline, does this dictate the best arrangement for a cur-riculum? How are cognitive structures related to structures of the disci-plines? Do the disciplines as they now exist represent all of human knowledge or even its most important component?[18] This debate still rages today, as we saw in the discussion of Adler's *Paideia Proposal* and of McPeck's view of critical thinking.

In addition to concerns about the material they teach, educators should also be interested in the products of educational research on pedagogy. Since the mid-1980s, much work has been done on small-group and co-operative learning. The topic has become so important that some states have even mandated (or strongly recommended) the use of small-group learning in the standard subjects. How can teachers sort through and eval-uate the host of results and recommendations made by researchers?

It is one task of philosophy of education to analyze the concepts used in research and to raise questions about its premises and conclusions. In my work, even though I am enthusiastic about students working together and learning from one another, I have raised several questions about the specific recommendations on small-group learning that are so popular today.[19] For example, must all groups be heterogeneous, or are there still uses for ability groupings? What kinds of tasks are suitable for heteroge-neous groups? For homogeneous groups? What is the relation between in-dividual and group learning? Should groups remain intact or be regularly reconstituted? Why? What goals are sought through group work (cogni-tive, moral, affective)? How are they best met? What is the role of teach-ers in facilitating small-group work?

It is often hard for teachers to resist the latest "findings" of educational research, and certainly an open and experimental attitude should be en-couraged, but teachers should ask the hard questions we have been dis-cussing in this chapter: Do the researchers' claims correspond to what we regularly observe in schools? Do their premises, methods, and conclusions hang together in a convincing way, or are there contradictions in their ac-counts? Are their accounts authoritative, and who should count as an authority in this particular area? (For example, well-trained empirical researchers sometimes know very little about the subject—say, mathematics—that their "subjects" are studying. This may or may not be a problem, but in some cases it is clearly something to be concerned about.) How did the researchers come to their problem? Is it part of a well-established program with a history, or is it merely ad hoc? What difficulties do they report? Is there an obvious ideological bias in the work? Is any bias honestly disclosed? Does the work serve the interests of researchers better than those of the participants or targets of research?

Teachers also need to be aware of debates that arise over knowledge as cultural capital.[20] It seems indisputable that certain forms of knowledge—the subjects usually associated with college preparation—have been used to exclude large numbers of people from various material goods. Recognizing this, some theorists have recommended that all students should have access to these privileged forms of knowledge. But notice that this is an ethical argument; it has to do with social justice, not the epistemological adequacy of the material. This is the kind of problem I warned about in the introduction—one for which this text's organization is not entirely satisfactory.

However, it is enlightening to look at the issue from an epistemological perspective. What makes algebra, geometry, and Shakespeare more adequate as school subjects than carpentry and machine work? One could argue that college preparatory mathematics and literature are superior to practical and problem-oriented curricula because they are formally organized and legitimated by authorities in the disciplines. But this argument really will not do. In order to accommodate the mass of students now forced to take college preparatory mathematics, textbooks and teachers have to present material that is, from an epistemological perspective, inadequate. Often the axiomatic nature of mathematics is not discussed at all, and even in geometry, proof has been greatly reduced. Logical connections are not made, and it is not unusual for students to complete three or four years of college preparatory mathematics with little or no sense of the real importance of the great theorems and ideas. Thus we cannot claim epistemological superiority—or even adequacy—for the disciplines as they are now taught in schools.

In contrast, many courses in carpentry, mechanics, retail selling, cooking, hair care, and television repair are both well organized and adequate with respect to the knowledge required in actual work. From the perspective of traditional epistemology, we could make a strong argument that the best practical courses are epistemologically superior (that is, better grounded in reliable knowledge) to the weak mathematics courses widely offered.[21]

But remember that there are epistemological views outside the tradition of justified true belief. If we argue that knowledge is both a source and tool of power, it is reasonable to recommend that all students have access to the knowledge once reserved for a few. The difficulty here is that such recommendations are too simplistic. First, if the knowledge associated with privilege is just that—knowledge with an elitist stamp of approval on it—then members of the dominant group are likely to shift the locus of their power to something else. After all, it is claimed that the knowledge is important as capital, not as knowledge in the epistemological sense. Therefore, it does not really matter whether people have this particular knowledge; what matters is that what they acquire is recognized as important. Distributing elite knowledge more justly will not in itself effect the redistribution of a society's material goods, and the effort may well act against redistribution by causing (1) a redefinition of elite knowledge, (2) deprivation of knowledge that could be genuinely useful to oppressed groups, and (3) a widespread sense that society has "tried" and that the failure of groups who must do the ill-paid work of society is their own fault.[22]

This topic is of such current importance that we will return to it in the chapter on social and political philosophy. For now it may be useful to reflect on the epistemological issues and views discussed in this chapter and ask yourself whether they help in analyzing the problems of access to knowledge. Does it matter whether the material students learn is epistemologically adequate in the traditional sense? Does it matter whether the material is adequate in the Deweyan sense? Does it matter whether it is adequate in the postmodern or critical theory sense?

Constructivism

Constructivism—variously described as a philosophy, an epistemology, a cognitive position, or a pedagogical orientation—currently dominates mathematics and science education.[23] One of its basic premises is that all knowledge is constructed; knowledge is not the result of passive reception. This premise is common to all forms of constructivism and is also a basic tenet of cognitive psychology. Few scholars today would reject the notion that knowers actively construct their own knowledge. A question does arise, as we shall see, as to whether every knower constructs his or her knowledge in an entirely idiosyncratic way or, of necessity, uses a cognitive machinery common to all human subjects. But the cognitive premise is not the one that brings forth the strongest objections. It is the description of constructivism as an epistemology that invites attack.

Constructivists in education trace their roots, as we have seen, to Piaget. His version of constructivism sought to identify the structures of mind underlying cognitive behaviors characteristic of each stage of mental development. Piaget described an abstract "epistemological subject"—a structure resembling a machine program that can account for the cognitive behaviors we observe. His work was structuralist as well as constructivist. He related the structures of mind to abstract structures of mathematics, biological structures to cognitive structures, and structures of the intellectual development of the race to those of individuals.

His work appealed to many educators who believe that children must be active in their own learning. Educators began to distinguish "developmental learning" from "rote learning," the former being described as active and making a lasting difference in how students approach problems and new situations, the latter described as passive, temporary, and useless for further learning. Notice that in such a construal, there is already a theoretical contradiction: If *all* cognition (and even perception) is active, then even rote learning must be active. It, too, must represent some kind of construction. Today's constructivists are careful to distinguish between weak and strong constructions.

Constructivist teachers deemphasize lecturing and telling and encourage instead the active engagement of students in establishing and pursuing their own learning objectives. The move away from lecturing and telling cannot be defended on the grounds that they encourage passive learning, for the reason mentioned previously. But it can be defended on the grounds that observably active learning is "stronger" and that teachers need to know what and how students are thinking in order to facilitate their learning. Thus constructivist teachers often use methods adapted from Piaget's "clinical method." They begin by telling students, "Let me hear you think," and then follow up with prompts, challenges, variations on the initial problem, and questions about the general usefulness of the methods students have chosen.[24]

Objections to Piaget's constructivism have been raised both inside and outside the constructivist camp. We will consider those from the inside first and then examine those raised to the most popular recent versions of constructivism. Many educators sympathetic to constructivism have criticized Piaget's work for concentrating too heavily on the individual child's interactions with objects. These educators point out that most of us learn more from one another than from the direct manipulation of objects. Through interaction with others, we learn the basic questions of reflective inquiry: How did I arrive at this result? Does it work? What is it useful for? How can I be sure? How can I explain it to others? Are there viable alternatives? As others put such questions and challenges to us, we internalize their questions and develop the habit of asking them of ourselves. Further, we can complete many tasks with the help of others that we are, at first, unable to complete on our own. Critics of Piaget who feel that he neglected the social aspects of learning often draw heavily on Vygotsky, and many contemporary constructivists refer to this Vygotskian adaptation as "social constructivism."[25]

Radical constructivism departs even further from Piaget. It deemphasizes the epistemological subject and places the individual cognizing subject at the center of all construction of knowledge. Gerald Goldin remarks on this departure:

> It is interesting to note that in developing and arguing for the above ideas [that knowledge is constructed individually and that we can never conclude that two people have the same knowledge], radical constructivists are not in particularly close agreement with Piaget, from whom they trace their lineage. Piaget not only recognized "logical necessity," but also accorded an important role to "structure" apart from idiosyncratic construction by individuals.[26]

Basically, Goldin and other critics of radical constructivism object to the fact that, on the one hand, radical constructivists claim to take a postepistemological stance and, on the other hand, continue to make statements that sound epistemological. The key thesis to which objections are raised may be stated this way: "Coming to know is an adaptive process that organizes one's experiential world; it does not discover an independent, preexisting world outside the mind of the knower."[27] Many cognitive scientists and philosophers would agree with this statement if it were modified to acknowledge *some* role for an "independent" world. There is considerable disagreement over what Piaget believed on this. Glasersfeld, for example, says that when Piaget used the word *object,* he meant the object as constructed by human cognition so that when he said, "The object allows itself to be treated," he was already referring to an object of cognition.[28] I do not agree. It seems to me that Piaget accepted the distinction between the object itself and what we can know about it. For Piaget, knowers are constrained by both the general structures of mind we all possess and by the nature of the objects we encounter. He would agree, of course, that coming to know is an adaptive process and also that we do not *discover* a preexisting world (and many philosophers part company with him right there), but I find no evidence that he would reject the *existence* of an independent world.

Let me try to make this a bit clearer. Consider Glasersfeld's brief discussion of "real world" objects:

I can no more walk through the desk in front of me than I can argue that black is white at one and the same time. What constrains me, however, is not quite the same thing in the two cases. That the desk constitutes an obstacle to my physical movement is due to the particular distinctions my sensory system enables me to make and to the particular way in which I have come to coordinate them. Indeed, if I now could walk through the desk, it would no longer fit the abstraction I have made in prior experience.[29]

Most of us would want to say that the distinctions our sensory systems have made in prior experience can be traced at least in part to something in objects like desks, tables, and chairs. The very notion of a sensory system implies things to sense. As several critics have pointed out, if radical constructivists are just saying that our perception and cognition are theory-laden, that all knowledge is mediated by our cognitive structures and theories, then they have lots of company among contemporary theorists. However, if they are saying that there is no mind-independent reality, then they seem to be arguing a line long ago rejected.

Postmodern thinkers might raise very different objections to radical constructivism. First, if the position really is postepistemological, why talk about the nature of reality at all? Why answer challenges that arise, supposedly, from the certainty of mathematics and other traditional problems? Radical constructivists should, like Wittgenstein, just set epistemology aside as the "philosophy of psychology."[30] The concept of "viability" that constructivists use to explain how knowers accept or reject various beliefs can be confined to use in empirical studies. It would be enormously useful to teachers, for example, to know what leads students to revise misconceptions or to hold tenaciously to ideas that do not seem to enhance adaption. Viability does not have to be construed as an epistemological concept. To do so invites the sort of criticism advanced by Suchting, namely that "viable" is not clearly different from "verified," "confirmed," and other epistemic terms usually taken as correlates or substitutes for truth.[31] Thus an internal battle for constructivists is to decide whether their theories are or are not epistemological.

Second, as we have seen, postmodern thinkers have raised serious objections to the idea of a *constituting* subject. From postmodern perspectives, human beings are not autonomous subjects who create their own realities, and there are even questions about the ways in which knowledge is constructed. As *situated* knowers, much of what we know has been constructed in a very weak sense. We are products of our times and situations—in short, we are *constituted* subjects. As subjects, we retain some agency and our cognitive processes may very well be constructive, but we do not construct reality. In one sense, postmodernists might argue, constructivists have retained and even emphasized a central feature of Cartesian epistemology that they should have rejected or at least challenged.

For teachers, it may not matter whether constructivism is or is not an epistemology or, if it is, whether it is adequate. As a cognitive position, it is clearly strong, but it is not unique. Constructivists might profit from a careful study of Dewey's work, which lays out in considerable detail an active view of learners. They should also study Piaget's work closely. Do Dewey and Piaget differ on important matters? Both are thoroughgoing interactionists; both place knowers and the known in one world of potential experience. But Piaget, in keeping with his Kantian roots, posited cognitive structures that describe mental activity in each stage of development, whereas Dewey preferred to work with visible behaviors, spoken intentions, and observable consequences. Also, Piaget was interested primarily in development, not education. Dewey was so thoroughly concerned with education that he placed the philosophy of education at the center of all philosophy.

Educators should also keep in mind that one can adopt many of the practices recommended by constructivists without being a constructivist. Similarly, one can be a constructivist without using every pedagogical strategy blessed by the parent doctrine.

In conclusion, as you become immersed in constructivist theories, you might ask of them the kind of questions we raised in the previous section: (1) Do their recommended materials meet the special criteria advanced by constructivism; that is, do they call forth powerful and viable constructions? (2) Are there serious questions about constructivist research? Do some concepts need clarification? Are alternatives neglected? Are there inconsistencies? (3) Is attention given to the sociology of knowledge? Are students encouraged to question the importance of what they are learning? Are they learning something about the connections between knowledge and political power?

SUMMARY QUESTIONS

1. Should true opinion count as knowledge? Why do we often credit students with knowledge when they have only true opinion?
2. Are there circumstances under which we might say someone has knowledge even though what he or she believes is false?
3. What kind of statement might provide an adequate foundation for knowledge? What other sources might we consider to anchor our knowledge?
4. Do we need a concept of truth?
5. Why might philosophers prefer a historical account of the development of knowledge to the traditional conception of justified true belief?
6. What are the strengths and weaknesses of Dewey's "forward-looking" epistemology?
7. How does an "epistemological subject" differ from an actual, concrete subject?
8. In what ways do standpoint epistemologies challenge traditional epistemology?

9. Is epistemology entirely separate from psychology?
10. In choosing subject matter content, are there values more important than truth?
11. What are the advantages and disadvantages of "disciplinary" knowledge?
12. Is cultural power a more important criterion for knowledge than its status as justified true belief?
13. How do radical constructivists differ from Piaget?
14. What is meant by a *constituting* subject? By a *constituted* subject?
15. Constructivism dominates theoretical discussion in math and science education. Why do you think this has happened?
16. How do Dewey and Piaget differ in their epistemological positions?

INTRODUCTION TO THE LITERATURE

For a general, highly readable introduction to epistemology, see Roderick M. Chisholm, *Theory of Knowledge,* 3d ed.; for Dewey's theory of knowledge, see *The Quest for Certainty;* for a discussion of coherence theories, see Keith Lehrer, *Theory of Knowledge;* and for an introduction to constructivism, see Jean Piaget, *Insights and Illusions of Philosophy.*

CHAPTER 7

Philosophy of Social Science and Educational Research

In the last chapter, we saw that the search for an absolutely reliable foundation of knowledge, although fascinating, has led most philosophers to conclude that there is no such foundation. Even observation, perhaps the most basic of scientific activities, is thought now to be theory-laden. In educational research and other forms of social science, doubts have also arisen about the exclusive use of the quantitative methods so familiar in the physical sciences. We will begin with a brief discussion of the debate in philosophy of science over the nature of scientific knowledge; next we will look at the debate over quantitative and qualitative research in education; and finally, we will try to apply some of the thinking of the first two sections to particular cases of educational research.

How Does Science Grow?

In the discussion of knowledge as justified true belief, we referred briefly to the work of Karl Popper. Popper's basic idea is that we can never be fully justified in accepting a particular scientific belief—not if by *justified* we mean that a belief is totally confirmed by the evidence. The best we can do, Popper says, is to show that test after test has failed to refute or falsify our claim. Indeed, according to Popper, this is the way science grows. It does not grow by gross accumulation but by a series of focused attempts to shake the various claims put forth. Some claims are rejected;

some are revised; some are refined and entrenched. But even those that become entrenched may one day be refuted.

Popper's insistence that science can only proceed through careful attempts to falsify its own claims has led many scientists and philosophers to regard "falsifiability" as a criterion by which scientific and nonscientific claims can be separated. From this perspective, *scientific* claims must be stated in such a way that it is clear what sort of evidence would falsify them. If, for example, we claim that the trajectory of a particle fired from a spiral tube will be a curved or spiral one, it is clear that the observation of some other path—a line tangent to the tube's curve at the point of escape—will refute the claim.

In contrast, how can one falsify something like Freud's claims about the workings of the unconscious? The inherent difficulty in such work has led some scientists and philosophers to question whether Freud's work should be regarded as science at all. A recent manifestation of this problem is seen in the controversy within the American Psychological Association (APA) over recovered memories. Some psychologists insist that repressed memories of early sexual abuse can be and have been recovered from the unconscious of victims through appropriate psychoanalytic methods. They offer as evidence the suffering that led patients to seek help in the first place and the memories themselves. Other psychologists argue that the "memories" may have been created by the process itself, and the initial sufferings—far from serving as evidence of the validity of the memories—should cast doubt on what is recovered. This is a fascinating debate involving several beliefs that are fairly well entrenched and that, in this instance, clash with rather than support each other.

First, as we noted in our discussion of epistemology, many scholars today believe that memory and, indeed, all mental processes are constructive; that is, these scholars do not believe that objects and events are somehow stored as exact images in memory. Every act of remembering is an act of construction and can thus be affected by present events and moods. If this constructivist premise is accepted, it is hard to argue that recovered memories of childhood sexual abuse (or anything else) are necessarily accurate.

Second, however, social scientists and psychiatric workers now believe that incest and other forms of sexual abuse of children are much more widespread than once believed. Further, there is evidence to support this belief. Thus, although memories may be subject to reconstruction, there are strong reasons to believe that many children have suffered abuse, repressed the memory, and suffered emotional disorders as a result. We know that child abuse, in many forms, is a reality; we have seen it. We can still admit, however, that "child abuse" as a concept is a social construction, and our description of it has changed considerably over time.[1] For example, many people today believe that spanking is a form of child abuse, and many school districts (and whole states) now forbid corporal punishment in schools. Some years ago, this judgment would have been thought ridiculous.

Third, scientists, like all of us, are influenced by ethical and political beliefs, and these play a major role in the present controversy. One side wants to ignore such beliefs and concentrate on the science involved: Memory is a constructive process, and "recovered" memories may be distorted; they may even be entirely concocted. At the very least, we should examine the process by which the memories were recovered before we take any accusation seriously. The other side accuses the first of perpetuating the arrogance and domination of male science—refusing to believe victims (mainly female) and demanding "objective" evidence in situations where personal suffering should be accepted as the strongest possible evidence.

You can see from this example that there are some difficulties in applying Popper's falsification scheme. If one scientist presents a case of recovered memory, how can it be falsified? In principle, it surely can be. We need only find evidence that the events described in the "memory" did not happen. But as we attempt to do this, we may be accused of blaming the victim, of upholding a system that protects males, and even of supporting a system of corrupt science. Further, scientists do not usually pursue one such case as detectives and lawyers must. Any attempt to do so may exacerbate the accusations just mentioned.

One of Popper's followers, Imre Lakatos, recognized some of these difficulties and tried to refine Popper's ideas and better describe the process by which science proceeds.[2] He suggested that scientists are not usually so concerned with the acceptance or refutation of a particular hypothesis but rather with the effects of certain results on the parent theory currently guiding their research. Refutation of a particular hypothesis generated by a theory will lead scientists to tinker with the theory, not discard it. Normally, they will revise or adjust peripheral concepts and rules. They will not change the core concepts, which, Lakatos said, lie in a "protective belt." Thus we do not learn a lot about the workings of science simply by studying individual investigations. We must analyze *programs* of research. Then we see more clearly how scientists react when their individual conjectures are refuted. When a program of research guided by theory x is *progressive*, x is capable of generating many hypotheses, and x itself is not threatened, although its surface contours may change. However, a program is *degenerating* when its workers spend most of their time responding to refutations and patching up the holes in x. Then the core of x is threatened, and the whole program may collapse.

In the next chapter, we will see how Kohlberg's developmental theory of moral reasoning may be evaluated from a Lakatosian perspective. In general, Lakatos's approach is valuable for educators because it draws our attention to programs of research. The sheer volume of educational research can be overwhelming, and there is strong evidence that teachers pay little attention to it. However, if you learn to look at programs of research, you can get a sense of how vigorous a particular chain of research is, and this may help you to decide whether to reject it or to study it more seriously.

If we examine the controversy over recovered memories from a Lakatosian perspective, we get some sense of why political and ethical beliefs may play such an important role. At the very heart of the position that claims the truth of recovered memories is the notion of an unconscious that has a certain integrity. What would psychoanalysis be, how would it function, if this notion were rejected? How can it be protected if the other side shows convincingly that many recovered memories are actually new constructions or amalgams of past (perhaps innocent) events and present constructs? On the other side, what is the future of social science itself if it can be shown convincingly that the standard criteria of evidence are contaminated with political bias?

Another way of looking at the APA controversy is to regard it as a paradigm clash. In 1962, Thomas Kuhn introduced the notion that science grows through revolutions.[3] Although many critics have pointed out that Kuhn is less than clear in his use of the word *paradigm,* a Kuhnian paradigm seems to consist of a basic theory, set of concepts, and ways of working that guide a particular branch of science for some interval of time. A paradigm, Kuhn said, gives rise to a coherent tradition of research; it attracts "an enduring group of adherents," and it is "sufficiently open-ended to leave all sorts of problems" for its workers.[4] While a paradigm holds sway, scientists are engaged in what Kuhn calls "normal science."

When anomalies accumulate or something unexpected is discovered or invented, a revolution may occur. The old paradigm gives way to a new one: Its basic theories are discarded or assimilated, its concepts are revised and new ones are added, and its ways of working may be drastically changed by the accessibility of new tools.

Of course, before one paradigm actually replaces another, there may be a fairly lengthy period of "paradigm clash." During this time, it is not clear which paradigm will succeed. Often, heated words are exchanged, political issues invade scientific discussion, sides are chosen for reasons of politics, ethics, or power, and the defending paradigm may be fully occupied trying to patch up its theories or methods. Sometimes, of course, a new paradigm fails or is assimilated to the older, stronger one. But Kuhn's attention was on successful revolutions, such as those initiated by Copernicus and Galileo, and the changes they induce.

Few scientists and philosophers would argue against Kuhn that such remarkable changes never occur. The history of science shows in fact that they do. But Kuhn has more to say on the subject. He claims that two paradigms—let's call the old one A and the challenger B—are often incommensurable: "The normal-science tradition that emerges from a scientific revolution is not only incompatible but often actually incommensurable with that which has gone before."[5] In mathematics, incommensurability means that two sets of numbers—the rationals and irrationals, for example—cannot be expressed as integral multiples of one unit of measure. Thus, in the strictest sense of incommensurability, B could not be expressed entirely in terms of the theories, concepts, and rules of A, nor A in B's terms. Kuhn however, puts the case more broadly:

> To the extent that two schools disagree about what is a problem and what a solution, they will inevitably talk through each other when debating the relative merits of their respective paradigms. In the partially circular arguments that regularly result, each paradigm will be shown to satisfy more or less the criteria that it dictates for itself and to fall short of a few of those dictated by its opponent.

Kuhn then adds something that seems obvious from our discussion of the APA debate:

> Paradigm debates always involve a question: Which problem is it more significant to have solved? Like the issue of competing standards, that question of values can be answered only in terms of criteria that lie outside of normal science altogether, and it is that recourse to external criteria that most obviously makes the paradigm debates revolutionary.[6]

Is truth itself then relative to a paradigm, and if so, how is it that successive paradigms—at least in the physical and biological senses—seem to give us so much more technical power? Kuhn suggests that workers in A cannot adequately criticize the work of those in B (or vice versa) because they work in different worlds. In psychology, for example, Skinnerians and Freudians operate in totally different traditions. Skinnerians reject the notion of the unconscious; for Freudians, the notion lies at the very core of their paradigm. Is it, then, impossible for one group to criticize the other?

Here, it seems to me (but not, apparently, to Kuhn), the idea of meta-domains and metalanguages might be useful. Surely there is a scientific domain that lies beyond (or encompasses) paradigms. Although A and B disagree about what should count as evidence, they presumably agree that scientific work requires presentation of some sort of evidence. Presumably they agree also that counterexamples and entailments that lead to contradictions must be addressed. Therefore, discussion is not impossible.

Many philosophers and scientists readily acknowledge this metascience domain and invoke discussion in it to attempt to adjudicate between A and B. However, the difficulties grow when we acknowledge the questions of value mentioned by Kuhn. Must scientists step out of the domain of science to decide which problems are important? Must they consider the effects of their work on individuals and communities? Have these problems always been there but denied by scientists who have insisted on the objectivity of science? Some scientists argue that they are not responsible for the uses to which their science is put. Science is employed to advance knowledge. Discussion of how its products are used belongs to the domain of politics or moral theory. Can this sharp separation be supported, or can we find difficulties in it?

A Debate in Educational Research

In the last three or four decades, there has been a fiery debate within educational research over the merits of quantitative versus qualitative methods. Many educational theorists regard this debate as a genuine paradigm clash. The quantitative model held sway and might well be thought of as the one that guided "normal science" for many years. This model is often referred to as the "naturalistic" model, but it must be understood that "naturalistic" here has a different sense from the one we used in talking about Dewey's "naturalistic" philosophy. It refers more simply and directly to the model of the natural sciences. *Naturalistic* social science, then, is social science modeled on the natural sciences.

The quantitative or naturalistic paradigm has three main features: (1) It is theory-driven; (2) it proceeds by testing hypotheses; (3) it aims for generalization.[7] These criteria have been used to define educational research, and models that reject them have been challenged. As we move into this discussion, it will be clear why "naturalistic" may be a better descriptive term for the standard paradigm than "quantitative." Not all of standard science is quantitative, although insofar as its eventual aim is hypothesis testing, it is necessarily quantitative. But in the stages preceding hypothesis testing, it may look very like qualitative research. Indeed, in the years before qualitative research was widely accepted, most qualitative studies were labeled "exploratory." Thus, something like qualitative research has long been part of naturalistic studies but with certain constraints: The initial phase was considered preliminary and exploratory (not the main event); its purpose was the refinement of hypotheses and operational definitions (not often the generation of hypotheses, since these were supposed to be derived from theories); and the interpretive ("discussion") phase was confined largely to interpretation within the parent theory and suggestions for the removal of anomalies through the use of more powerful or meticulous methods.

It is not surprising, then, that the first wave of qualitative research to be accepted was regarded as exploratory. Gradually, from a confluence of forces, a new paradigm arose. Anthropologists introduced methods that were very different from the experimental methods of the psychologists who had long dominated educational research. Some sociologists began using methods that caused an internal battle in sociology; for example, they questioned whether hypotheses had to be derived from theories.

Educational research was affected by all these battles in the disciplines and usually made its judgments locally. Thus, an ethnographic study would be accepted by a faculty whose anthropologists affirmed both the study and the qualifications of its author. A non–theory-driven sociological study might be accepted by one faculty but rejected by another.

The methodological battles within the social sciences contributed to a growing feeling within the educational research community that the naturalistic model (the model of the physical sciences) was inadequate for the study of education. Several theorists have suggested that the aims of social science are different from those of naturalistic science. Whereas naturalistic science aims at explanation in terms of prediction and control, social science aims at understanding. Educational research in the naturalistic mode can rarely tell us that a particular pedagogical method—say, one of teaching multiplication—is significantly and generally better than another. Qualitative methods—ethnographic studies, case studies, historical summaries, even powerful anecdotes—can help us understand why a method works with some children and some teachers in some situations and fails to do so with others. Then individual teachers can ask themselves how nearly their own situation and professional characteristics fit those described in the research reports.

In educational research, the questions directed at studies in the new mode have sometimes boiled down to one: Is this science? Even if we have reservations about the adequacy of the word *paradigm* or the concept *revolution* (and my use of *paradigm* does not signify total acceptance), I think we have to acknowledge that what has happened in educational research has all the earmarks, except possibly one, of a scientific revolution. The one possible exception is that the end is still in doubt; there may or may not be a total displacement of one paradigm by another. But all the signs of paradigm *clash* are there: the accusations of A that B is not doing *science;* the accusations of B that A is inadequate, outdated, and hopelessly bogged down in trivia; the introduction of new language; arguments that talk past one another; the ambiguous use of once-standard terms; frequent reference to the social domain of value—regarded by one as outside science and by the other as containing science.

Influence has flowed in both directions. Important figures long associated with the standard paradigm have acknowledged qualitative aspects previously ignored in naturalistic science; qualitative researchers have polished their work on category schemes to increase the possibility of generalization. Thus quantitative methods have become more qualitative and vice versa. It may be that what some think of now as a "qualitative" paradigm will not displace the old but, rather, that a new paradigm incorporating the best of each will emerge.

This result—an amalgam of qualitative and quantitative—is perhaps more likely if a form of incommensurability is recognized. Consider a mathematical analogy. The rational numbers and the irrational are demonstrably incommensurable. One cannot find a common unit of measure in which to express both rationals and irrationals. No matter what unit is selected, for example, one cannot lay off 4 and $\sqrt{2}$ in integral multiples or divisions of that unit. (One can *construct* some of the irrationals. For instance, construct a unit square; the diagonal, then, has measure $\sqrt{2}$, and that length can be marked off on a number line where the length of the square's side is used as 1.) Although the two systems are incommensurable, together they form the real numbers—a system considerably more powerful and useful than either of the two components. Similarly, if qualitative and quantitative modes, or parts of them, really are incommensurable in some important sense, their combination should yield a power that neither of them alone possesses.

Of course, this kind of resolution of incommensurable systems will not always work. There probably is no way to unite two theories that include mutually contradictory statements. For example, it seems impossible to combine Skinnerian and Freudian theories—one denying and the other asserting the existence of the unconscious.

Resolution also depends on what we mean by *incommensurable,* and on this a great deal of work still needs to be done. Attempts to establish commensurability here, I think, have merely muddied the waters. For example, when Elliot Eisner uses terms like *referential adequacy* and *structural corroboration* as substitutes for *validity* and *reliability* (standard terms in the naturalistic model),[8] it suggests that one set can be described in terms of its differences from the other. Commensurability means that there is a common unit of measurement or, stretching things as Kuhn did, a common unit of meaning. The very promise (and threat) of a new system depends on its incommensurability with the old.

Incommensurability of scientific paradigms does not imply the impossibility of cross-paradigm criticism as many philosophers seem to think.

Rather, it means that scientists have to step out of their narrow scientific frames of reference into the larger social domain and use ordinary, "natural" language to ask questions about purposes, uses, meanings, and significance. This, of course, does imply a recognition that science is not entirely self-contained or entirely self-correcting.

It may well be that as we study the incommensurability question more closely, we will describe incommensurability in terms of purposes and uses instead of technical terms and concepts within competing modes. Several educational theorists, from both camps, have begun to talk this way. Lee Cronbach, for example, has pointed out that policymakers generally need information that is very different from that needed by parents. On the issue of effectiveness of Catholic versus public schools, for example, Cronbach notes that policymakers need information at a high level of generalization; parents, on the other hand, need to evaluate *this* Catholic school against *that* public school.[9] It may well be that one mode of research is better designed for a particular purpose than the other, or it could be that both modes are useful to both groups in different ways. Similarly, qualitative researchers have emphasized ways in which their work can contribute to the work of naturalistic scientists: It can produce new concepts, generate hypotheses, find problems, and even generate theory. At one level, then, the debate has quieted down. A new paradigm has begun to encompass the two rivals.

At another level, however, the debate is heating up. Qualitative research has been extended into "narrative research," and again the challenge has arisen: Is this science? Before we get into the debate itself, it is worth noting that a possible answer to this is, No, this work is not science. It is an application of the humanities to education and important in its own right. Then, of course, narrative researchers would have to show that their methods, sources, modes of reporting, and the like are compatible with those generally accepted in the humanities. This would be by no means a trivial task.

However, the issue is not cast that way right now. It is, rather, a legacy of the quantitative-qualitative debate. Is this new mode a legitimate offspring of qualitative research? D. C. Phillips raises the question whether we should be concerned with the truth of the narratives used in educational research and responds that, at least sometimes, we should be so concerned.[10] Surely, when something important hinges on the truth or facticity of a narrative, we should be concerned. But what are these occasions?

Phillips uses the example of a mathematics teacher who tells a story about how he produced what is deemed a successful calculus lesson. If the teacher's story is not true (not confirmed by relevant epistemological justification), readers of the casebook in which his story appears may be misled. But, of course, teachers are often misled by contemporary naturalistic research as well. What is true by these standards today may be false tomorrow. I am not sure, therefore, that truth is so important in this example, although it may be in others. Of course, we have a moral interest in truth-telling, and every researcher should be honest about the status of his or her work as report, philosophical fiction, or speculation. But if the confessed purpose of a narrative is to encourage readers to "try looking at it this way," the truth of the account may not be of primary importance.

What seems unarguable is that researchers should be forthcoming about the purposes and limitations of their work. Readers of the calculus teacher's story should be cautioned that it *is his* story and that other explanations might be more accurate or more useful. Readers should be invited—and they usually are—to interpret the story in light of their own experience and, where ethically and practically feasible, to test its recommendations in their own experience.

Narrative research, as part of the hermeneutic tradition, invites interpretation and reinterpretation. It puts far more responsibility on the readers or users of research who must play an active role in constructing meaning for themselves. This is not to say—although some radical advocates of hermeneutics *do* say—that there should be no interest in what the author or researcher means, and researchers still bear responsibility to convey their intentions, interpretations, and conclusions as clearly and coherently as possible.

I will conclude with an example I have used in other places,[11] and this may effectively illustrate both my points and the one that worries Phillips. Suppose we advocate that science teachers begin a unit on evolution by telling a wide range of creation stories before and perhaps even after telling the scientific story of evolution. Approaching the unit this way is motivated by the recognition that human beings in all times and places have asked and attempted to answer questions about the origins of the universe and life, especially human life. It provides a wonderful opportunity to acknowledge stories from many different cultural and religious perspectives. And the criteria used by narrative researchers can be used to evaluate the stories: Are they plausible, gripping, or compelling? Relevant to the likely readers' predicaments? These are clearly very different criteria from those used in standard science.

But, Phillips would want to ask, which one is *true?* Surely we would not want to leave students with the idea that all are equally true and that they may choose the one they like best. My response is this: When we tell the scientific story, we should also discuss the criteria by which scientific studies are usually judged. How deeply we go into this must depend on the maturity of our students. They may be able to see that some of the creation stories (perhaps all) fail on the criterion of evidence demanded by science. We still do not have to say "and this one is true." Rather we should say that the best scientific thinking of our day accepts this view.

Has my example inadvertently shown that narrative accounts cannot in themselves be science since, by my own account, they are judged on different criteria? I think this is clearly the case. But that admission does not entail that narratives cannot be used effectively in scientific investigation, nor does it imply that the narratives so used must themselves be true. It does suggest that narratives must be recognized *as narratives* and judged accordingly. It also suggests that there is plenty of work for philosophers and researchers to do in analyzing the differences between narrative itself and the various uses of narrative. It suggests also that we might profitably make distinctions between research uses and pedagogical uses of narrative.

The debate over what constitutes legitimate educational research is also heated at the policy level. Government agencies have recently put tremendous emphasis on randomized experiments as the gold standard for educational research. This is a model borrowed from medical (especially drug) research, and its aim is to find the best method by which to accomplish educational aims.[12] The exclusive use of this model has many faults. First, it ignores the crucial fact that the model has limitations even in the testing of drugs; a given drug often has differential effects, working as predicted for most patients but failing or even harming some others. Second, education is very different from medicine. Usually, physician and patient share one goal—treating or curing the patient's ailment. In contrast, participants in education (teachers, students, parents) have various purposes, different aptitudes, different personalities, and different backgrounds. These differences interact with every method implemented and make the whole enterprise enormously complex. Consider just one factor: the relation between doctor and patient may have little effect on the efficacy of a prescribed drug, but the relation between teacher and student may crucially affect the way a pedagogical method is received.

Third, insistence on one form of scientific research is short-sighted and sacrifices the significant contributions of other forms. What we should insist upon instead is that every piece of research conform to the highest standards of the form it represents and that the method chosen be appropriate for the stated problem.[13]

Fourth, insistence on the use of randomized experiments neglects ethical problems that arise as we arbitrarily assign students to one or another "treatment." If teachers know their students well, and I have argued that they should,[14] they also know that some methods may be less than effective and even harmful with some students. Why should we pretend that children and teachers are interchangeable units to be considered as mere collective variables in an experiment? Many of us find this attitude deeply troubling.

Finally, not only is the randomized experiment just one form of scientific research, but *scientific* research is just one form of educational research.[15] Recognizing this, educational theorists might reconsider their insistence that all forms of educational research be "scientific." Perhaps it is enough that certain forms induce a multiplicity of meanings and, in rare cases, even wisdom.

Some Examples

Through all of your professional life, you will rightly be concerned with the results of research and its effects on your work. For years educational researchers and theorists have deplored the fact that so few teachers pay any attention at all to the products of research. Often the complaint is that teachers do not *use* research. However, I am not urging you to use research but, rather, to explore it critically. Even if you do not accept everything said by Popper, Lakatos, Kuhn, and others (few philosophers accept any one account fully), the methods of criticism stated or implied in their work may be helpful in evaluating research.

In the next chapter, as we look at Kohlberg's developmental model of moral reasoning, we will find Lakatos's notion of progressive and degenerating paradigms useful. In the chapter on critical thinking, we saw that it was useful to understand both of two competing theoretical positions before trying to criticize either one. Recall that both groups of theorists agree that critical thinking must have an object, must be "about something." But one group uses subject matter largely as a source of examples to fill out chains of formal or informal reasoning. The other insists that subject matter is the very heart of critical thinking and that the rules and habits emphasized in the other program actually grow out of intelligent work in a discipline. As you learn more about the programs in critical thinking, you may disagree with parts of both of them. For example, I would teach some formal logic because many students (by no means all) find it both useful in mathematics and fun. I would also give students lots of opportunities to apply logic informally to problems in everyday life. I agree with those in the second camp when they say that logical rules and habits of mind grow out of disciplined activity. With Dewey, however, I agree that disciplined activity does not have to center on the traditional disciplines. Any activity pursued regularly and intelligently should give rise to the desired habits.

In the chapter on epistemology, we examined the constructivist movement and, again, saw that it was possible to criticize it from within a particular view of constructivism, across views of constructivism, or from without. In every case, however, robust criticism requires understanding of the aims, methods, and concepts of the miniparadigm or program under investigation. An important and justified complaint raised by Ernst von Glasersfeld against Wallis Suchting's devastating critique of radical constructivism is that Suchting made no attempt to understand the program as a whole or what it is trying to accomplish.[16] For teachers, it is especially useful to understand the varieties of constructivism—Piagetian biological/individual constructivism, social constructivism, and radical constructivism—and what each has to contribute to classroom practices.

Now let's consider how some of the ideas from philosophy of science might be applied to another popular educational movement—cooperative learning. Group work in a wide variety of forms is enormously popular in current educational theory; indeed, it is even mandated in some state curriculum frameworks. Some models of cooperative learning are closely linked to social constructivism. The underlying belief is that students learn from social interaction as much as or more than they do from individual manipulation of objects. Attempts to articulate what one knows and to understand what others are saying are important—perhaps central—in developmental learning. Other models are based on the belief that cooperation within teams that compete with each other provides an increased incentive to learn. Still others offer models of cooperative learning to advance an understanding of democratic processes or to accomplish status equalization among classmates.

Philosophers interested in a critical examination of cooperative learning and research on cooperative learning might ask whether the various models incorporate contradictory beliefs in addition to their avowedly different aims, whether the results thus far announced induce the need to "patch up" or explain anomalies between what is predicted by the theory and what has been observed, and whether talk across models is leading to the strengthening of some central claims and/or the revision of others.[17] Criticism might proceed from the outside and challenge the basic notion that group work is more effective academically than individual work, or it might try to show that the advantages of group work are limited more severely than its advocates acknowledge. Criticism from the inside might be directed to issues already identified. It could be aimed at the defense of a model, the destruction of a model, or the refinement of a model that can incorporate the best features of several others. In the latter case, we should surely want to ask: Are the current programs of cooperative learning part of one paradigm, or are they in some important ways incommensurable? Do they use terms in the same ways? Do they share basic premises? Are their methods compatible?

Before leaving this brief discussion of educational research and philosophy of science, I should mention that feminist and postmodern philosophers have launched powerful critiques of science as it has been conducted under what is sometimes called "Cartesian epistemology." The feminist criticisms will be discussed in Chapter 12. Here I will just say, by way of preview, that feminists have challenged the traditional notion of objectivity, the detachment of subject and object, the tendency to objectify (make into objects) human beings in social science, an emphasis on method that smacks of "methodolatry," and a denial of the influence of social and political power on the inner workings of science.

SUMMARY QUESTIONS

1. A recent survey report says that education has improved over the past five years—at least if we measure improvement by the percentage of academic courses students are taking. Is this claim falsifiable? Is it subject to interpretation?
2. Is there a major difficulty with Popper's falsifiability thesis?
3. How can constructivist premises be used to cast doubts on "recovered" memories?
4. Is the subjective report of suffering the strongest possible evidence of sexual abuse?
5. What are the characteristics of a progressive program of research? A degenerating one?
6. According to Kuhn, what characterizes normal science? What happens when a revolution threatens?
7. Does Kuhn's thesis imply relativism?
8. If we accept the thesis that Freud's claims are true relative to his entire psychoanalytic framework, should we accept claims about the influence of the planets on individual lives as true in relation to astrology? How are the cases different?
9. In what areas should science accept the fact that science is embedded in a social context? In what areas should it resist the influence of the larger culture, if it can?
10. What is meant by *incommensurability*?
11. Are science and religion incommensurable? In what sense?
12. What do we mean by "naturalistic" social science?
13. What criteria characterize naturalistic educational research? Can one or two be discarded while the other(s) is (are) retained?
14. What are the dangers of "going native"—that is, of becoming an insider in another culture or paradigm? What are the advantages?
15. In what ways does it seem right to say that the social sciences, in contrast to the natural sciences, aim at "understanding"?
16. What are the strengths of qualitative research?
17. What kinds of questions seem more appropriate for quantitative than for qualitative research?
18. As a policymaker, what might you want to know about a large district's schools? As a parent, would your needs differ? How?

19. Can you think of uses for narrative research? What is narrative research?

20. Should educational research emphasize randomized experiments? Why or why not?

21. Is there a kind of paradigm clash in the critical thinking movement? What premises lie in the protective belt of each camp?

22. Where would you start in criticizing constructivism?

23. Are overt signs of activity necessary for active engagement? Can listening, for example, be active?

24. Should teachers be urged to *use* research? Is there an alternative that is preferable from a professional perspective?

25. Consider the questions on cooperative learning toward the end of the chapter. Any one of these raises issues for teachers and philosophers to analyze.

INTRODUCTION TO THE LITERATURE

A good general introduction is found in D. C. Phillips, *Philosophy, Science, and Social Inquiry.* The articles I have cited in my note 7 by Firestone and Peshkin may interest students with a serious interest in educational research. One of the most important works is, of course, Thomas Kuhn's *The Structure of Scientific Revolutions.* Peter Winch's *The Idea of a Social Science* is especially valuable for those interested in social science. For a compelling account of mathematics from a Lakatosian perspective, see Philip J. Davis and Reuben Hersh, *The Mathematical Experience.* For an overview of the problems of educational research, see Ellen Condliffe Lagemann and Lee Shulman, *Issues in Education Research.* Relevant articles often appear in *Educational Researcher* and in *Science and Education.*

CHAPTER 8

Ethics and Moral Education

E thics, like epistemology, is a center of heated debate in current phi-losophy. Just as critics of Enlightenment epistemology attack its quest for certainty and the exclusivity that accompanied it, critics of contempo-rary ethics object to its formalism and separation from the problems of real life. Too many philosophical discussions have concentrated on the na-ture of ethical theories and their adequacy (metaethics), and too few have attempted to give any guidance on how we should live our concrete lives. Critics also attack the notion of universalizability in ethics; that is, they object to the premise that whatever one person is morally obligated to do in a particular situation all others in comparable situations must also be obligated to do. This premise, which we will discuss in the section on Kantianism, has often been taken as the very essence of the moral. A third center of criticism extends a comparable objection in epistemology. It at-tacks the emphasis on an abstract individual and the reliance on processes that make all real individuals into exemplars of this abstraction.

Before launching our examination of prominent ethical theories, I should mention that some philosophers make a distinction between ethics and morality. In everyday life, we often associate *morality* with personal life, particularly sexual habits and rules. However, *morality* as used by philoso-phers has a much wider range of meaning, referring to how we should con-duct our lives and, especially, how we should interact with others. Many philosophers define *ethics* as the philosophical study of morality. Others use the two terms synonymously, and that is what I will do in what follows.

We will begin our discussion with a brief sketch of pre-Enlightenment ethics, concentrating primarily on Aristotle because there is currently such an impressive revival of interest in his approach. Then we will look at Enlightenment ethics and post-Enlightenment approaches. After that, we will examine current approaches to moral education that run parallel to the schools of moral philosophy.

Pre-Enlightenment Ethics

Aristotle's approach to ethics and moral life is currently enjoying a great revival of interest. In part, renewed interest can be traced to our present longing for an ethics connected to real life, one that acknowledges our cultural and social situatedness. Aristotle, unlike Plato, who conducted much of his discussion on ethics through ideal settings and thought experiments, concentrated his analysis on the real community in which he lived. He wrote extensively on themes familiar to all of us: friendship, the management of bodily appetites, good and ill fortune, intellectual life and contemplation, social interaction, and the management of material goods. Aristotle was deeply concerned with virtue and the identification of exemplars. His *Nicomachean Ethics* is devoted almost entirely to a sophisticated analysis of the good life and the virtues required and nurtured by it.[1]

Because virtue is central to the good life as Aristotle described it, and because virtuous persons—persons of good character—exhibit virtues in every aspect of their lives, children should be trained to respond virtuously to life's demands. One becomes virtuous, Aristotle held, by behaving virtuously. When we discuss moral education, we will say considerably more about character education that traces its roots, at least in part, to Aristotle.

Some philosophers have complained of Aristotle's ethics that those subscribing to it will be hard put to criticize their own society. All the standards and models of virtue emerge from that society; therefore, it is difficult to see how critics can recommend significant changes. On one level, we might respond that few societies live up to their own ideals, and thus there will always be work for critics and moral educators who see their society falling far short of its own ideals and models. But defenders of Aristotle want to insist on more than this. They want to defend the notion that societal transformation is possible within an Aristotelian framework. Aristotle himself said that human beings persistently seek better ways than their ancestors have bequeathed them and that a characteristic of a good society's exemplars is that they go beyond their traditions and seek fuller, richer descriptions of the good. Martha Nussbaum has argued this in support of Aristotle.[2] It is not at all clear, however, to many of Aristotle's critics that this is really so. There have been and still are theocratic communities that label any and all changes heretical and adhere dogmatically to their traditions.

Defenders of Aristotle have argued that the development of his ethic does not depend entirely on his particular society. He did attempt, they say, to identify common human situations and to name the virtues that arise in each one. For example, all human beings fear pain, death, and losses of various kinds, and situations that induce such fear require courage. Is this not the case in all times and places? One might acknowledge this and still express concern about particular expressions of courage. If the courage of the warrior becomes the ideal, as it did in Homeric times, might not this virtue drown other virtues in its wake? Clearly, some forms of courage are compatible with compassion, humility, and gentleness, and others are not. Plato, too, wrestled with the problem of how to produce warriors who would be fierce and ruthless with their enemies and gentle and generous with their own people. Perhaps, suggest some of Aristotle's critics, we need more than virtue to guide our ethical life. Aristotle's answer to the problem is that the person of virtue must know when and how to exercise each virtue.

A major concern for critics of virtue ethics is the possible relativism of such ethics. Like epistemologists in their quest for certain foundations of knowledge, moral philosophers have sought to anchor moral life and ethical discussions in something universal and certain. Ethical/moral relativism is the doctrine that moral values, including conceptions of the good and the right, are relative to particular societies or communities. What is good in one society may be a matter of indifference or even evil in another. Further, there is no way (critics of relativism say) to adjudicate between one value system and another. However, defenders of tradition-bound ethical approaches insist that ethical traditions are maintained by the exercise of virtue and that, over time, they are vindicated by their rigor and explanatory power. Alasdair MacIntyre, for example, says: "The rival claims to truth of contending traditions of enquiry depend for their vindication upon the adequacy and the explanatory power of the histories which the resources of each of those traditions in conflict enable their adherents to write."[3] Although most moral philosophers have tried hard to avoid relativism in the past, current debate suggests greater interest in competing traditions and far less in universal approaches to ethics.

It may be useful to consider two examples here, one from Aristotle's time and one from our own. Why did Aristotle not see the evils of slavery? His ethic of virtue does nothing to challenge the practice. To be sure, it decrees that a virtuous master will treat his slaves humanely and that a virtuous slave will obey his or her master and work diligently. But the goodness of a slave, who, for Aristotle, was a human being with certain distinctive and disabling characteristics, was very like that of a good horse or a good weapon—it served well the functions to which it was assigned. Would another sort of ethic, an ethic of principle, have led the Greeks to condemn slavery? This is an interesting question; the answer is unclear. Many of Aristotle's contemporaries felt that slavery could be defended best, if at all, on the grounds of expediency. (Their argument was a form of unarticulated utilitarianism—that the happiness or well-being of Athenian citizens depended on the otherwise perhaps unjustifiable pain of a few.) But Aristotle went beyond expediency. He attempted to *justify* slavery. Would another sort of ethic have blocked this attempt? It is worth thinking about.

One could argue, as many naturalists and relativists do, that a society needs the example of another society that has freed itself of a particular evil and finds itself better as a result. Of course, the "better" society has to explain why it is better and how it is better as the result of its reform. The society still mired in its evil may then begin to question itself, and if it decides to change its ways, it will probably construct its own rationale for doing so. But the principles included in the rationale may have had little or nothing to do with the motivation for change. Slavery in the United States was both defended and condemned on Christian principles. Indeed, it was maintained with only slight discomfort under the principles of the Constitution.

Consider next a current example. In some parts of Africa, excision of the external female genitalia is still practiced. When feminists from all over the world get together to discuss this problem, some want to condemn the practice as contrary to a universal and absolute principle prohibiting the infliction of unnecessary pain. Others, perhaps misunderstanding the doctrine of relativism, insist that we must not intervene in the moral systems of other peoples. "It is right for them even if it is wrong for us." And so the horror of mutilation, infection, and lifelong discomfort is allowed to continue. If you are distressed by this result, you may agree with those who condemn relativism.

But a relativist does not have to react this way. She may well respond with sensitive investigation into reasons for the practice, exploration of alternatives with those inside the society who are already uneasy with the practice, and persuasive arguments demonstrating why abolition of the practice leads to a better society. One does not need an absolute principle to urge moral change, and one does not have to accept practices that induce pain and humiliation just because they are judged right by another group of human beings. Thus the charge of relativism may not be the most serious charge that can be brought against an ethic of virtue.

Another kind of complaint against virtue ethics seems to me more important, and that is that it leads to elitism. As Aristotle described the virtues and as the approach is described today by MacIntyre,[4] the danger is quite clear. Virtues and excellences arise in the diligent pursuit of certain practices. These practices or complex tasks are instituted and recognized by the society, and they require a continuity of thought and action through planning, executing, monitoring, and evaluating. Different practices demand different excellences and even different virtues. Some people, because of the positions they hold, have opportunities to develop virtues and excellences that are highly prized; others do not. A hierarchy of virtues tends to induce and maintain a hierarchy of status and privilege. Many societies have tried to justify this result by arguing either that certain virtues *earn* people the opportunity to enter practices where further virtues will be called forth or that the privileges accorded to the most virtuous hardly compensate for the burdens they assume for the rest of society.

Concerns about elitism (and even totalitarianism) are most vigorous when ethics clash at the level of social theory or policy. In recent years, there has been a growing discontent with individualism and the various forms of liberalism. Communitarians, many tracing their roots to Aristotle, have charged that liberalism has placed too much emphasis on the rights of abstract individuals and not enough on the duties, loyalties, and reciprocal contributions of actual individuals in actual communities.[5] I will say more about this important dispute in the next chapter in the discussion of social theories and educational policies. Here it is enough to know that contemporary philosophy is expressing both a renewed interest in Aristotle and a deep concern over the evils that sometimes accompany emphasis on the community and its demands.

The great merit of Aristotle's ethics, as I said at the start, is its connection to everyday, real life. Aristotle did not confine his philosophy to the analysis of abstruse language or the elaboration of a formal system. Instead, he addressed questions of concern to all human beings in the actual conduct of their lives. As we will see in the next major section of this chapter, Aristotle's legacy is also powerful in contemporary moral education, and we will revisit his ideas in that context.

It sometimes strikes beginning philosophy students as odd that in most discussions of epistemology and ethics, writers move from Plato and Aristotle immediately to the Enlightenment. We skip over the Middle Ages as though nothing interesting happened in all these centuries. But the Middle Ages are quite fascinating from an ethical perspective. First (confining ourselves to the Western tradition), they were a time of ethical orthodoxy. There was one Church and one faith—challenged often by heresies but accepted without question by the masses of people. Medievalists argue over the extent of the Church's authority in the ethics of everyday life. Some say that the Church dominated all of social and political life; others insist that its role was more limited. In any case, the ethics of the Middle Ages was one of authority and deference to practice. In some ways, it was characteristically Aristotelian: Each class had its special virtues and privileges, tradition guided all practices, and training in the appropriate virtues and excellences was preferred over reasoning and analysis.

Second, the point of the ethic was to *order* life on earth, not to better it. People accepted the miseries of life as inevitable, and they also seemed to believe that there would be a real reckoning in the next world. One did one's duty, accepted one's place, endured one's sufferings. As part of a Christian orthodoxy, suffering was even exalted. Great suffering on earth would, for the righteous, lead to great rewards in heaven. Thus suffering became a virtue even in love; unconsummated longing was glorified in courtly love.[6]

The tendency toward this kind of ethic—one of order, obedience, tradition, and acceptance—is strong even today. The revival of fundamentalism in all the major religions threatens a return to ethics of orthodoxy. The Enlightenment brought with it the wonderful idea that human beings might have a hand in their own destinies, that an adequate ethic would make life better here and now, and that human beings are *subjects, agents*—not just vessels for divine intervention. The debate between these two very different ethical orientations is illustrated today in the Catholic

Church between orthodox views of charity as works done through obedience and the grace of God and liberation theology with its tremendous emphasis on human initiative.[7] The debate is also illustrated in a conflict long present in Protestantism: Is the main purpose of the church salvation or social improvement? In the first case, we find an ethic of orthodoxy; in the second, an ethic more consonant with Enlightenment thought.

Enlightenment Ethics

The Enlightenment brought the promise of freedom from the authority of the Church and an invitation to human beings to exercise reason in the conduct of their lives. Although philosophy certainly reflects this trend, ordinary life was more affected by the Calvinism and Puritanism that broke the hegemony of the Catholic Church. Indeed, in Crane Brinton's *History of Western Morals*,[8] Kant is mentioned several times only in passing, and yet his ethical approach has been one of the two dominant ethics in moral philosophy.

Kant has been both revered and reviled as the philosopher who elevated individual human rationality over all forms of authority in ethics. His categorical imperative puts ethics on a logical base: So act that you can (logically) will that your decision be made law; that is, act in a way that you can, without contradiction, insist that all others in similar situations should also act. From this basic principle, Kant deduced several absolute rules for human conduct, including his well-known prohibition of lying. One cannot, Kant argued, logically will that others should follow one's decision to tell a lie, because the result would be a breakdown in the whole concept of truth-telling and lying. An example Kant used has induced considerable criticism. Kant argued that we are not justified in lying even to a would-be murderer about the whereabouts of his intended victim. We are not responsible for what the murderer does with our information. Indeed, if we lie, we may even accidentally lead the murderer to his victim, and then we *would* bear a responsibility, because we had willfully told a lie. From the Kantian perspective, we are responsible for our choices, and our choices are moral if and only if they are logically derived from the absolute principle of duty.

Kant's ethic is one form of *deontological* ethics; such ethics emphasize duty and attempt to describe its scope and its relation to other ethical concepts. In some ways, this philosophical ethic matched the religious (Calvinist) ethic of the times. Its elevation of duty over love was certainly compatible with the Calvinist/Puritan ethic. Deontological ethics (derived from the Greek "deon," meaning law) may be contrasted with *teleological* ethics, which emphasize the ends sought and the likely consequences of our actions.

Kant's ethical approach has several dramatic effects: It emphasizes human rationality; it enhances the notion of autonomy and individualism; it guides ethics into abstract studies with an emphasis on logic; it makes possible (or claims to make possible) the derivation of absolute principles; once these principles are established (for example, "Do not steal"), an ethical agent must not argue from the immediate consequences of an act because these are irrelevant in judging it right or wrong; it leads to an emphasis on the *right* (procedural aspects of ethics) rather than the *good* (the context or ends sought in ethical action). In the next chapter, we will see that Kantianism has also provided a partial base for some of the most prominent social theories of the twentieth century.

The absolute principles of Kantianism are, for the most part, compatible with traditional Christian ethics, but its methods are not. According to Kant, agents are justified by the proper application of the categorical imperative, not by blind obedience to the laws of God. Human beings become the legislators of their own laws through the exercise of reason. This does not mean for Kant what it came to mean for some later philosophers. Because human reason is God's gift, according to Kant, its proper use should culminate in principles acceptable to God. We do not legislate idiosyncratically. Using reason rightly, we should all arrive at the same place. Indeed, a feminist complaint about epistemological and ethical individuals described in Enlightenment ethics is that they are not individuals at all but abstractions drawn from the experience of middle-class European males.

Kantianism not only moved ethics away from the Church's authority (although not away from belief in God or Christianity); it also deemphasized tradition. What has been pronounced good by the community must now be put to a rigorous logical test. Exemplars of virtue no longer set the standards, although they may, of course, be admired if their acts meet Kant's imperative. Every person must make his or her own ethical decisions, and to have moral worth, they must be made and enacted out of a sense of duty; that is, an ethical agent must choose to do the right *because* it is right, not because he or she is led to do it out of obedience to authority, inclination, or love.

Critics of Kantianism are numerous. Many contemporary philosophers challenge the universalizability criterion that is at the heart of Kantianism and has even been declared by some to be the very hallmark of the moral. Some challenge Kantian claims to universality at the level of content. They object that absolute principles cannot be derived from the categorical imperative—that, in fact, visions of the good are smuggled in as theorists attempt to do pure derivations. Others challenge universality at the level of method. These thinkers insist that even the form of practical reasoning is not universal but tradition-bound.[9]

Many object to the grimness, the Puritanical tone, of ethics of duty. Most of us prefer to be the recipients of acts done out of love, care, or inclination rather than duty. Recognizing this, Kantians have shrunk the moral universe. Those things that are done out of love are often considered not to be *moral* matters at all, and a considerable literature has been devoted to the problem of separating moral issues from other issues of value. Because the demands of duty are so strict, the field of its application has been reduced in another way: Kantians have greatly emphasized negative duties over positive. As ethical agents, we are constrained *not* to do things that will interfere with the free agency of others, but we are not often required to perform positive acts to help or to enhance another's growth. Such acts are "supererogatory" or above and beyond the call of duty. In Kant's language, they are "imperfect" rather than "perfect" duties.

We will return to the Kantian tradition in the next chapter, where we will consider Rawls's theory of justice and apply some of that thinking to problems in education. We will also revisit Kantian ethics in the final chapter on feminism.

Utilitarianism

In contrast to Kantianism, utilitarianism insists that a vision of the good must precede determination of what is right. For utilitarians, happiness is the greatest and most obvious human good, and an ethic should guide us toward producing as much happiness as possible. In its simplest form, utilitarianism seeks the "greatest good for the greatest number." But utilitarianism, like Kantianism, has produced a vast and sophisticated philosophical literature. Classical utilitarians do not speak of "maximizing" happiness; rather, they direct us toward optimizing the ratio of happiness over pain. Obviously, we cannot always maximize happiness—or even define what such maximization should look like—but we can see to it that we raise the numerator (happiness) and reduce the denominator (pain). Instead of defining the duty of ethical agents in terms of doing what is right (determined by Kant's logical process), utilitarians define the right in terms of optimizing this ratio of happiness to pain.[10]

Utilitarianism, like Kantianism, is a comprehensive ethic; that is, it speaks to both individual behavior and the moral behavior of whole societies. Again, like Kantianism, it is very much a product of its times. Kant severed the bonds of human rationality to authority. He did not reject God, but he insisted that the individual's God-given capacity to exercise logic and moral intuition must replace obedience to authority. In social theory, as we will see in the next chapter, he paved the way for liberal individualism. Utilitarianism, in contrast, responded more directly to the social conditions of the time. In the England of John Stuart Mill, masses lived in misery while a few lived in great comfort. It was exactly the time for sensitive thinkers, already liberated from the Church's authority, to consider ways to relieve such misery. Readers might get some sense of the misery through fiction—Anne Perry's Victorian mysteries and Ken Follett's *The Man from St. Petersburg* come to mind.[11] Utilitarianism seems to be a fully appropriate response to the depiction of pain presented in these novels.

There are, of course, several variations of utilitarianism. Each has grown out of criticism of the parent doctrine. First, we must be concerned with how happiness should be defined. Is happiness mere pleasure, and is pleasure to be defined as that which pleases any given individual? Most thoughtful utilitarians reflect some of the thinking of virtue theorists on this issue. They, like Aristotle, see happiness as something distinctly human. It is not mere animal pleasure, and as a person becomes better and better educated, he or she is likely to reject earlier views of happiness in favor of those that emerge from more careful examination and reflection.[12] Thus, happiness could require of some people acts that others might regard as mere sacrifice.

Second, many utilitarians adopt rules that look very like those of Kantians. Known as "rule utilitarians," these people use the utilitarian principle to derive rules of conduct. Thus both Kantians and utilitarians find stealing to be a bad thing. Kant would press individual moral agents to consider whether it is logically consistent to allow stealing; can we *logically will* the act we are contemplating (stealing) to be obligatory or permissible for all others in a similar situation? Utilitarians would ask, instead, whether stealing is compatible with producing the optimal ratio of happiness over pain in the whole society. Although both ethics condemn stealing as a general practice, most thinkers find utilitarianism more sensitive to circumstances. It is at least conceivable that social conditions might be so horrible that the rule against stealing could be suspended under the terms of the utilitarian principle. In contrast, Kant thought that rules condemning stealing and lying were absolute.

Many students are amazed (and turned off) when they hear that Kant insisted we should not lie even to the would-be murderer who asks about the whereabouts of his intended victim. Philosophical study creates many instant utilitarians with this bit of Kant's writing. But consider: Kant did not say that we should simply hand over the victim in the name of truth. We can rally round and protect the victim; we can sacrifice ourselves; we can fight to the dying breath. If we were to convert the world to Kantianism, all forms of subterfuge would be eliminated. Even war would be impossible.

In the real world, however, most of us would defend a decision to lie to a murderer or to steal from a millionaire to prevent a child's starvation. Utilitarianism has enormous practical appeal. But consider some of its complexities. Should we consider killing one person if we can thereby ensure twenty years of happiness for one thousand people (for one million or one billion)? Most of us would say no to this—or, more thoughtfully, we might say that the example is silly, since there are no such guarantees. But puzzles of this sort have led to revisions of utilitarianism. Usually, life is given a value above all other goods. After all, there can be no happiness without life. Therefore, we cannot sacrifice anyone's life for the "greatest happiness."

But what if life is matched against life? What should we do in the infamous lifeboat problem? If the lifeboat is crowded with twenty people and only fifteen can possibly survive in it, what should we do? Here many of us would prefer that all of our companions be Kantians. We could be absolutely sure that no one would be pushed overboard; we would all have to wait and see, and we would prefer the death of all at the hands of nature to the murder of one. Scenarios like this one have pushed utilitarians to create a hierarchy of utilities and to introduce sophisticated revisions to block intuitively objectionable results. Indeed, the great utilitarian philosopher Henry Sidgwick argued that utilitarianism itself rests on basic moral intuitions, such as the one that murder is wrong.[13] Still, in the lifeboat case, where no value other than life is under consideration, utilitarians are pressed to save as many lives as possible by sacrificing some lives. Who should be put overboard? Those least likely to survive anyway? The least valuable to society? The oldest? These are all questions the utilitarian might have to consider. A Kantian, following an absolute prohibition against deliberate killing, would consider none of these questions. Thus, although utilitarianism has been repeatedly revised to conform more nearly to the intuitions noted by Sidgwick and others, utilitarians still face grisly decisions avoided by Kantians. Of course, utilitarians have accused Kantians of accepting avoidable tragedies and of a denial of responsibility for cases in which "all die" *because* of their unwillingness to break a rule. Kantians respond that such outcomes are not because of their refusal to act; the results are beyond their control as moral agents.

Whatever we think of utilitarianism, we have to face the fact that social policy is heavily influenced by utilitarian thought. Why, for example, do we not raise the minimum wage even when it is clear that people working forty hours a week cannot support families on it? The argument usually given is that raising the minimum wage would create hardships for many who can now afford services that would become inaccessible to them. Sometimes it is argued that such a move would actually eliminate jobs, but that argument begs the question. If people who *had* jobs could move above poverty, they would contribute to greater consumption and, possibly, to more jobs. A compassionate society would respond to those who lost jobs by either creating work or providing a subsidy. The most obvious reason for allowing a phenomenon like the "working poor" is that their hardship contributes to what John Kenneth Galbraith has called "the culture of contentment."[14]

As you think about educational policies, you may find many examples of decisions that are best explained by utilitarian arguments. A decision to invest educational monies in college preparation for as many as possible rather than to allocate some amount to very expensive vocational programs might be justified on utilitarian grounds. Similarly, a decision to maintain buildings where they will be "appreciated" and to ignore buildings where vandalism is frequent might also be justified by a utilitarian argument. But one might also argue on utilitarian premises that the greatest good for the greatest number would be achieved by giving all children preparation for college. As we will see, such a recommendation might be supported as well by a neo-Kantian argument on justice as fairness. It is rare when a particular decision can be traced to exactly one philosophical position.

Deweyan Ethics

Dewey's pragmatic ethics is, like utilitarianism, consequentialist; that is, an act is judged ethically acceptable or unacceptable according to the consequences it produces. Dewey differed with utilitarians, however, on several important issues. First, he thought it was an error to posit one greatest good, even one so obvious and desirable as happiness. Human beings desire a host of goods, and at any given time, happiness may not be the immediate good sought.[15] Further, a single definition of happiness may induce insensitivity to the views that others hold on happiness. Second, Dewey objected to the calculation inherent in utilitarianism. We cannot, Dewey thought, rank utilities and give them stable values. Human events and needs are dynamic; changing events bring new needs and interests.

Third, Dewey put much more emphasis on the *responsibility* of individuals and institutions than is usual in utilitarianism. For Dewey, the primary criterion of ethical behavior is willingness to accept responsibility for the full range of anticipated outcomes. A moral agent, like a problem solver in any domain, must explore the full range of possibilities and ask whether he or she is willing to take responsibility for each outcome. In this, Dewey closely resembles existentialist thinkers. But Dewey also insists on a public test. The outcomes must be acceptable, or at least better than identifiable alternatives, for all involved. One cannot be judged moral merely by his or her willingness to accept responsibility for a horrendous outcome. One must think through the problem not only from the perspective of others but, whenever possible, with their actual expressions of interest included in the problem-solving procedure. The insistence on a public evaluation of goods is similar to the utilitarian principle, but it does not result in permanent rules, calculations, or fixed hierarchies of value.

Critics of Dewey's ethics object that Dewey makes no distinction between fact and value or between moral values and nonmoral values. All problems can be approached in roughly the same way. Some irritant—some sense of something's being the matter—leads reflective thinkers to devise hypotheses, explore alternatives, equip themselves as fully as possible with relevant information, test their hypotheses, and evaluate the results. This approach, which is judged so powerful in many situations, may not be adequate for moral problems.

Consider this example. A ten-year-old boy captures a beautiful moth and brings it into his house in a jar. He plans to keep it. His mother, after admiring the beauty of her son's catch, asks some questions. Does the boy know the moth's living habits? What does the moth need to survive? Does the boy intend to kill the moth and start a collection of preserved creatures? The boy reflects on his mother's questions. He does not kill things deliberately. He has fish, turtles, frogs, hamsters, and a snake; he has learned to care for all of them. But he does not know how to maintain a living moth, and he is afraid that he may not be able to learn fast enough to keep this beautiful moth alive. He and his mother call the rest of the family together, and they make something of a ceremony around releasing the moth into the twilight sky.

Now, clearly, on Dewey's criteria, the boy has behaved in a morally responsible way. But notice that he could have killed the moth and still been credited with moral responsibility so long as he had followed the problem-solving procedures and accepted responsibility for the likely consequences. There may be no way, using Dewey's scheme, to secure the value most of us find "moral" in this story—namely, preserving the life of the moth. Dewey's approach is very like that of the existentialist Sartre, who would also associate moral behavior with personal responsibility.

We could, of course, insist that the case just considered does not involve a moral problem at all because it falls outside the domain of human interaction. Some philosophers would indeed say that although there are matters of value involved here, they are not *moral* matters. Let's put that aside for the moment. There are values involved. The boy apparently values the lives of nonhuman creatures. What secures this value? Dewey would not seek a fundamental principle from which to derive a rule against killing creatures unnecessarily, nor would he say that the boy's authentic decision itself justifies the act. Further, although some utilitarians apply their basic principle to animals as well as people, this line of attack would not be compatible with Dewey's thinking. Dewey might well accept a working rule that counsels against the unnecessary infliction of pain and death. But such a rule, established as the outcome of prior investigations and reflection, would always be open to further investigation. Further, the kind of thinking involved in establishing the rule would have been complex and forward-looking. What effects does such a rule have on the human community? On the individual moral agent? What other values are involved?

Dewey's method has great procedural power. If we know that we value x, then we can proceed to gather information and test alternative means for attaining x. As we proceed, we may uncover other values, say, y and z, that are threatened by some of the means we entertain for obtaining x. Then we must decide whether we can responsibly choose a means that may result in an outcome that sacrifices y or z. At bottom nothing in Dewey's method can tell us why we *should* value x, y, or z except another "if" statement: If you value x, then logically you should value x_1, x_2, x_3, and so on.

For many of us, this is not a deplorable result. As we saw in Chapter 6, the search for absolute beginnings—for fundamental premises—seems to be a lost cause. Even so, there is considerable discontentment with Dewey's approach. Virginia Held expresses a feminist concern:

> Few feminists identify ourselves specifically as pragmatists, but perhaps most of us could offer more support for pragmatism at its best than most pragmatists realize. We would, however, have to transform pragmatism as so far developed for it to be compatible with feminism. Since experience, as feminists understand it, is not limited to the perceptual experience on which Charles Peirce had theory rely, nor to experience as the predictor of future experience, as with William James, nor to the empirical, problem-solving experiences invoked by John Dewey, feminists may never be in large numbers feminist pragmatists the way many are socialist feminists. But it is experience all the same to which we constantly return.[16]

Held differentiates between moral experience and empirical experience. "Moral experience," for Held, involves more than observable events. It involves feelings. Among other things, "*moral* experience is the experience of accepting or rejecting moral positions for what we take to be good moral reasons or well-founded moral intuitions or on the basis of what we take to be justifiable moral feelings."[17] Held accepts the distinction most philosophers make: The *moral* domain, in contrast to other spheres of action, involves what we *ought* to do not for mere instrumental reasons but from a deep feeling of conviction.

We are not able to settle the disagreement here. Dewey would almost certainly reply that every domain of life involves in some way what we "ought" to do and that every ought is reasonably construed as an "ought if." But Held may be right that Dewey put too little emphasis on feelings. Probably at bottom, as Sidgwick observed of utilitarianism, pragmatic ethics, too, rests on an intuition. Pragmatists need to say more about how this intuition is connected to experience as they describe it. We will examine feminist ethics further in the next section and in Chapter 12.

Moral Education

Like so many of the other topics we have discussed, moral education is a huge one, and we cannot possibly treat it comprehensively here. We will look at four perspectives on moral education that run parallel to our discussion of ethics. In each discussion, we will try to "do" a bit of philosophy; that is, we will raise questions about premises, the need for clarification, apparent contradictions, and the like.

Let's begin with character education. As we noted in Chapter 1 and again in the first section of this chapter, one of Aristotle's great legacies is his lasting influence on moral education, and one reason his influence has lasted is that it has great practical appeal. Aristotle worked with the society at hand. He described the best people and the acts they found admirable, and from this descriptive work, he recommended a course of moral education. Children, he said, should be taught to behave virtuously. The virtues identified in the very best citizens were to be inculcated at appropriate ages in children. Virtue is as virtue does. When the virtues are well established, people can safely raise questions and engage in critical analysis of the society and its customs.

The Aristotelian tradition has been powerful not only because it is so commonsensical but also because it is largely compatible with the Hebraic tradition illustrated in the biblical injunction to "train up a child in the way he should go" and because it was consciously adopted by the Catholic Church. Thus, its weight has been augmented by at least two other powerful traditions.

Character education in the United States is presently experiencing a revival after a lapse in interest of several decades.[18] In Chapter 1, we mentioned that the Character Development League produced a curriculum for use in schools and homes. Its explicit intention was to inculcate thirty-one virtues that, it said, would culminate in a thirty-second integral virtue, character.[19] Teachers were given directions on how to approach the important task of character development, and the inculcation of specific virtues was assigned to particular grades. This way of approaching moral education strikes many in the United States today as very strange, but the method is still used in many other countries.

Character education, aimed at the inculcation of specific virtues, depends heavily on the identification and description of exemplars. The character lessons distributed by the Character Development League used biographical accounts as their centerpiece. Children were asked to describe exemplars in their own lives and to keep track of their own attempts to satisfy the demands of various virtues, but every lesson began with the story of some real person whose behavior was illustrative of the virtue under consideration.

Today modifications of the earlier approach to character education are of increasing interest. Several important literature-based programs of moral education have been developed. Most of these are not, however, aimed directly at the inculcation of specific virtues. Rather, they combine features of character education with those of more cognitively oriented approaches. Still it is fair to say that character education is enjoying greater interest today than in, say, 1950.[20]

What might philosophers say about character education? First, we might raise the issues already mentioned in our discussion of Aristotle. When virtues are identified within a particular society, they may escape critical examination. The courage of the warrior may, for example, be so admired that members of the society do not think (or dare) to criticize war itself. Honesty may be taken to a self-righteous extreme that ignores hurts inflicted on those who could do with a bit of prevarication. Aristotle himself felt constrained to defend slavery because it seemed necessary in a well-run society; he engaged in this defense even though some of his contemporaries saw the evils of slavery and faced up to its mere expediency.

Second, although philosophers do not themselves engage in empirical research, they look for empirical evidence when empirical claims are made. In keeping with this philosophical demand, we should ask what evidence there is that children raised by the character education method actually exercise the prescribed virtues. The evidence so far is not convincing. Several studies have shown that such instruction sometimes produces youngsters who are very well behaved in the presence of the authorities who instruct them but not so well behaved when the authorities are absent.[21] Further, there is worrisome evidence that when the method is carried to extremes and children are forced to exhibit certain virtues and forbidden to protest or even to express their pain, the results can be horrendous. Alice Miller has described how several members of the Nazi high command were raised, and she attributes their adult propensity to do dreadful things in the name of obedience to their rigid upbringings.[22] In rebuttal, of course, philosophers might examine Miller's work to see how convincing *her* evidence is.

A third concern philosophers might raise about character education is that, given its dependence on tradition and authority, it clearly implies a well-ordered society. In Aristotelian societies, there is widespread agreement on the roles and functions of each member of society. There may be subcultures, but these are subject to the rule of the larger society. It is assumed that there is consensus or near consensus on the values to be transmitted. When I was a child, for example, every school day started with "morning exercises": a reading from the Bible (usually Psalms or Proverbs), recitation of the Lord's Prayer, and the flag salute. It never even occurred to me that the few Jewish students in my classes might have been discomfited by the Lord's Prayer.

In today's society, many bemoan the loss of "traditional" values, but at least we are aware that subcultures have values that may be different from those of the dominant group and that these values are treasured. Recognition of the pluralism of values leaves us feeling a bit rudderless at sea, but this suggests the need for a careful analysis of the virtues described in character education programs and a dialogue on how various groups interpret them. Today's character education has incorporated some features from other approaches, particularly from the one we shall look at next.

Cognitive Developmentalism

Whereas character education traces its roots to Aristotle and the biblical tradition, Lawrence Kohlberg's cognitive developmental theory has Kantian roots. Its emphasis on moral reasoning, the primary place given to a single principle (Rawls's principle of justice), and its identification of "moral" with the right rather than the good are all compatible with Kantianism.

Kohlberg also drew on Socrates and Plato to justify his concentration on moral reasoning rather than moral behavior, and he drew on John Dewey to support many of his recommendations for "just community schools."

Kohlberg was largely responsible for the creation and exposition of a theory concerning the growth of moral reasoning. His theory builds on Piaget's earlier ideas of moral growth and fits solidly in the camp of developmental theories. It describes three main stages of development, each with two substages; the three main stages are labeled preconventional, conventional, and postconventional.[23] In the preconventional stages (1 and 2), moral thinkers behave appropriately from fear of punishment or hope of reward; in the conventional stages (3 and 4), they recognize the demands and rules of their own culture and shape their behavior accordingly; in the postconventional stages (5 and 6), they move beyond the detailed rules of a particular culture and invoke a universal principle of justice.

A huge and fascinating debate has arisen around the substages of the conventional stage. Some research seems to show that the average male thinker attains stage 4, whereas the average female attains only stage 3. This revelation (which has been hotly contested)[24] led Carol Gilligan to challenge Kohlberg's theory. Because Kohlberg had used only male subjects in his initial research, Gilligan charged that the stages were constructed from biased data. Might it not be the case, for example, that stage 3—characterized by sensitivity to the reactions of others (the "good boy," "nice girl" stage)—can be the launching stage for a mature moral orientation that emphasizes care, response, and relation rather than justice? Stage 4, alleged to be higher than stage 3, might simply be an alternative route to moral development. Gilligan described what she called "a different voice" in moral reasoning, and because this voice was discovered in interviews with women, it quickly became identified with women.[25] Reasoning in the different voice requires attention to feelings and to issues concerning the quality of life. Reasoning in Kohlberg's scheme gives little attention to feelings and, some contend, puts matters of the good life outside the moral domain.[26]

We will spend considerable time on the theoretical aspects of this debate in Chapter 10. Let's consider here how philosophers might criticize Kohlberg's theory. Using the scheme we discussed in Chapter 7, we can criticize the Kohlbergian program from the inside, from the periphery, from a "neutral" outside position, or from another paradigm.

I.

Researchers on the inside of a thriving paradigm produce results that expand the usefulness of the parent theory. In addition to their production work, they tinker with the methods, minor subtheories, and conceptual definitions regularly used by workers within the paradigm. As we have noted, when a program's workers spend more time in fending off attack than on production, we fear that the program or paradigm may be degenerating.[27]

Kohlbergians have faced and are still struggling with several important objections to their claims. For example, does the empirical evidence bear out the claim that the stages are invariant? Here we must recall that stage theories have several common characteristics: (1) Development proceeds sequentially through the posited stages; (2) development is invariant—subjects must pass through *every* stage in order and there is no backward movement (except, perhaps, at the transitions where a subject may vacillate between, say, stages n – 1 and n); (3) the stages described are universal. Thus, if people who have tested at stage 4 later give stage 2 responses, the claim of invariance is threatened. Several researchers have suggested that responses may indeed be more situation-sensitive than Kohlberg realized. When anomalies have occurred, Kohlbergians have often responded by making ad hoc adjustments in their protocols and coding schemes rather than treating the anomalies as serious threats to the theory.[28]

Kohlbergians have also had to answer objections to their claim for the universality of the stages. If we find clear differences between genders or across cultures, we might well challenge the claim to universality. Gilligan's work drew attention to an apparent lapse of universality. If women and men in the same culture reach different levels at moral maturity, the theory cannot claim universality for its stages. Kohlbergians have to respond by either (1) accepting the centuries-old notion that women are morally inferior to men (on either biological or educational grounds) or (2) showing that earlier Kohlbergian studies were mistaken in their methods or conclusions. Not surprisingly, Kohlbergians chose the second response.[29] (In Chapter 12, we will take a historical look at the work of philosophers who unhesitatingly accepted the first response).

Criticism from the inside, then, concentrates on finding and removing errors as detected by the paradigm's own mechanisms. It protects the inner core of concepts, beliefs, and hypotheses.

II.

As we move to the periphery, we may find challenges to one or more of a theory's core concepts but not to all of them. Gilligan's challenge is of this sort. She does not challenge developmentalism itself, and it is not clear that she even challenges stage theory, although she might. Instead, she has suggested that there might be an alternative track of development—one hinted at by the different voice. If Gilligan is right, then Kohlberg's particular brand of developmentalism will be badly damaged, but developmentalism and even stage theory might survive.

Another challenge from the periphery preserves developmentalism but attacks stage theory. From this perspective, it may be that people do grow or develop morally and that the growth of certain key capacities or attributes can be tracked more or less sequentially, but the growth of these capacities and attributes does not cluster into stages.

Still another possibility is that the stagelike differences we often see are simply artifacts of cognitive development; children, for example, become increasingly able to handle rules and apply them appropriately. This might account for their movement from preconventional to conventional stages. Critics who argue this way accept a stage-theoretical description of cognitive development but reject a separate stage-theoretical description of moral development.

III.

As we have seen, there are reasons to doubt that any theory or critique can really be neutral. But a philosopher might try to look at the work within a program to assess whether most of it is productive or defensive. For example, Noam Chomsky's theoretical work on generative grammar and a competence theory of language rejuvenated the field of psycholinguistics. There was a tremendous burst of research activity. Unquestionably the paradigm was productive for a considerable period of time. The same can be said for a period of at least two decades of Piagetian research. Is the Kohlbergian program productive or defensive? Notice that answering this, in a time of doubt, may depend on how hard we look for productive or defensive studies. Again, the possibility of neutrality is questioned.

IV.

Finally, we might challenge the Kohlbergian program from the outside. We still have to understand what Kohlbergians are trying to accomplish; we also have to understand their vocabulary, methods, and schemes of interpretation.

We might, for example, challenge the notion that morality is properly described as developmental. Apparently, few people advance to the postconventional stages, and when they do, most are highly educated white males in Western cultures. Kohlberg concluded from this that the development of moral reasoning was slowed or prematurely cut off in some cultures by lack of appropriate experience. But if a pattern is truly *developmental,* it should emerge under merely adequate stimulation. If a particular kind and degree of education are required, this casts doubt on the developmental nature of the phenomenon. Again researchers have complained that Kohlbergians often interpret cross-cultural, gender, and class differences as cases of arrested development rather than counterexamples to the theory. Notice, however, that even if we could make this objection stick, we would only have shown that Kohlberg's scheme is not developmental. We would not have cast serious doubt on all theories of moral development.

What could effectively cast such doubt? Harvard child psychiatrist Robert Coles has purportedly suggested that moral development theories are false because children are morally better than adults! If that contention can be supported evidentially, developmentalism (at least with respect to morality) is a lost cause.

Another effective challenge is one that could show that responses to moral problems are more dependent on contexts than on personal attributes. If it can be shown that people who test at stage 4 under controlled conditions respond at lower levels under pressures in real-life situations, developmental theories would be badly shaken.

Still another important challenge comes from those who want to know whether there is a dependable link between moral reasoning and moral behavior. Kohlberg, in agreement with Socrates, accepted the premise that to know the good is to do the good. Evil, from this perspective, is always a form of ignorance. Many of us reject this. Pointing to the Nazi high command as examples, we notice that they were members of what was probably the best-educated generation in human history; yet they committed atrocities. They might even have been able to give high-level responses to Kohlbergian dilemmas; if they had been told what counted as "high," they almost certainly could have done so. Thus, moral educators might properly be hesitant to use exclusively a form of moral education that overemphasizes the cognitive.

Another very important question could arise from within or without. What reason have we to believe that Kohlberg's principle of justice really represents the universally highest level from which to launch moral arguments? Some philosophers and empirical researchers have suggested alternative construals of justice, and feminists have suggested that justice needs to be supplemented by (or even replaced by) care.[30] We might, that is, challenge the *content* of Kohlberg's stage theory. Under one kind of challenge, repairs could be made from within; something could be substituted for justice, or an alternative concept of justice could be used.

Under another sort of challenge, no substitution would do. Perhaps mature moral thinkers do not converge in their thinking toward one overriding principle. Perhaps, instead, they diverge into a multiplicity of sophisticated moral approaches.[31] Indeed, it seems likely—given the history of moral philosophy—that basic moral intuitions (which are incapable of proof) guide moral thinkers who move in a wide variety of directions as their thinking matures. Again, a challenge of this sort would, if borne out, cast doubt on the present description of stage theory and, perhaps, on developmentalism itself.

So far we have looked at contemporary manifestations of Aristotelian virtue theory and Kantian deontology. Using our parallel structure, we should now look at a program of moral education based on utilitarianism. One has been proposed by British philosopher of education John Wilson.[32] It sets out to teach students principles and how to apply them. Its goal is to produce individual, autonomous moral agents capable of identifying and applying the principles most likely to bring about the best effect.

Because this program of moral education has not been specifically implemented in the public schools of the United States, I will not go into details here. But we find roughly similar programs at many colleges. Wilson's basic idea is that we should actively and explicitly teach about morality. At the college level, many programs now include required

1966 Version (VC₁)	1975 Version (VC₂)

1966 Version (VC₁)

I. Choosing
  (1) freely
  (2) from alternatives
  (3) after thoughtful consideration
  of the consequences of each
  alternative

II. Prizing
  (4) cherishing, being happy with
  the choice

III. Acting
  (6) or doing something with the
  choice
  (7) repeatedly, in some pattern of
  life

1975 Version (VC₂)

I. Thinking
  (1) thinking on various levels
  (2) critical thinking
  (3) moral reasoning on the higher
  levels
  (4) divergent or creative thinking

II. Feeling
  (1) prize, cherish
  (2) feel good about oneself
  (3) aware of one's feelings

III. Choosing
  (1) from alternatives
  (2) considering consequences
  (3) freely
  (4) achievement planning

IV. Communicating
  (1) the ability to send clear
  messages
  (2) empathy—listening, taking in
  another's frame of reference
  (3) conflict resolution

V. Acting
  (1) repeatedly
  (2) consistently
  (3) acting skillfully in the areas in
  which we act (competence)

FIGURE 8.1   Values Clarification Program
Source: Barry Chazan, *Contemporary Approaches to Moral Education* (New York: Teachers College Press, 1985), p. 48.

courses in ethics, and the motivation for such courses is often, at least implicitly, utilitarian. We teach ethics and moral philosophy because doing so is likely to increase the ratio of happiness over pain. Similarly, if we examine educational policy at the K–12 level, we find that much of it is guided by utilitarian thinking.[33]

Is there a moral education program based on Dewey's ethical theory? There is one that claims to have roots in Dewey's thinking. The Values Clarification program reflects some of Dewey's ideas: It makes no distinction between valuing in the moral domain and other domains; it emphasizes the process rather than the content of valuing; and it insists that values are manifested in action—that is, it is illogical to say we value something if that something plays no role in how we live our lives.

In *Values and Teaching,* Louis Raths, Merrill Harmin, and Sidney Simon put great emphasis on both freedom of choice and thinking.[34] Consider Figure 8.1. It seems that the second edition moves even closer to Dewey in its insistence on critical thinking in the analysis of consequences and the consideration of alternatives.

However, some of the commercial materials produced by advocates of values clarification oversimplify the processes described in *Values and Teaching.*[35] Too often, teachers are advised simply to ask students about their values—not to probe deeply for the sort of analysis recommended by both Dewey and the originators of values clarification. You might want to read both the original materials and several critiques before making a judgment about values clarification. Remember, too, that John Dewey gently chided some of his disciples for becoming too permissive in the name of progressive education.[36]

Values clarification is also subject to some of the criticisms leveled at Dewey's own moral theory: Should there be no distinction between the moral domain and others? Can we teach valuing as a mere process—must there not be content, specific values to be taught? Are there no stable, universal principles to guide moral action?

Volumes have been written on moral education, and we have barely scratched the surface here. But we have seen how theories of moral education parallel or reflect theories in moral philosophy, and we have worked through a critical analysis of one theory of moral education. In Chapter 12, we will revisit moral education from a feminist perspective.

SUMMARY QUESTIONS

1. Would another approach to ethics have counseled Aristotle against trying to justify slavery? Is this concern relevant to our present consideration of Aristotelian ethics?
2. What is gained in the move to Kantian ethics? What is lost?
3. If imperfect duties cannot be logically derived from the categorical imperative, why do (you think) some of us feel them so keenly?
4. If we can surely save one hundred worthwhile lives by sacrificing one noncriminal but apparently worthless life, should we do it? How can you support your decision?

5. Should we continue to vaccinate against pertussis (whooping cough) when a (significant) number of children die from the vaccination?

6. Should we make a distinction between fact and value?

7. Should we make a distinction between moral values and nonmoral values? Why or why not?

8. Can there be a feminist pragmatism?

9. What is the feminist argument against pragmatism?

10. If utilitarianism and pragmatism both depend ultimately on a moral intuition, what is it?

11. Should we depend on the injunction "Train up a child in the way he should go"? Why or why not?

12. Can you defend Kohlberg's dismissal of character education as a "bag of virtues" approach?

13. What might stages 4, 5, and 6 look like if they were constructed under the guidance of Gilligan's "different voice"?

14. Is a principle of justice the highest principle from which to launch ethical argumentation?

15. Do you believe that "to know the good is to do the good"? Why?

16. What might a utilitarian program of moral education look like?

17. Consider the two statements: (1) A values x and (2) A should value x. Can Values Clarification make a distinction between the two statements? Should we make a distinction?

18. How does the Values Clarification program fall short of Dewey's expectations? How does it attempt to meet them?

INTRODUCTION TO THE LITERATURE

For a comprehensive overview of approaches to ethics, see Peter Singer, ed., *A Companion to Ethics.* There is no better introduction to virtue ethics than Aristotle, *Nicomachean Ethics,* or to utilitarianism than John Stuart Mill, *Utilitarianism,* or to Kantianism than Immanuel Kant, *Grounding for the Metaphysics of Morals.* A good introduction to Dewey's view is found in *Human Nature and Conduct.* On moral education, see Lawrence Kohlberg, *The Philosophy of Moral Development.* For a good overview of approaches to moral education, see Barry Chazan, *Contemporary Approaches to Moral Education.*

CHAPTER 9

Social and Political Philosophy

The problems of social and political philosophy are of particular interest to many educators and policymakers today. Since the days of Socrates, philosophers have been concerned with the concept of justice, and different views of justice give rise to different views on matters central to education such as equality and equity. For the past two centuries, liberalism—particularly individualistic liberalism—has dominated Western political philosophy. By "liberalism" here, I am referring to a philosophical tradition that includes both liberals and conservatives as we identify them today. Both are concerned with liberty and equality, but liberals tend to put greater emphasis on equality and conservatives more on liberty. In contrast to the liberal tradition's focus on individuals (their liberties and equality), another tradition emphasizes the community, how individuals are developed within it, and what these individuals owe to their community. Although this philosophical tradition goes back at least as far as Aristotle, it has enjoyed a tremendous revival, as "communitarianism," just since the late 1970s. The debate between liberalism and communitarianism is one of the liveliest in today's philosophy. After a brief introduction to the current debate, we will look closely at problems of educational equality and equity.

The Current Debate

We saw in the last chapter that under the influence of Kant, ethics became highly individualistic; that is, ethics was liberated from the authority of the church, ruler, and even community and was thought instead to rest on the individual's "good will" and logic. Each moral agent was to decide what he should do according to the categorical imperative: So act that you can logically will that your act should become law; that is, act so that you can logically will that all others in similar situations will be bound to do what you have chosen. This led to the enormously influential universalizability criterion. Many philosophers came to use universalizability as the main test of the moral; moral decisions, as contrasted with other kinds of decisions, *had* to be universalizable. That notion has come under increasing challenge in recent years.

For present purposes, it is important to understand why Kant's approach has been called "individualistic" and why the notion is somewhat paradoxical. Before Kant, Descartes had already put great emphasis on individual knowers who were described as working toward dependable knowledge through the procedure of systematic doubt. Knowledge was thus liberated from authority and placed firmly on a rational base. But notice that the "individual" thus described is a generalized rational agent—not a real, full-bodied individual with attachments, emotions, and community affiliations. Descartes, of course, recognized the real nature of human beings, but knowledge claims were to be tested against the model of generalized rationality. Method became king and replicability the law of the kingdom of knowledge. Thus, in one sense, the individual (as general rationality) became the very heart of knowledge production; in another sense, the individual disappeared.

Similarly, in Kant's ethic, the individual—as the general mechanism of practical reasoning—became central, but the individual—as actual, embodied person—became irrelevant. The individual as a richly complex, social being was reduced to a reasoning machine. Thus we have a paradox: great emphasis on autonomy but a remarkable uniformity prescribed for the products of that autonomy.

Interestingly, even though the individual described by Kant seems hardly to be an individual at all, Kantianism and utilitarianism (which posits an impartial, individual calculator) together increased theoretical and practical interest in individual rights. Indeed, a main complaint against individualistic liberalism is that it has carried the doctrine of individual rights too far. Critics object that it has become difficult to talk about the rights or legitimate demands of a community today. All of our attention has been focused on the rights of individuals.

Of course, there are important differences between neo-Kantianism and utilitarianism, but both have contributed to the emphasis on individuals versus communities and on rationality defined in terms of well-defined procedures. John Rawls, who locates himself in the Kantian tradition and whose *Theory of Justice* has been enormously influential, separates himself from both utilitarianism and communitarianism in an early passage:

> Each person possesses an inviolability founded on justice that even the welfare of society as a whole cannot override. For this reason justice denies that the loss of freedom for some is made right by a greater good shared by others. It does not allow that the sacrifices imposed on a few are outweighed by the larger sum of advantages enjoyed by the many. Therefore in a just society the liberties of equal citizenship are taken as settled; the rights secured by justice are not subject to political bargaining or to the calculus of social interests.[1]

It is clear how this passage separates Rawls from utilitarians, but notice that it separates him from communitarians also in its insistence that certain "rights" are settled, that they are not subject to political bargaining. Most communitarians would insist, to the contrary, that the things we call rights are products of real negotiation or a consensus of beliefs in actual communities. Some rights, of course, we have held to for so long and tested so well that we have come to think of them as inviolable and even "natural."

Communitarian thinking about rights is both descriptive and prescriptive. It describes how certain ethical products—rules, customs, procedures—arise from the moral life of communities, and it prescribes how we should think and act in building and critiquing moral communities. "Rights," communitarians believe, do not precede community building. They are outcomes of a shared sense of what is good.

The liberal position, particularly as it is laid out by Rawls, puts great emphasis on procedures. Rawls builds his theory of justice on a strategy he calls "the original position." In the original position, all participants are fully rational persons, but they have no idea what their actual positions in society will be. They must create the rules by which they will live. Now what rules would you choose if you might turn out to be one of the least advantaged people in the society? Persons in the original position are behind a "veil of ignorance" with respect to their talents, affiliations, projects, loves, and weaknesses. They know nothing of their own character or personality. What rules will they choose?

Rawls gives a first formulation of the two principles that he says would result from deliberation in the original position and later adds "priority rules" to fill out his conception.

> The first statement of the two principles reads as follows.
>
> First: each person is to have an equal right to the most extensive basic liberty compatible with a similar liberty for others.
>
> Second: social and economic inequalities are to be arranged so that they are both (a) reasonably expected to be to everyone's advantage, and (b) attached to positions and offices open to all.[2]

Rawls then undertakes to describe what is meant by "basic liberty," "everyone's advantage," and "open to all," and we will consider the second and third expressions when we discuss equality and justice in schools. Rawls builds a comprehensive and fascinating theory of justice on this technique. The underlying assumption, in the tradition of Locke and Rousseau, is that individuals somehow exist before communities and that they enter a "social contract" when they form communities and societies. Notice, however, that one could reject this assumption at the descriptive level and still insist that, as a *technique,* it prescribes the best way to build a theory of justice. Of course, if we take that position, we then face the difficult task of showing how this theory, built entirely on abstract hypothetical conditions, can be applied to life in real societies.

This last observation is the crux of the communitarian argument against Kantian and Rawlsian liberalism. The persons deliberating behind the veil of ignorance are not real people, and what emerges can be no more than hypotheses for real people to try out.[3] Rawls and Kant depend too exclusively on rationality and the procedures that grow out of purely logical processes. In contrast, real people are affected by all sorts of things that are not strictly logical. Thus, communitarians insist that a concept of the "good" precedes discussion of what is "right," and the debate between liberals and communitarians is often cast as one over the priority of the good and the right. From one perspective, a shared sense of the good must precede any discussion of procedures; from the other, procedural right must precede construction of the good.

In the hyperrationality of Rawls, we see the "individualist paradox" again. The individual is sacrosanct, his or her rights are "settled," and yet he or she is not recognizable as an individual. Rawls himself says that only one person is really needed in the "deliberation" behind the veil of ignorance because all thoroughly rational persons would have to agree!

Although utilitarian thinking differs from Kantianism in positing the priority of the good (usually happiness) over the right, it resembles Kantianism in the feature criticized by communitarians. It, too, strips persons of their identifiable social characteristics and reduces them to utilities. The only way to favor one individual or one group over another is to calculate the utilities. For example, it might be possible under utilitarian policies to favor the young over the old in distributing certain goods because the net ratio of happiness over pain thereby would be increased. Again, the thinking encouraged by utilitarianism is hyperrational; it is not the sort of thinking most of us do in moral situations. Remember this now familiar caveat: Utilitarians could acknowledge that ordinary people do not think this way but could still insist that they *should*. They would defend this recommendation by pointing to the utilitarian principle and its grounding in reality; people really do, after all, prefer happiness to pain.

Dewey's position among social theorists is an interesting one. He was clearly not a utilitarian, although he was certainly a consequentialist; he rejected utilitarianism because he thought it was a mistake to posit one greatest good and because he objected to the sharp separation of means and ends. For Dewey, ends are always ends-in-view, not finalities, and because means involve accomplishing something, they are not easily separated from ends and must be subjected to a similar ethical analysis.

Some scholars label Dewey a "pragmatic liberal" and others (in more recent years) a "democratic communitarian." By the first, writers intend to convey Dewey's sympathies for just procedures as they are often described by liberals but, at the same time, his insistence that their efforts be tested in real communities. Justice, for Dewey, is located in consequences, not in procedures that predate deliberation and reflection. Dewey separated himself from the whole social contract tradition. Indeed, he thought (mistakenly) it was quite dead: "The fact that man acts from crudely intelligized emotion and from habit rather than from rational consideration, is now so familiar that it is not easy to appreciate that the other idea was taken seriously as the basis of economic and political philosophy."[4]

By the second label, "democratic communitarian," contemporary writers intend to separate Dewey from forms of communitarianism that promote hierarchy, elitism, and exclusivity. Some communitarians make the mistake of assuming that communities are somehow fixed. They put great stress on acknowledged common values and on traditions. Dewey, in contrast, always insisted on a dynamic view of community. Community is always under construction in Dewey's view, and it must pass a democratic test: A *democratic* community cannot be assessed entirely from within. We must evaluate the number and quality of its connections with other communities. For Dewey, as we saw in an earlier discussion, community depends on the desire to communicate and the commitment to continue inquiry. For many other philosophers and educators who embrace a form of communitarianism or Aristotelianism, community precedes communication. In contrast to Dewey, these thinkers hold that people must be taught the values and mores of a community before they can communicate effectively. In education, this view is usually translated into a recommendation for transmission of values through a common curriculum.

The ethic of care, which was discussed briefly in the last chapter and will be analyzed more deeply in the discussion of feminist theory, is in many ways compatible with Dewey's democratic communitarianism.

Dewey always believed that true democracy requires face-to-face relations at some level. Similarly, the ethic of care begins its theorizing with basic human relationships. As thinking moves into the social arena, it still remains tightly connected to the actual conditions and desires of real people. It may ask questions that carry it outward into the world of strangers without universalizing. For example, it may ask, What if this were one of my own children? Questions of this sort need not lead to uniform, impartial answers. To the contrary, they should suggest thought experiments in which family membership is expanded to include children with many different characteristics, aptitudes, and interests.[5] In such thought experiments, we do not strip either our imaginary children or ourselves of our individual and social characteristics, and we recognize that our recommendations are products of our situation and standpoint. Thus, although we can surely create a set of social and educational recommendations that considers people outside our own narrow circle, we recognize that the set can always be expanded or revised as new voices join in the experiment.

Dewey suggested a similar question, although he did not follow it with a systematic thought experiment: "What the best and wisest parent wants for his own child, that must the community want for all its children. Any other ideal for our schools is narrow and unlovely; acted upon, it destroys our democracy."[6] This passage raises questions about the "best and wisest" parent. What would such a parent want? Further, suppose the parent has many different children. Will he or she not want different things for different children? In all such thought experiments, we have to be careful not to abstract so completely that we lose all real human qualities; we should not generalize so far that we "totalize" or assimilate all others to our own scheme of things; and yet we do not want to collapse into a narrow and selfish scheme in which we tell only our own story, serve only our own interests, and recognize only our own values.

Although I have given just a thumbnail sketch of important positions in current political philosophy and of the one I intend to use in my analysis, perhaps these will be sufficient to launch a discussion of justice and equality in education. As we proceed in that discussion, we can add to the background as needed.

Justice and Equality in Education

I have organized this part of the chapter around problems of inequality. Are the observable inequalities in U.S. schools allowable under the views of justice and care that we have considered so far? First, we will consider inequalities in resources—in physical facilities, instruments, maps, books, and the other paraphernalia of education. Second, we will look at inequalities in relationships. Is there anything schools can or should do for children who have no academically competent, loving adults in their lives? Third, we will ask what is meant by inequalities in the curriculum. Should all children have the same curriculum, or should they be allowed to make well-informed choices according to their own interests?

Inequalities in Physical Resources

In 1991, Jonathan Kozol once again drew to our attention this nation's disgraceful neglect of many of its urban children.[7] When we read Kozol's description of urban schools—windows boarded up, faulty heating systems that leave some rooms in shivering cold and others in stifling heat, toilets that do not work, sewage backing up into kitchens and cafeterias, paint peeling from walls and ceilings, rooms so crowded that teachers have to count on high absenteeism to seat the children who do show up— we surely know that this is not what we would want for our own children. These conditions, which Kozol calls "savage inequalities" because they contrast so sharply with the conditions of richer schools, represent, for many of us, a clear case of injustice.

Could anyone argue otherwise? One could argue along the following lines. A certain amount of inequality in any society is necessary to promote the general welfare. After all, we would hardly seek equality if it meant misery for all of us; that is, if the only way to achieve equality were to accept a situation in which everyone is (equally) miserable, most of us would reject it. What we want is as much equality as we can achieve consistent with the greatest possible general welfare. Of course, people differ on the combinations that will move them from indifference to seeking a change in one direction or the other. Some of us will tolerate considerable hardship to achieve equality; others will shrug off rather dramatic inequalities in order to produce an increase in the general welfare. Indeed, when a substantial part of the population is content, social change is very hard to effect.[8]

Utilitarian thought can support a scenario in which some people live in comparative misery, but it would not allow huge numbers to suffer, and the best of it would not allow even a small number to suffer horribly for the mere hedonistic happiness of many. For example, it would put such a high value on life that the loss of even one life could not be outweighed by an accumulation of petty pleasures spread over a vast majority. Thus we find that there is often police protection (guards, locks, metal detectors, and the like) in schools where most of the horrible conditions described by Kozol exist. Similarly, there is at least one medical facility in even the poorest areas that must by law treat life-threatening emergency conditions in the indigent. Almost everyone is outraged when a child is killed in school or someone dies after being refused medical treatment.

But, as I said, utilitarianism can support a scheme in which most of the inequalities described by Kozol exist. Assuming there is just so much money to spend on education, how should it be spent so as to achieve maximum effect? If the children in community A break the school's windows, scribble on its walls, stuff objects into its toilets, urinate on its stairways, and behave in a generally destructive way, why should money be spent on repair? That money can be more effectively used in purchasing science equipment and books for children in community B, who will not destroy what is bought for them. Using a strictly economic argument with achievement outcomes as the only value considered, one need not even question the values in community A; that is, one need not argue that A's people are somehow deficient or that they deserve the conditions I have described. One simply calculates the costs and likely benefits.

In contrast, Rawls's concept of justice as fairness would probably not defend such inequalities. Behind the veil of ignorance, citizens would legislate to protect themselves in case they turned out to be among the disadvantaged. This, of course, is a theoretical claim; real people behind a theoretical veil of ignorance—a mere strategy—might behave very differently. For example, one might argue fatalistically, "I sure hope I'm not one of those poor clods, but if I am, I shouldn't have the right to spoil things for others. I'll just have to work harder!" Such a possibility underscores the abstract nature of Rawls's scheme. His rational, autonomous thinker is an abstract entity.

But Rawls has an important provision in his theory of justice that might block the inequalities described by Kozol. "The intuitive idea," Rawls writes, "is that the social order is not to establish and secure the more attractive prospects of those better off unless doing so is to the advantage of those less fortunate."[9] This idea, part of Rawls's second principle, is called the "difference principle." To support the inequalities we have been discussing, a Rawlsian would have to show that the extra funds invested in the education of well-off children somehow benefit the least advantaged.

Before applying the difference principle, however, a Rawlsian would have to be sure that the conditions of the first principle—"each person [has] an equal right to the most extensive liberty compatible with a similar liberty for others"[10]—have been met. If education is construed as a "fundamental right," then it would seem virtually impossible to claim that the first principle has been met under present conditions, because education would be included in the set of basic liberties.

However, opponents could argue, and indeed have argued, that financial resources do not determine the quality of education, that class size does not affect how teachers teach, and that the low number of students taking college preparatory courses in poor schools is a result of poor student attention and ability, not a sign of neglect or the curtailment of a basic liberty. What could we do to demonstrate convincingly that children living in the schools described by Kozol are deprived of a basic liberty?

Our problem here points up the difficulties in trying to apply a sophisticated, abstract theory to a real social problem. If people are not moved to care for these children simply upon hearing the story of their plight, it is doubtful that any argument will move them.

But let's persist for a bit with the argument. Suppose we could justify the contention that Rawls's first principle is somehow satisfied. Then we must ask whether the observable inequalities are allowable under the second principle.

Let A be the advantaged group and L the least advantaged group. If A and L now have equality with respect to basic liberties, anything further that benefits A must also benefit L. It may seem impossible to argue that increased benefits to A could also benefit L, but in fact many policymakers have argued this way. For example, they claim that large expenditures in so-called lighthouse districts help us to engage in responsible educational experiments, and what is learned there can benefit all schools. Or, for another example, higher investments in the education of A will produce the professional people, scientists, and policymakers needed to improve the condition of L. The assumption here is that well-educated members of A will contribute to the welfare of L.

All of this is debatable, but the most difficult part of the argument is the first. Under what conditions is the first principle met with respect to education? Is education even relevant to the first principle? And is it to be considered under the difference principle? Rawls said little about education in *A Theory of Justice,* but he did write:

> Now the difference principle is not of course the principle of redress. It does not require society to try to even out handicaps as if all were expected to compete on a fair basis in the same race. But the difference principle would allocate resources in education, say, so as to improve the long-term expectation of the least favored. If this end is attained by giving more attention to the better endowed, it is permissible; otherwise not.[11]

As we have already seen, it is possible to argue—and people have done so—that education of the better endowed is indeed likely to raise the long-term expectation of the least advantaged. Cynics might say that the term gets longer and longer. Critical theorists insist that such a scheme merely perpetuates the plight of the disadvantaged and that very plight ultimately becomes necessary for the employment and well-being of professionals drawn from the ranks of the "better endowed."

But Rawls goes on to say something that will interest us in the next two sections of this chapter. Referring to society's decision on how to allocate educational resources, he writes:

> And in making this decision, the value of education should not be assessed solely in terms of economic efficiency and social welfare. Equally if not more important is the role of education in enabling a person to enjoy the culture of his society and to take part in its affairs, and in this way to provide for each individual a secure sense of his own worth.[12]

Two points in this paragraph need further discussion. First, we have no trouble agreeing with Rawls that the value of education must include matters beyond economic efficiency and social welfare, and more will be said on this later. But second, we need to ask what it means for a person to be able to enjoy "the culture of his society" and thereby "secure a sense of his own worth." Does it make sense today to speak of "the" culture? And is there one society within which everyone can secure a sense of self-worth?

Setting aside these important questions momentarily, we have to assess Rawls's theory as highly abstract. Taken seriously, it would probably require a society to remove at least some of the inequalities Kozol has described. But it leaves much room for argument. Further, even though Rawls himself insists that self-worth is an important goal of education, many policymakers tie the allocation of resources strictly to learning outcomes. They want to be assured that more money spent will result in higher test scores, and so the most frequently used arguments for reducing inequalities center on economic efficiency and social welfare—graduates must be prepared to hold better jobs, help the nation compete, and contribute to the economy through greater consumption.

Kenneth Strike points out that Rawls's later work is not so abstract; it insists on the political practicality of justice as fairness.[13] But a review of a very recent essay by Rawls raises the charge of abstractness anew:

> Rawls, perhaps the most admired philosopher of all in the English-speaking world, turns in the longest essay and also the most abstract. Although his language is uncluttered, he piles one hypothesis upon another to make a brittle intellectual structure that, it seems, would not withstand the faintest tremors of political life on Earth.[14]

In contrast, Dewey's approach can be traced to face-to-face community life. If there is a major difficulty with his approach, it is the fact that important political decisions are no longer made in such communities. Dewey himself recognized this difficulty in the 1920s.[15] When he wrote that the "community" must want for all its children what the best and wisest parents want for their own, he had in mind a social collectivity in which face-to-face communication is possible. In such a community, the conditions noted by Kozol would be visible and open to appeal. Today, minorities and the poor are increasingly isolated in their own geographic communities, and communication breaks down between these isolated units and those in which political decisions are made.

If Dewey had lived past the 1960s, he would almost certainly have been a strong advocate for the kind of campaign conducted by Martin Luther King, Jr. From Dewey's perspective, the civil rights movement was a powerful attempt to build community outward, to form the connections required by democratic methods, and to force face-to-face meetings. It would be difficult indeed to face the parents and children of East St. Louis, Camden, and the South Bronx and say in person, "This is all you deserve."

Building and rebuilding community is one method to be used in addressing inequalities. Dewey would say that we must act in direct communication with one another. But as important, we must use the method of intelligence in our interactions—not the methods of authority and tradition. We must ask what the consequences will be not only for the children now suffering deprivation but also for our own children and, as Dewey insisted, for our democracy itself.

Again, as in the applications of utilitarianism and Rawls's theory, we may find it possible to neglect the removal of inequalities if it can be shown that the consequences of such action are unclear. If property is still destroyed, if achievement does not increase, if teenage pregnancies are not reduced, how can we justify pouring in more money? It is perhaps not surprising that so many critics shout, "Money is not the answer!" A follower of Dewey would argue that it is reasonable to "give money a chance." We should provide adequate resources (those we would want for our own children) and watch carefully over a longer period of time to see if the predicted desirable outcomes are achieved. Of course, Dewey's followers would also argue that we should look for more than higher test scores when we assess consequences.

Care advocates approach the problem quite differently. First, the *conditions,* not the money spent, represent the real inequality. We ask the question, "If these were my children, would I permit such conditions to exist?" The obvious answer is no, and the "no" is unqualified. In an article written in response to *Savage Inequalities,* I said that all children must have adequate and attractive school facilities.

> We demand this not because "children can't learn" in horrid conditions but because it really is savage to allow children to live in unsafe, unhygienic, and unattractive places. Well-to-do parents provide decent environments for all their children—bright and dull, ambitious and lazy, good and bad. Surely the community owes all its children a decent *living* environment for at least the school day.[16]

And I stressed the point that we "provide safe and attractive environments for our own children because we love and accept responsibility for them, not merely so that they can learn math and reading."[17] This approach invites no argument in defense of miserable conditions. They must be changed. But what else is required? After facilities have been repaired and adequate supplies distributed, what else must be done?

Inequalities in Basic Relationships

When the problems of poor children are considered, their family relationships are only rarely mentioned. School reform efforts do mention the importance of family involvement, but little discussion centers on the quality of relationships needed for the healthy intellectual, moral, and emotional development of children. This neglect is the result of two main habits of mind: First, many theorists are reluctant to pronounce on the quality of relationships in cultures other than their own; there has been a healthy move away from the arrogance of earlier times when professional workers did not hesitate to describe environments different from their own as deprived. Second, traditional theories have concentrated on the public aspect of lives, not that domain usually considered "private." Feminist theorists have helped to collapse the distinction between public and private, and feminists often begin their moral theorizing with the basic parent-child dyad. However, aside from feminist thought, it is rare for philosophers of education to consider basic relationships at all.

At an intuitive level, we know these relationships are vital. All of us admire stories of successful people who endured great hardships but persevered with the encouragement of a parent or other adult to get an education. In every such story, there is some adult who cared enough to spend time with a child, express his or her belief in the child's capacities, and provide the emotional support necessary to maintain the child's growth and confidence.

The psychologist Urie Bronfenbrenner put the case this way: "In order to develop, a child needs the enduring, irrational involvement of one or more adults in care and joint activity with the child." I would describe such involvement as "nonrational" rather than "irrational," but Bronfenbrenner made his point when he explained, "Somebody has to be crazy about that kid."[18] In the absence of such passionate love, some adult has to care at least that the child will survive and become a decent person.

Martin Buber made relationship the very heart of education. He wrote that every child longs for the world "to become present to" him or her through communion:

> The child lying with half-closed eyes, waiting with tense soul for its mother to speak to it—the mystery of its will is not directed towards enjoying (or dominating) a person, or towards doing something of its own accord; but towards experiencing communion in the face of the lonely night, which spreads beyond the window and threatens to invade.[19]

Buber saw teaching, as well as parenting, as a matter of relationship, and "the relation in education," wrote Buber, "is one of pure dialogue."[20] Children need to know that someone will listen to them and care what happens to them. Recall what Buber said (Chapter 4):

Trust, trust in the world, because this human being exists—that is the most inward achievement of the relation in education. Because this human being exists, meaninglessness, however hard pressed you are by it, cannot be the real truth. Because this human being exists, in the darkness the light lies hidden, in fear salvation, and in the callousness of one's fellow-men the great Love.[21]

I have quoted from Buber at some length because we rarely hear such language in education texts today, and yet we know at some level that he is right. Although the language is missing from policy statements, it is often heard in teachers' accounts of their classroom experience.[22] We know that teachers are not just conveyors of instructional treatments, managers of classroom activities, distributors of resources, lecturers, and disciplinarians.

The relationships in poor children's lives are not necessarily poorer than those of wealthy children in the senses we have been discussing. But realistically, we have to recognize that an impoverishment of spirit often accompanies financial poverty. People may work hard with little return; they may suffer the denigrations of "being helped"; they may feel helpless because they cannot provide for their children as they would like to do. And deep inside they may doubt that their children's efforts in school will ever pay off. Thus, even where love characterizes the relationship, poor parents may not be able to "present the world" as their wealthier counterparts do. In heroic cases, they have exactly the effect described by Buber—meaninglessness, darkness, fear, and callousness recede. In ordinary cases, however, poor parents may become for their children the living representation of meaninglessness and helplessness.

In a society like ours where so much depends on success in school, children not only need continuous love and warm companionship from adults; they also need adults who can present the world effectively. Because so many parents, despite their love, cannot provide models of what it means to be educated, teachers must serve this function in the lives of those children. They must represent whole persons, not just instructors, in their relations with students. Students need to see that the possibilities advertised as inherent in education are *real* possibilities for their own futures. This need suggests that teachers and students should stay together, by mutual consent, for several years. Time should be spent on the development of trust so that the advice, care, and instruction given by the teacher will be received by students with understanding and appreciation.

In an earlier chapter, we contrasted analyses of teaching that concentrate on epistemological issues with other accounts that focus more on personal relationships and the skills required for everyday living. In Ntozake Shange's novel, Betsey learned far more from the servant girl, Carrie, than she did from her teachers, and the learning was aimed at skills and attitudes that matter in real life. But Carrie could not help Betsey with the kind of learning we are today so eager to provide for all children. Our analysis of relationships and their importance suggests that policymakers give far more attention to the ways in which teachers connect with students as individuals—to what teachers can mean to students and not simply to the academic material teachers are supposed to get students to learn. Any feasible form of compensatory education must address the problem of unequal relationships in the lives of poor children.

Although educational policymaking has so far not been greatly influenced by philosophical analyses of relation and relatedness, some has been affected by the growing emphasis on community. Many educators are drawn to communitarian thought—sometimes only at a superficial level. The call for community is growing, and many educators are writing about community and how to develop it.[23] Philosophers and educators who write about caring and relatedness are often grouped with communitarians because of their attack on features of classical and contemporary liberalism.[24]

Here we must be very careful. Communities, depending on how we define them, can be created for many different reasons and sustained by a wide variety of methods. They can be as self-serving, exclusive, and demanding as individuals. They can be coercive as well as cooperative, unforgiving and punitive as well as protective. Indeed, when we attack liberalism—from a communitarian perspective or any other—we should keep in mind the observations of Stephen Holmes that David Horowitz recently pointed out:

"Every anti-liberal argument influential today," as University of Chicago's Stephen Holmes observes, "was vigorously advanced in the writings of European fascists," like Giovanni Gentile and Carl Schmitt, including the critique of "its atomistic individualism, its myth of the presocial individual, its scanting of the organic, its indifference to community . . . its belief in the primacy of rights, its flight from 'the political,' its decision to give abstract procedures and rules priority over substantive values and commitments, and its hypocritical reliance on the sham of judicial neutrality."[25]

Because fascists have advanced such critiques, the critiques are not necessarily wrong. Even fascists can be right on some things. But the interest of fascists in community should lead educators and philosophers to consider the foundations of community carefully. Built only on the foundation of common beliefs and aims, a community can be either good or bad, wise or foolish.[26] Built on an underlying concept of relatedness and guided by continuous reflection, it may be safe from the perversions of fascism. This latter possibility, however, suggests the need for serious study of relations and relatedness.

Some of the most difficult and abstruse philosophy has been written, paradoxically, to elucidate the concept of relation.[27] Without lengthy analysis, it may be enough for present purposes to say that the caring relation as a mode of being underlying community should prevent two of the most common evils associated with community: It should prevent our failing to respond to people outside a given community, and it should stop us from committing cruel acts against those within the community who cease to believe or threaten secession. Notice that I have not proved—or even argued in any depth—that communities built on caring relations will be free of such evils. I have merely stated the possibility and leave it for you to consider further.

Curricular Inequalities

In Chapter 4 I mentioned Mortimer Adler's *Paideia Proposal* and its recommendation that all students should have the same curriculum at least through grade twelve. On the face of it, such a proposal seems aimed at equality, and indeed Adler argues that the same education for all is a requirement of democracy. But is it?

Suppose that we were parents of a large heterogeneous family. Some of our children have genuinely academic interests; they find the usual subjects quite fascinating. Others of our children have mechanical talents; some have artistic talents; some have athletic talents; still others have "people" talents.[28] Should they all have the same education? I quoted John Dewey earlier, "What the best and wisest parent wants for his own child, that must the community want for all its children. Any other ideal for our schools is narrow and unlovely; acted upon, it destroys our democracy."[29] What would the best and wisest parents want for their very different children?

It is highly unlikely that Dewey would endorse Adler's proposal, even though Adler suggests by juxtaposing quotations from Hutchins and Dewey that Dewey might do so. In all of his educational writings, Dewey insisted that the content of study is not nearly so important as the method of inquiry and the level of thought invoked in its pursuit. There is nothing in any subject itself that is inherently "good for the mind." Mind is entirely a dynamic affair, and "intelligence" should be applied to *doings,* not to some unseen and stable capacity. Therefore, to a large extent, children can be allowed to pursue subjects and topics that genuinely interest them. These interests, employed wisely, will lead to knowledge and attitudes that are adequate for personal fulfillment and for citizenship.

Freedom to pursue individual interests under the careful guidance of competent teachers does not imply the absence of common learnings. Dewey believed that common problems arising in the associated living he recommended for schools would necessarily induce common learnings. Indeed, he even argued specifically for geography in the curriculum, but he saw geography as the study of the earth as "man's home," not as the memorization of place names and figures. This perspective on geography opens it up to a wide range of approaches and concentrations, and it makes the memorization of facts and figures both unnecessary and unproductive. Instead children learn what facts and figures they need as they pursue their inquiries and try to solve problems.

Although he disagreed strongly with Rousseau on the separation of "natural" man from man as citizen (on this Dewey agreed with current critics of liberalism), he affirmed Rousseau's stand on the education of children with different interests. In the following passage, we hear both Dewey and Rousseau:

> The general aim translates into the aim of regard for individual differences among children. Nobody can take the principle of consideration of native powers into account without being struck by the fact that

these powers differ in different individuals. The difference applies not merely to their intensity, but even more to their quality and arrangement. As Rousseau said: "Each individual is born with a *distinctive* temperament. . . . We indiscriminately employ children of different bents on the same exercises; their education destroys the special bent and leaves a dull uniformity. Therefore after we have wasted our efforts in stunting the true gifts of nature we see the short-lived and illusory brilliance we have substituted die away, while the natural abilities we have crushed do not revive."[30]

Thus, plans such as Adler's cannot find support in Dewey's work. The best and wisest parents do not define equal education as identical education. But if children do not receive identical educations, will not one form of education be better than another? Will not some children be better prepared than others to claim the goods of society?

This is a major dilemma for critical theorists. If society and education were so designed that each individual could pursue his or her own interests without penalty, critical theorists would have no quarrel with Dewey. But society has organized the schools and their curriculum by class interests, not by individual interests. As Michael Apple comments: "The decision to define some groups' knowledge as the most legitimate, as official knowledge, while other groups' knowledge hardly sees the light of day, says something extremely important about who has the power in society."[31]

The knowledge that Adler wants all children to have has long been identified with the privileged classes. Is it a generous gesture, then, to insist that all children should acquire such knowledge? Or will such insistence merely allow those in power to say that equal opportunity was provided but many people were not bright enough or ambitious enough to profit from it? A plan under which all children must study exactly the same subjects regardless of interest seems unquestionably to favor those who are either interested intrinsically or whose families make extrinsic interests so important that they override the natural interests of children. (Recall our earlier discussion of how inequalities arise in basic relationships.)

In commenting on recommendations for a national curriculum and national standards, Apple expresses the same concern: "I want to argue that behind the educational justification for a national curriculum and national testing is an ideological attack that is very dangerous. Its effects will be truly damaging to those who already have the most to lose in this society."[32]

One could argue, of course, that the people about whom Apple is concerned, having so little to begin with, really have the *least* to lose. A system that insists on including them cannot possibly make their situation worse. This is the heart of the dilemma for critical theorists. The critical response has to be that enacting a system purporting to improve social conditions is worse than doing nothing if it both fails to change those conditions and, in its failed attempts, justifies the status quo. This is what Apple fears—that in the interests of national competitiveness and the privileged classes, children of the poor will be more rigidly ranked and more firmly stuck in their lower places than ever before:

> The "same treatment" by sex, race and ethnicity, or class is not the same at all. A democratic curriculum and pedagogy must begin with a recognition of "the different social positionings and cultural repertoire in the classrooms, and the power relations between them." Thus, if we are concerned with "really equal treatment," as I think we must be, we must base a curriculum on a recognition of those differences that empower and depower our students in identifiable ways.[33]

I would go further and insist that the starting point has to be provision for individual interests as Rousseau and Dewey saw them. Education organized around a finite number of broad talents and interests, augmented and filled out by serious inquiry into common human problems, stands the best chance of achieving a meaningful equality.[34]

However, the school's role is limited. Today the school can only help some to escape poverty at the expense of those who do not. *Some* people must do the work that is done now by the "working poor." Why should these people live in poverty? If everyone were well educated as defined by Adler or by the proposed national standards, this work would still have to be done. If the work is valuable, it should be decently paid. This problem is beyond the control of schools, but as we study it, we see the great error of supposing that inequality can be removed by forcing everyone to study the same curriculum.

The best the school today can do (and society seems unwilling to support even this) is to provide adequate facilities for all children, long-term caring relationships that support intellectual development, and differentiated curricula nonhierarchically designed. Given the preceding analysis, we can find many reasons to predict that these measures are unlikely to be adopted.

SUMMARY QUESTIONS

1. Why are the Cartesian and Kantian notions of the individual paradoxical?
2. Are there such things as rights? What is their source?
3. Is "the original position" best thought of as a real description or as a strategy?
4. What is meant by the complaint that liberals give higher priority to "right" than "good"?
5. Dewey admired utilitarians for their emphasis on consequences. Why was he not a utilitarian?
6. Why is Rawls accused of neglecting the political?
7. Is there just one good—happiness—that humans seek? Can it be measured?
8. On what matters do fascists and communitarians agree?
9. Why is Dewey sometimes called a "democratic communitarian"?
10. How might Dewey describe the "best and wisest parent" to whom he referred in The School and Society?
11. How should we define equality in schools?
12. Should we spend more on the education of the disadvantaged than the advantaged? How can we justify such a decision?
13. Can utilitarians avoid the following? It is ethically permissible to allow 15 percent of the population to live in poverty (not starving) if their condition ensures the prosperity of the other 85 percent.
14. In trying to achieve equity in schools, should we prescribe the same curriculum for all students?
15. Is community always a good?
16. Why do children need an adult who both cares for them as individuals and can serve as a model of an educated person?
17. What is the role of trust in education?
18. Is The Paideia Proposal democratic or elitist?
19. Should we support the drive for a national curriculum? Will it promote equality?
20. How can schools provide for individual differences?

INTRODUCTION TO THE LITERATURE

For the liberal perspective, see John Rawls, *A Theory of Justice;* for a communitarian critique, see Michael Sandel, *Liberalism and the Limits of Justice.* Dewey's astute anticipation of the liberal-communitarian debate appears in *The Public and Its Problems.* For a dramatic description of inequality in U.S. schools, see Jonathan Kozol, *Savage Inequalities.* For a nontraditional approach to schooling and equity, see Nel Noddings, *The Challenge to Care in Schools.* On community building, see Thomas Sergiovanni, *Building Community in Schools.*

CHAPTER 10

Problems of School Reform

In this chapter, we will apply material from previous chapters, especially the one on social/political philosophy, to an analysis of terms that figure prominently in the school reform movement that has dominated education for the past decades. Among these terms are *equality, accountability, standards,* and *testing.* Educators, parents, and policymakers use these terms daily, but they rarely stop to ask exactly what is meant by them or where significant disagreements might arise if the terms were subjected to analysis. This is a task for which philosophy is well suited.

Equality

Americans seem to love the word *equality.* Our Declaration of Independence declares that "all men are created equal," but the founders themselves did not really believe this. Few believed in the equality of blacks and whites or of women and men. In the Declaration itself, reference is made to "the merciless Indian Savages," and American Indian populations were slaughtered by whites for more than a century after independence. What could the writer and signers of the Declaration have meant by *equal?* To those involved in creating the Declaration, it seems to have meant that all free citizens were political equals, but even this is questionable, given property owners were privileged over those who did not own property. Perhaps it meant simply that, in the new nation, there would be no royalty or hereditary nobility. We can't settle that issue here, but these early contradictions should warn us that *equality* is a complex concept.

Today, it is generally accepted that equality refers to a right to equal treatment before the law. Even on this, debate continues over the rights of citizens versus noncitizens and of prisoners of war versus unlawful combatants. It seems also that wealth plays a role, and the poor often receive less than adequate legal advice. However, this is more a failure of implementation than of interpretation or definition.

But there is another sense of *equal* that has always interested educators. Are children equally capable of learning what our schools require of them? Some early behaviorists came close to believing that external conditions entirely determine what children can and will do,[1] but most people have long believed that children are born with different capacities and inclinations. As we saw in the last chapter, both Dewey and Rousseau believed that children have very different talents and interests and that they should not be subjected to a uniform, standardized curriculum. Charles W. Eliot, long-time president of Harvard University, went so far as to say: "If democracy means to try to make all children equal or all men equal, it means to fight nature, and in that fight democracy is sure to be defeated. There is no such thing as equality of nature, of capacity for training, or of intellectual power."[2]

Recognizing natural inequalities does not, however, imply the sorting function that Eliot went on to recommend. We need not sort children into groups that will become, differentially, professionals, managers, industrial workers, and day laborers. The educational objective would be to help children to make well-informed choices among a set of rich, attractive curricula. But if we design curricula for different "capacities," will not the (unintended) effect be the same as sorting? In fact, that was one result of offering a variety of curricula in our high schools, and many educators today deplore the effects of "tracking." Another effect, rarely mentioned, was that many more students actually enrolled in and graduated from high school. If we place these results side by side, we find ourselves on the horns of a dilemma. On the one hand, it seems clearly wrong to consign large numbers of children (usually poor and/or minority children) to curricular tracks that will limit their occupational choices. On the other, it also seems wrong to ignore the interests and talents of children and force them all into one track (or out of school entirely). Indeed there is growing alarm that our current insistence on doing this, in the name of equality, may be increasing the high school dropout rate.

Can this dilemma be resolved? We might try resolving it by making a distinction between equal outcomes and equal opportunities.[3] It may seem odd, given our knowledge of individual differences, that the dominant choice at the beginning of the twenty-first century is for equal outcomes. Policymakers, through the No Child Left Behind Act (NCLB), have decided that all students should meet "the same high standard" set by each state. The outcomes specified are measured by scores on standardized tests, and this method of evaluation requires standardized curricula.

When we look honestly at the history of education in the United States, we must admit—much to our shame—that we have badly served our poor and minority students. This is not a new shortcoming. Educational critics documented and decried the problem in the 1960s,[4] and little has been done to improve conditions for these students. Clearly, there is some justice in demanding now that schools achieve roughly the same results with all students. NCLB requires that test results be disaggregated by race, gender, and special educational categories, and that every designated group meet the established standard. At the level of groups, it seems entirely reasonable to expect that the average black child should do as well as the average white child, but it is absurd to demand that special education students and students new to the English language should be held to the same standard as students in regular classes. If special education students could do as well as general students, they would not be in special education.

Putting that odd requirement aside, why should we not demand that black students do as well as white students? One reason offered for the racial gap is that educators have been guilty of expecting less from minority students—the "soft bigotry of low expectations." It is right to raise our expectations of black children. But much more must be done. We know from years of research that test scores are highly correlated with parental income and educational attainment. Simply demanding equal outcomes—"no excuses"—is not enough; something must be done about inputs and opportunities.

Before turning to a discussion of equal opportunity, however, we should say a bit more about the effort to achieve equal outcomes and why so many educators have reservations about that effort. First, as Eliot said, people differ in their capacities. In general, a demand for equal academic outcomes is unrealistic. But we should maintain a reservation here. It may be both realistic and democratically essential to demand that certain minimum standards be achieved by all (or almost all) students. What should these standards be, what methods should be used to achieve them, and how should their achievement be evaluated?

A popular slogan today is "all children can learn." The intent of the slogan is to remind educators that they should not decide on the basis of race, gender, economic status, or any other extraneous factor that some children cannot be expected to learn. But the slogan, as it is stated, is empty. What is it that all children can learn? Surely it is not true that all children can learn whatever the school decides to offer. When we add an x to the slogan—"all children can learn x"—we may rightly decide, depending on the x, that some children cannot learn it or that they will have a very hard time doing so. Then, too, we have to answer the question, Why should they learn x? and we rarely bother even to ask the question.

When we force all children to take exactly the same courses, we are likely to increase, not decrease, differences. Those students who have the appropriate talent, are attracted to the material, and have adequate resources to support them are likely to do well. Those lacking in interest, talent, and resources are doubly cheated. They experience failure in work they have not chosen, and they are deprived of courses at which they might do well.

Another objection arises when we try to achieve equal outcomes by equalizing test scores. The curriculum may become impoverished. Certainly a curriculum that concentrates almost exclusively on preparation for standardized tests bears little resemblance to the rich traditional curriculum recommended by Adler. Objections to Adler's curriculum have already been raised; sameness ensures inequality, not equality. But at least Adler's curriculum appeals to some students, and it is undeniably rich in content. I experienced such a curriculum in high school, and I loved Latin, history, mathematics, and literature. But many of my classmates hated this curriculum, and they were cheated. Today, in schools that emphasize the specific content that will appear on standardized tests, it can be argued that all children are being cheated.

Before embracing equal outcomes as the educational goal to be achieved, educators and policymakers should spend some time analyzing and discussing the outcomes they want to equalize. Surely, we do not want to make all people alike, even if this were possible. It is admirable to work toward a system in which all students can experience success, but success for one student may be very different from the success of another.

Still, although individuals should be free to make choices that fit their interests and talents, we might expect roughly equal outcomes for groups of students defined along racial, ethnic, and gender lines. Why should black students, for example, do less well on any measures we hold to be educationally important? We can argue consistently that any child should be able to select proudly an academic, vocational, or commercial course of study but that no one curriculum should hold a disproportionate number of children from any one group. If it does, and especially if that curriculum is not as rich and respectable as other curricula, then there is clearly some injustice operating.

It may be impossible to pursue equal outcomes without providing equal opportunities, and so we cannot make a simple choice between equal outcomes and equality of opportunity. Some who have made the choice for equal outcomes argue that the same curriculum and the same expectations for all define equal opportunity. If all students are required to study academic subjects and if we expect all students to succeed at them, we have provided equal opportunity. Most advocates of equal outcomes will concede that some students will need extra help, and they agree that for opportunities to be genuinely equal, such help should be given.

But can the schools alone provide equal opportunity? We have already noted that school success and the economic/educational status of parents are highly correlated. It is unrealistic to demand equal outcomes from poor and rich, from the educationally privileged and those who are not. Those who recognize economic differences as strong influences on school success are often advocates of affirmative action, because they believe that educational and economic advancement for parents will translate into more likely educational success for their children. This is a powerful argument that puts greater emphasis on the well-being of groups and the society at large than on rules of strict fairness among competing individuals. It should also be admitted that a form of affirmative action for whites operated implicitly in the United States for many years.[5] Although both the advancement of groups and strict fairness for individuals are important values, it may be—as Isaiah Berlin reminded us[6]—that we cannot promote both at the same time. Sometimes we have to choose between cherished values; we have to decide which is more important for the well-being of the whole society at the time of decision.

A host of environmental factors affects the school success of children. Children who suffer from lead poisoning, asthma, vision problems, and toothaches are unlikely to engage energetically in schoolwork.[7] A just society would do something to remove the worst of these inequalities, and it would do so not only so that children could learn better but, simply, because it is the right thing to do.[8]

It is probably a mistake to make a choice between equality of outcomes and equality of opportunity. The two are inextricably linked. Just as we had to ask what outcomes were to be equalized, we now must ask what opportunities we have in mind when we advocate equal opportunity. Should every student have an opportunity to enter Harvard?[9] What would this mean? Should equal opportunity mean that everyone has an opportunity to make a fortune? If, instead of focusing on a single explicit goal for which equal opportunity should be provided, we think in terms of helping all children develop physically, intellectually, emotionally, and morally, we should see that inputs must be considered as well as outcomes.

Because it is the right thing to do, we should provide all children with safe, healthful, and intellectually rich environments. Because we are preparing students for life in a liberal democracy, they must have choices, but the choices should be well informed, not capricious. No child should be assigned or relegated to a course of study on the basis of test scores. Rather, she or he should be able to choose any course of study the school offers with pride and confidence. But notice the list of "shoulds" in this paragraph. To make them real possibilities, we would have to make vocational courses as rich and respectable as academic courses.[10] We would have to work on producing citizens who have a Whitmanesque respect for all honest occupations and talents. We might have to sacrifice some alleged individual rights and freedoms for the greater good. (What are these rights and from what are they derived?) And, because these goals and the methods to reach them are so complex, the problems we have discussed here must remain open to intelligent debate.

Accountability

The demand for accountability came to education from the business community. Businesses commonly hold employees accountable for their performance, and that performance is almost always in some way related to profits. Similarly, some people think that educators should be held accountable for their performance and its effectiveness in producing student learning.

However, even in business there is more to consider than profits or the "bottom line." There should be concern for the quality of products, the well-being of workers, and the use of ethically justified methods and procedures. In education, the issues are far more complicated. Schools hold multiple essential aims, and they must promote both the growth of individuals and the health of our liberal democracy. Schools are organized to help children learn a wide variety of subjects and skills, and they are also charged with creating citizens through both the teaching of specific knowledge and patterns of socialization compatible with democratic life.[11]

The history of education reveals a continuing debate on the aims of education. It is a discussion in which every generation must engage. Today too many policymakers emphasize narrow aims. Supposing that the question of aims has long been settled, they focus on standardized test scores as the main indicator of student and teacher performance. But responsible educators have long warned that the aims of education cannot justifiably be so constrained. In 1918, for example, educators produced the *Cardinal Principles Report*, recommending seven great aims of education:

1. Health.
2. Command of fundamental processes.
3. Worthy home membership.
4. Vocation.
5. Citizenship.
6. Worthy use of leisure.
7. Ethical character.[12]

Few would suggest that the schools should abandon any of these aims, although—by ignorance, laziness, and short-sightedness—we have in fact abandoned several of them.

Aims-talk should be revived in our schools. We may virtually all agree that schools and educators should be held accountable, but we should press the question: accountable for what? And right on the heels of that question must come a thorough discussion of how the agreed-upon aims should be accomplished. If we accept responsibility for the achievement of certain ends, must we not also accept responsibility for the means we choose to attain them?

Consider the one great aim now mandated by federal law: the proficiency of every student on certain standardized tests. Some of us question the wisdom of elevating that aim over all others. But, if we accept it, how should we go about achieving it? Does it matter how we do it? George Orwell described in chilling terms how the prestigious independent school he attended got young boys to learn Latin and history.[13] Most people today reject the methods suffered by Orwell—corporal punishment, isolation, shame, tedious repetition, pernicious competition, and constant coercion. At least, we reject some of these methods, but many schools still employ shame, tedious repetition, pernicious competition, and constant coercion. Not long ago, I heard a school superintendent tell his teachers that he "didn't care how" they got their students to do better on the crucial tests—stand them on their heads in the back of the room, if that will work, he said—just do it. Although he was almost certainly joking, his teachers were rightly appalled.

Few educators would talk so irresponsibly, but many are willing to subject students to daily labor on boring worksheets designed to prepare them for tests. Many students are thus deprived of art, music, field trips, and drama. This scripted, narrowly academic activity occurs more often in schools serving poor and minority students than in more affluent schools. Can the practice be justified as a means of helping poor students do better? Would more affluent parents permit their children to be so instructed?

In the last few paragraphs, I have used the words *responsible* and *responsibility*. Without rejecting *accountability,* we might consider what is gained by using the richer vocabulary of responsibility. *Responsibility* and *accountability* point in different directions. We are *accountable* to a supervisor, someone above us in the hierarchy, but we are *responsible* for those below us. This is not the only way to interpret the words, of course, but it conveys an important point. A sense of responsibility in teaching pushes us constantly to think about and promote the best interests of our students. In contrast, the demand for accountability often induces mere compliance. What will satisfy our superiors and the letter of the law? It's worth noting that a similar thing often happens in business. The demand for accountability with respect to profits tends to lower concern for the real quality of products, workers' welfare, and integrity in business dealings. The problem is not entirely solved by a shift in vocabulary, but such a shift enriches our thinking and may lead to more enlightened practice.

Emphasis on responsibility draws our attention again to inputs. We are responsible not only for specific academic outcomes but also for what we offer, the methods we choose, and the quality of the relationships we build. We recognize—as Dewey and Rousseau recommended—that children have different interests and talents, and it is our responsibility to nurture them, not to produce a standard product.

How might we increase a sincere sense of responsibility in teachers? Most teachers enter the profession with a keen sense of responsibility. To sustain it, we must find ways to encourage caring relations between teachers and students. One way to do this is to allow teachers to work with the same students for three years instead of the now typical one year. It takes time to develop relations of care and trust; that time should be granted, but it should not be coerced. When teachers and students are forced to stay together against their will, the benefits aimed at are likely to be lost. We must continually ask what we are aiming at and whether our methods are likely to facilitate or undermine our efforts.

Standards

In an article highly critical of the mode of school reform called the "standards movement," Roger Shattuck claims that the movement is a sham, a disgrace. There can be no standards without a specific curriculum, he writes.[14] Many thoughtful educators agree with Shattuck that the standards movement is a mistake, but the reasons for agreement differ from Shattuck's.

Must content be specified before standards are established? It depends on what we mean by *standard*. Diane Ravitch—along with many others—writes about content (or curriculum) standards.[15] The word *standard* in this context refers to a model curriculum; the stated standards are the curriculum. This mode of curriculum construction has a history. In the 1960s, some curriculum workers recommended that every curriculum be stated in the form of behavioral objectives.[16] A behavioral objective states exactly what a student will do, under what conditions, and to what level of proficiency. It is this last criterion that most people think of as a standard and, with this understanding, Shattuck is clearly right. Content must be specified before a level of proficiency can be established. But if we think of a standard as a model that provides an exemplar, then the so-called "content standards" may be regarded as the specified content—as a standard curriculum.

An important argument against a curriculum defined as a set of standards, behavioral objectives, or competencies is that such a curriculum is, by its very nature, impoverished. The idea that schools should teach all and only that which they expect every student to learn is fundamentally deficient. A contrary view—one familiar to those who went to school before 1970 or, more recently, attended an independent school— is that the curriculum material available should be comprehensive and richly varied. From this curriculum, students would select and master different subsets of material. The available or presented curriculum should be far more extensive than the material mastered by any one student or group of students.

This way of construing curriculum has several attractive features. The massive amount of material that might be mastered encourages students to structure what they learn and, it has been argued, the cognitive power of such structuring far outlasts the impressions of specific tidbits of information in long-term memory. Second, the challenge of gathering and arranging the curriculum appeals to creative teachers. What will be presented is always open to new treasures. (I, for one, can't imagine teaching a closed, entirely specified curriculum.) Third, it provides for individual differences among both students and teachers.

But, of course, this approach to curriculum construction makes the setting of standards (as measures of performance) a complex activity. Certainly, the subject itself has considerable bearing on the standards to be set. What does it mean, for example, to understand algebra? What does one have to do to show that understanding? Should we establish one set of standards for those who expect to use algebra in their future work or studies and a different set for those who may never use it? If some students will never use it, why do we force them to study it? If we have answered this question satisfactorily, does the answer guide us in the setting of standards? One can see that subject, students, available materials, and the repertoire of teachers all affect the setting of defensible standards.

Are there some subjects or skills for which universal standards should be established? It seems clear, for example, that all students should learn to read or, in agreement with the *Cardinal Principles,* that all should have "command of the fundamental processes." But what are these fundamental processes, and what does it mean to have command of them?

Some educators and policymakers fear that a realistic analysis of the sort I suggest here will inevitably lead to "low expectations" for some students. In particular, they fear that teachers may hold low expectations for poor and minority students. I share that fear. We should not decide what students will be able to do on the basis of race, ethnicity, gender, or economic status. However, that fear should not be relieved by forcing all students to meet the "same high standards." Realistically, that simply will not happen. Further, if we respect all healthy talents and interests, we should not force students to compete for success on uniform material.

There is another meaning of *standard* that should at least be mentioned. Sometimes people speak vaguely of standards in an effort to say that—somehow—things should be better. Students should learn more. Teachers should work harder. We should have higher standards. We could start our discussions with this vague plea and then move to the sort of analysis I have suggested. The starting point, then, would be basic agreement that "we" can do better. But what will we mean by *better*, and who will be the judge?

You can see that the way we talk about things is crucially important. Changes in vocabulary can be revolutionary or reactionary. Richard Rorty has gone so far as to say that "what matters in the end are changes in the vocabulary rather than changes in belief, changes in truth-value candidates rather than assignments of truth-value."[17] The change from behavioral objectives to competencies to standards is reactionary. Its purpose—explicit or implicit—has been to retain an approach to curriculum that is strongly resisted by many. Each change in vocabulary tries to make the underlying concept more appealing to a wider audience. *Competency* is more easily grasped than *behavioral objective*, and *standard* is a word with more appeal than *competency*. The basic concept, however, has not budged. In the next chapter, we will examine some changes that could be revolutionary. The language we employ greatly affects what we do.

Testing

The choice of vocabulary is powerful in directing what we do. Choosing *accountability* instead of *responsibility* points us toward testing as a means of showing authorities that we have accomplished what is expected. Once that choice is made and the connection between accountability and testing firmly established, we are inclined to dismiss aims that cannot easily be measured by tests. When some of us press for aims such as aesthetic appreciation, worthy home membership, and caring for one another, someone is likely to ask, But how do you measure that? It is not that there is no way to evaluate our success with them, but such aims are not rightly measured by tests. Should we drop valuable aims because we cannot create tests to measure them? Perhaps worse, should we work to create tests to measure them?

The deliberate choice of vocabulary sometimes facilitates policies that would otherwise be highly questionable. For example, some policymakers have used *equality* as a reason for forcing special education students and limited English speakers to take the standardized tests required of all regular students. If they were not required to take the tests, the argument goes, those students would feel left out. *Equality* demands that everyone take the tests.

Testing itself becomes infected by the vocabulary surrounding it. *Equality* forces tests on everyone and every subject. *Accountability* demands equality of outcomes on every test. And *standards* define both the curriculum and what appears on the tests. Because there must be equality of outcomes, the whole process of schooling becomes standardized. Tests are now regarded, as field trips and special programs once were, as privileges—experiences offered in the interests of children.

Can a test be an educational experience in the truest sense? If the questions are explored freely and with intellectual curiosity, a test can provide an educational experience. Consider a question that appeared on a Florida state test: What are the angles in a 3-4-5 triangle? Governor Jeb Bush was stumped when a high school student put the question to him. Proudly, the student announced her own answer: 30 degrees, 60 degrees, and 90 degrees. But the student was wrong! Think of the fascinating discussion that could be triggered by this little story. Space prevents a full presentation of the possibilities, but here are a few: a demonstration of why the student's answer is wrong, discussion of the test maker's mind—how wrong answers ("distractors") are generated, calculation of expected value when one guesses, a review of related mathematics, consideration of a variety of ways to get the right answer, and a reminder of the simplest way—draw and measure.

The problem with today's testing movement does not lie with the test itself. If a test question prompts the sort of thinking suggested above, it can be the basis for a full, rich lesson. Problems arise when tests are rushed through just for the sake of a score and then are linked to high stakes—the promotion of students, the pay of teachers, and even the jobs of administrators. But notice how this use of tests is an almost inevitable result of a movement guided by the vocabulary of accountability, equality, and standards.

In closing this chapter, I'll point out another effect of restricted vocabulary associated with high stakes testing. Tests are now frequently used to decide whether a child should be promoted or retained in grade. There is convincing evidence that retention rarely improves a child's performance (often the child does worse), and its effect on self-esteem is devastating. When I argue this case, a listener may respond by saying, Oh, you're for social promotion? My answer: No. I'm for doing something constructive, positive.

Our vocabulary has restricted our thinking to just two possibilities: retention or social promotion. If you're against one, you must (however reluctantly) be for the other. But why should we be restricted to these two choices—both so harmful? Why not promote such children but place them in very small classes with a loving teacher who will work with them for, say, three years? Why not do careful, patient diagnostic work that will address social and emotional problems as well as academic problems? In doing this, we would not use a nose-to-the-grindstone approach; we would not deprive these students of art, music, drama, physical education, and field trips. Rather, we would provide the sort of rich experience every good teacher and parent prefers. We would teach the whole child.[18]

SUMMARY QUESTIONS

1. What might the signers of the Declaration of Independence have had in mind when they endorsed the expression "All men are created equal"?

2. In what ways are people equal? In what ways are we inevitably unequal?
3. Can we achieve equal outcomes without providing equal opportunities?
4. What does it mean to have an equal opportunity?
5. To whom should teachers be accountable?
6. For what should they be accountable?
7. Is *responsibility* a more powerful concept than *accountability* for education?
8. How does vocabulary direct what we do? Can you give some examples?
9. What does the slogan "All children can learn" mean? How might it be better phrased to capture its meaning?
10. What is a standard?
11. Can a curriculum be laid out as a set of standards?
12. What is gained by doing this? What is lost?
13. Should we expect all students to "meet the same high standards"?
14. What is the purpose of testing?
15. Should tests carry high stakes? All tests? For whom?
16. What are some alternatives to retention and social promotion?

INTRODUCTION TO THE LITERATURE

For a philosophical analysis of equal opportunity, see Kenneth Howe, *Understanding Equal Educational Opportunity*. For a clear description and cogent defense of standards, see Diane Ravitch, *National Standards in American Education*; also Ravitch, *Left Back: A Century of Battles over School Reform*. See Alfie Kohn, *The Case Against Standardized Testing*, for an opposing argument. For a discussion of the importance of aims-talk in education, see Nel Noddings, *Happiness and Education*.

CHAPTER 11

Multiculturalism and Cosmopolitanism

In the last chapter, we took a critical look at the current movement for school reform, especially at the problems related to standardization and testing. We cannot fault the expressed goal of the movement that has been under way for almost three decades—to reduce the achievement gap between white and minority students—but the methods so far chosen have been questionable. We turn now to what may be a more hopeful approach. Viewing education through a wider lens, we see the possibility of goals that are larger and more important than test scores.

Multiculturalism

Valerie Ooka Pang provides a useful definition with which to start our discussion: "Multicultural Education is an academic discipline that holds a range of views from total school reform to curriculum infusion to societal change."[1] From Pang's perspective, the purpose of education is to help people understand the social and cultural aspects of the world in which we live and learn. "It is a people-centered and a culture-centered framework in education."[2] As such, it is an education for *all* students, and its purpose is to bring us together, not to separate us and cause divisiveness.

Pang's definition makes multicultural education sound reasonable, even innocent. But the discipline is loaded with thorny problems and questions. How should we describe the cultures included in "multicultural" education? Joel Spring, for example, distinguishes among "dominant, immigrant, and dominated cultures."[3] The use of these labels arouses some immediate concerns. Multicultural education must help us to understand both similarities and differences among cultures because cultures hold very different political positions. It does not aim simply at bringing people together under one common culture. Spring writes: "*Multicultural education* programs have four important goals. The first is to build tolerance of other cultures. The second goal is to eliminate racism. The third goal is to teach the content of different cultures. And the fourth goal is to teach students to view the world from differing cultural frames of reference."[4]

Opponents of multicultural education express some fears. Virtually all agree that racism should be eliminated and that it is good to teach something about other cultures, but should we teach *approvingly* about other cultures? Should we encourage students to look at the world from the perspective of other cultures? Would not such an approach deny the superiority of America's Western European heritage? Might it serve to divide and disunite us?

Arthur Schlesinger, Jr., expresses such a fear: "The new ethnic gospel rejects the unifying vision of individuals from all nations melted into a new race [Americans]. Its underlying philosophy is that America is not a nation of individuals at all but a nation of groups, . . . that ethnic ties are permanent and indelible. . . ."[5]

Pang and other multiculturalists would argue that Schlesinger misunderstands the fundamental definition and aims of multiculturalism. Multiculturalism is not to be equated with ethnic studies, although such studies might be included under the general aim to understand other cultures. Nor does it strive to elevate ethnic identity above "American" identity. Although Schlesinger is mistaken about the premises and aims of multicultural education, his concern is worth heeding. Without careful implementation and continuous reflection, it might indeed have a divisive effect. This possibility should be discussed openly and respectfully in all of our teacher education classes.

If cultures are distinguished as Spring identifies them, there are further worries. Surely there will be tension between "dominant" and "dominated" cultures, and we'll need to say much more about these two categories. But let's first look at what might be an easier case—that of immigrant cultures. Although Spring does not mention "preserving an original culture" as one aim of multicultural education, it may be implied by his third and fourth goals, and this is one of Schlesinger's fears—that immigrants will retain and favor their original identities. However, a well-reasoned and practiced form of multicultural education should make this unlikely. People can retain a lasting love for their original culture and still become loyal, dedicated Americans.

Jane Addams led the way in showing how to accomplish this dual dedication. She rejected the simple assimilation model that is implied in Schlesinger's comments about "individuals from all nations melted into a new race" and instituted a form of education that would help people to succeed as Americans (to "assimilate") *and* to retain pride in their original culture. To accomplish the latter, she encouraged immigrants to preserve and demonstrate the skills acquired in their homelands. In implementing procedures to do this, Addams was particularly concerned with the maintenance of family ties. She wanted the children of immigrants to understand and appreciate the skills of their parents, even if these skills were not highly valued in the new world. She set the example herself by establishing a museum in which artifacts from the original cultures were displayed and in which women were invited to demonstrate their skills for others.[6] It is a lovely story.

Addams's model is one that can be used in any community to honor and support its immigrants, but it represents only a part of what multicultural education seeks to achieve. How might we present and discuss "dominant" and "dominated" cultures? These labels might be acceptable in American schools when discussing the period of European world colonization, but when "dominant" is used to describe white American culture in today's world, objections are voiced. There are those who accept "dominant" in the sense of "best" or "exceptional," but they do not want to admit that some cultures are *dominated* by the dominant. They prefer to think that poorer countries are helped, led, and uplifted and, of course, this is to some degree true. Both stories should be told.

Some opponents of multicultural education fear not only the divisive effects but even more the possibility of losing the central culture that they define as American. From this perspective, it is permissible to teach about other cultures, but it is *not* permissible to treat them approvingly unless they agree with our own basic political premises. These opponents believe that students should not be encouraged to look at the world through these questionable cultural lenses.

Such worries are decades-old. In the 1960s and 1970s, controversies raged over a social studies program designed for fifth and sixth graders. *Man: A Course of Study* (MACOS) was created with substantial financial support from the National Science Foundation. It was hard to find a publisher for MACOS because of its innovative content, the equipment required, and fears about its profitability. But the main objections against MACOS came from people who claimed that it endorsed cultural relativism and even secular humanism.[7] In 1975 the controversy was taken up in Congress, and the result spelled the end of government support for innovative curricula.

There is more than a little irony in this story. On the one hand, many of the government-supported (but not endorsed) curricula were among the most creative and intellectually challenging programs ever produced in the United States. On the other hand, the idea of government sponsoring the creation of curricula that might be chosen for use in public schools raised fear that the federal government might play too large a role in education. In Congress, Representative John Conlan (R-Ariz.) declared that curricula such as MACOS represented "an insidious attempt to impose particular school courses and approaches to learning on local school districts—using the power of the Federal Government to set up a network of educator lobbyists to control education throughout America."[8]

One wonders what Representative Conlan might say about the role of the federal government in today's education.

Much of the debate over multicultural education today centers on bilingual instruction. Some argue that children should be taught first in their native language and then, transitionally, in English. Others insist that immersion in English is the most effective strategy both to learn the language and, more generally, to become fully assimilated American citizens. Again, there are plausible arguments on both sides of the issue. Certainly, there is something positive in helping students preserve the language of their parents and, as Addams recognized, it is also vitally important for people to learn the main language of the country in which they dwell.

Perhaps the most generous way to accomplish these goals is to add another: to provide dual-language instruction to all students. English-speaking children learn Spanish, for example, and Spanish-speaking children learn English. By encouraging them to help one another, we also reduce the possibility of dominant-dominated relationships. Bilingualism becomes not simply a method of teaching English to non-native speakers but an ideal for all students.[9]

One of the most difficult challenges for multicultural education is how to approach the study of subcultures within the United States. There is widespread agreement that education should help to eliminate racism, and—depending on how it is defined—most people agree that social justice should be discussed and promoted in schools. But the problems associated with subcultures that are not defined by language can be especially difficult. For example, there are frequent arguments over how to address homosexuality, and some critics believe that the subject should not be discussed in schools. Stories about families headed by two women or two men have been banned in some schools, and it is even difficult to discuss the problems experienced by homosexual teachers.[10] An important philosophical question centers on the definition of "subculture." What differences define a subculture?

Objections to multicultural education are based on both political-ideological differences and on religious differences. Some Christian groups have been vociferous in opposing any curriculum material that threatens what they take to be the very foundations of the nation. Although it is certainly the case that the United States is a Christian nation in the sense that most of its population identifies as Christian, it is *not* the case that the nation was founded on Christian principles. George Washington himself denied this.[11] The nation was founded on principles articulated in the Enlightenment, the Age of Reason. Notice that this does not mean that those principles are antithetical to Christianity.

Today there are valiant attempts to prevent the persecution of Muslim Americans. Opposition to Islam has reached disturbing levels, and it is heartening to hear many reasonable Americans speaking out strongly against this trend. However, when defenders of the rights of minority groups (dominated cultures) say that such behavior is "not American," it is time for a history lesson. Consider the treatment of Native Americans throughout our history, of blacks in the post–Civil War era, of Chinese laborers on our western frontier, of German Americans during World War I, of Jews with respect to club membership and college admission, of

Japanese Americans during World War II. Our principles were there, written down for the whole world to see, but we did not always live by those principles.

It is understandable, even desirable, for students to be proud of their American heritage. It is also understandable that some critics of secular education fear that a beloved tradition will be lost if students are encouraged to criticize their nation's failings, to understand other cultures, and to appreciate a full range of religious perspectives. Are these tasks that public schools should undertake?

Cosmopolitanism

Although multiculturalism is an academic program directed at schools, one of its aims reaches well beyond classrooms—to produce people with cosmopolitan attitudes.[12] Cosmopolitanism—a perspective that regards the whole world as a focus for citizenship and mutual concern—has a long history. Diogenes, Seneca, and Marcus Aurelius expressed a cosmopolitan attitude derived from their Stoical philosophy. The Stoic philosophy had two main aims: to make human life orderly through self-control and to encourage a sense of cosmopolitan citizenship. Although that philosophy was initiated by the Greeks, most of what we know about it comes to us from the Romans. Despite the philosophical efforts of Stoicism, both the Greeks and Romans were almost perpetually at war; the Stoic attitude had little influence on the actual politics of city-states and nations. Even under the "gentle emperor," Marcus Aurelius, war was continual and Christians were persecuted.

In modern times, a "cosmopolitan" personality has been much admired in most social circles. To be "at home" anywhere in the world is the mark of a cosmopolitan. However, when the cosmopolitan attitude displaces national identity and allegiance, society's judgment often turns from admiration to disdain or even condemnation. When Thomas Paine declared, "My country is the world; to do good is my religion," he was condemned by many Christians as well as nationalists.[13] Perhaps it is because cosmopolitanism is often identified with secularism as well as world citizenship that it is so vigorously opposed.

Drawing on the Stoics, Martha Nussbaum makes a strong argument for cosmopolitan education. Its advantages, Nussbaum writes, include learning more about ourselves, making headway in solving international problems, recognizing moral obligations to the rest of the world, and learning to make sound arguments that depend on distinctions other than national identity.[14] All of these goals are shared by multicultural educators.

Critics sympathetic with the goals outlined by Nussbaum (and endorsed by multiculturalists) nevertheless find problems with cosmopolitanism. Benjamin Barber, for example, points to the "thinness" of cosmopolitanism. He argues that the concept does not have anything close to the emotional impact of national patriotism. Of course, as Virginia Woolf and many eloquent pacifists have argued, nations have instituted all sorts of ceremonies and rituals to arouse national sentiments—parades, memorials, battle re-creations, fireworks, speeches, hymns, and heavily edited history. Nothing quite like this supports cosmopolitanism—hence its thinness.

But Barber also suggests that the cosmopolitanism urged by Nussbaum is somehow not quite necessary; it is built into the American ideal. Barber writes, "America's civic nativism is . . . a celebration of internationalism, a devotion to values with cosmopolitan reach."[15] But it could be argued in response to Barber that he has confused cosmopolitanism with exceptionalism—the doctrine that America is the "city on the hill" and the "light of the world," destined to lead the world to true universal ideals. Evidence of this confusion is revealed when Barber says that cosmopolitanism has "gotten America in trouble (in Mexico under Wilson, in Vietnam under Kennedy, Johnson, and Nixon . . .)."[16] Defenders of cosmopolitanism and multiculturalism would respond that it is American exceptionalism, not cosmopolitanism, that has caused the trouble. Too often, they argue, we have "generously" insisted on imposing our values on other people, believing that cosmopolitan values are already realized in the American Constitution and laws.[17]

The Educator's Dilemma

If we believe that Nussbaum is basically right in claiming that our moral obligation and human concern should not end at national boundaries, how should we balance our teaching so that the patriotism we are called upon to encourage does not threaten our relationship with people all over the world? Are patriotism and cosmopolitanism necessarily opposed? And where does exceptionalism fit in? Is the United States *exceptional* in its possession of universal principles that should be accepted by the rest of the world? Is it the duty of the United States to defend and to promulgate these principles worldwide?

We might suggest what Jean Bethke Elshtain has described as "chastened patriotism."[18] Such patriotism celebrates national identity but recognizes faults and shortcomings in a nation's practices. It is willing to learn from others, and it encourages an attitude that tries to see the world from the perspective of others. One can be rightly proud of the principles embedded in our founding documents and yet profoundly sad that we have so often failed to live up to them.

Without pretending to solve the problems involved, we can help students to explore difficult questions: Do we as Americans demonstrate the universal values embraced by cosmopolitanism? Should immigrants to America give up their ethnic culture and give first priority to being American? Should we be open to learning from others whose values are different from those we have been taught to accept? Should we be critical of some of these values?

Whatever position we take on the value of patriotism, we should help students understand the practices that support it: ceremonies, memorials, parades, pledges, religious rituals, and competitions. On this last, educators might encourage students to examine the competitive emotions aroused by many sports. What role might the attitude of playing-to-win have in sustaining war and domination?

In looking at our school culture since the *Brown v. Board of Education* decision (1954), have we lost the desire for racial integration? Northern schools are today more segregated than they were before *Brown*. On the one hand, it is good to recognize that black children can learn without the influence of white peers, and some all-black schools are exemplary. On the other hand, is not integration a value in itself? For example, might schools rightly insist that, at least once a week, the composition of school lunch tables be established by lottery rather than choice? What else might be done to encourage students from all ethnic groups to get to know one another?

Some critics have argued in opposition to Nussbaum's thesis that today's Americans have too little community and national interest.[19] They suggest that we need stronger local attachments, not weaker ones. Critics also argue against Nussbaum's claim that national identity is morally irrelevant in making critical moral decisions.[20] On the contrary, they insist, our deepest conceptions of morality are established within close, inner circles, and the quality of that early immersion advances or deters moral action in the wider world. In this connection, it might be argued that educators and policymakers are not entirely in agreement on the basic description of what it means to be a citizen. Our concept of citizenship has always been identified with a particular nation and its government. Since there is no global government to which we owe allegiance, how shall we define "global citizenship"?[21]

The challenge to today's educators is to find a way to prepare well-informed citizens who can listen to and analyze the arguments advanced for patriotism, American military leadership, multicultural education, and cosmopolitanism without attacking one another. To do this with generosity and without indoctrinating is a task worthy of Socrates.

SUMMARY QUESTIONS

1. Compare the amount of federal intervention in education today with that of the 1960s and 1970s. Is there a difference in the nature of the intervention?

2. How might we promote racial/ethnic integration within a particular school? What might we do to promote it across schools?

3. Does multiculturalism tend to divide us or unite us? How might you respond to Schlesinger?

4. How might a well-developed program in multicultural education help to reduce the achievement gap?

5. Is there a danger of promoting relativism in teaching about other cultures?

6. Are there values or practices that should be condemned even if they are accepted in other cultures? Is it morally acceptable, for example, for a culture to deny education to girls?

7. How might we balance discussion of national principles and our failure to live by them? Is there a danger that students will become cynical?

8. Does a commitment to cosmopolitanism undermine patriotism? Can we achieve a balance between the two attitudes?

9. How might we describe a "chastened" patriotism?

10. Can the notion of America as a "melting pot" be defended?
11. How would you criticize or defend the notion of American exceptionalism?
12. How would you criticize or defend bilingual instruction?

INTRODUCTION TO THE LITERATURE

For an introduction to multicultural education as an academic discipline, see Valerie Ooka Pang, *Multicultural Education: A Caring-Centered, Reflective Approach;* also Sonia Nieto, *The Light in Their Eyes: Creating Multicultural Learning Communities.* For a taste of the vigorous debates over cosmopolitanism, see Martha Nussbaum, *For Love of Country?* The problems involved in promoting global citizenship are discussed in Nel Noddings, ed., *Educating Citizens for Global Awareness.*

CHAPTER 12

Feminism, Philosophy, and Education

This chapter will serve three purposes: It will revisit some of the problems considered in earlier chapters and thus serve as a review; it will elaborate some feminist themes merely hinted at previously; and it will extend a particular feminist view, the ethic of care, and use it to examine some basic ideas in education.

Feminist Critiques of Philosophy

One of the great contributions of contemporary feminist thought is its powerful criticism of traditional philosophy. In Chapter 1, we discussed Jane Roland Martin's criticism of Plato's recommendations for education.[1] Her strongest objection centers on Plato's neglect of the tasks and values traditionally associated with women. Plato, in an argument that was remarkable for his time, took the position that women were not, by their sex alone, unqualified to be guardians of the republic. However, in the selection of guardians, only those traits and competencies long associated with male public leadership were sought. Plato held that some highly talented women could develop these traits and competencies, but he scorned the traits and competencies usually identified with women. To become a guardian, a woman had to become like a man. Clearly, even today, some feminists take a similar position—highly valuing work done in the public sphere and devaluing work in the home and neighborhood community.

Martin objects that such an approach entirely neglects the central importance of "reproductive" work—bearing and raising children, caring for the ill and elderly, maintaining a home, and responding to the physical and psychological needs of families. All of these tasks are brushed aside by Plato. Indeed, his female guardians were to be relieved of these jobs, and their children were to be raised by other, presumably lesser, women.

In contrast to Plato, Martin would educate both female and male children for both "productive" and "reproductive" life. Like other feminists, she wants girls to have opportunities in mathematics and science, but she also wants boys to learn care, compassion, and connection. She wants to put a higher value on women's traditional tasks, not simply liberate the "most able" women from them. Her argument raises a crucial social issue. If all able women become like traditional men, who will raise the children, care for the ill and elderly, and maintain supportive home environments? Martin is not, of course, arguing that women should stay home and accede to their continued exploitation. Rather, she wants us to realize how vital these traditional tasks are and to prepare all of our children to do them well. I have argued along similar lines in suggesting that much of the school curriculum should be organized around themes of care: caring for self; caring for intimate others; caring for strangers and global others; caring for plants, animals, and the natural environment; caring for the human-made environment; and caring for ideas.[2]

One can argue as Martin and I do without being an essentialist. An *essentialist* is one who holds that men and women have essential natures, natures that are essentially different. Contemporary followers of Carl Jung are essentialists. They posit essential masculine and feminine traits, strengths, and weaknesses. However, they also urge a balance—men must accept guidance from their "anima" or feminine aspect, and women must listen to their "animus" or masculine spirit.[3]

Many current feminists abhor the essentialist position because they believe it has long been used to exclude women from the public and professional world. Further, some believe that it is simply wrong, that biological evidence does not support it,[4] but the scientific argument rages on. There is no question about the political use of essentialism; the doctrine has not worked for the betterment of women.

Recognizing the harm done in the name of essentialism, most feminists reject the position. However, one can argue that centuries of experience have left their mark on women's ways of thinking and on the values they espouse, and not all of these ways and values are to be rejected as part of the legacy of oppression. This observation underscores Martin's point that we must think about our values and include them in our designs for education. Many contemporary feminists have become almost phobic over the word *essence*. However, even John Dewey allowed its use insofar as it refers to an enduring quality or attribute and not one fixed for all time in an unchangeable nature. Most feminists find the word too inflammatory, but if I were to use it, I would use it in the Deweyan sense. Indeed, I think it would be remarkable if thousands of years of very different experience did not produce some enduring differences between males and females. But that is not to say that these will endure forever, that they are not subject to alteration through education, or that there is no overlap between males and females in their manifestation. Nor is it to say that one set of traits is superior to the other.

Having mentioned essentialism and the fiery debates it triggers, I should now say more about the educational philosophy of Rousseau. As we saw earlier, Rousseau recommended an education for boys that would, so far as possible, preserve their natural freedom and goodness and, at the same time, make them into solid, independent citizens. For girls, Rousseau recommended an education for chastity, docility, and subservience. You can see how this fits an essentialist theory. If women are, by nature, intellectually inferior and dependent on men, then their education should be designed to help them make the most of their nonintellectual gifts, particularly the special charm that grows out of their weakness. Because they must please men in order to live comfortably and with some respect, they must be taught how to do this. Above all, they must be chaste, and yet they must be sexually alluring to their husbands. They must be able to converse sensibly, but they must not express what seem to be original ideas. They must spend considerable time on their appearance so that they will have a "natural" look. Whereas boys were to be educated for freedom,

> girls should be restricted from a young age. . . . They will be subjected all their lives to the most severe and perpetual restraint, that of propriety; one must impose restraint on them from the start, so that it will never be a hardship for them, so as to master all their fantasies and

make them submit to the wills of other people. . . . This habitual restraint results in a docility in women which they need all their lives,
since they will always be in subjection to a man or to men's judgments,
and will never be allowed to set themselves above these judgments.[5]

Susan Okin, after reviewing these comments and those suggesting that
Sophie and her peers be nevertheless schooled in coquetry so that their
husbands will not be tempted to wander, remarks, "Sophie is indeed to be
both concubine and nun."[6]

Perhaps you can see from this brief discussion why so many feminists
shun essentialism. One of the earliest feminists, Mary Wollstonecraft,
protested that women are not naturally (or essentially) docile, empty-
headed, vain, frivolous, and less fair-minded than men.[7] She insisted that
women had been made that way by their education, both formal and informal. Give women a chance, Wollstonecraft argued, and society might
find women every bit as intellectually and morally capable as men. Further, she said, women need the same education as men if they are to run
complex households efficiently and raise sons as well as daughters. Notice
that one could accept the basic ideas of essentialism and argue that
women's gifts far outweigh their weaknesses. Many Jungians argue this
way, and some feminists even argue that women are, by virtue of essential
traits, superior to men especially in the moral domain.[8] However, I think
it is clear that claims of superiority do not carry far when they are made
from a position of subordination, and such claims merely sidestep the
hard work of identifying and valorizing those qualities we want to promote. Let's continue the discussion of feminism's influence on philosophy
and education by revisiting some of the major topics discussed earlier.

Epistemology

As we have seen, traditional epistemology—an epistemology that has
searched for or claimed a foundation for all knowledge—has been attacked from several perspectives, and foundationalism seems to be on the
defensive. Pragmatists, postmodernists, and feminists all reject the notion
that knowledge can be firmly anchored in an antecedent set of premises or
conditions. Most of us no longer believe that truth can be derived from

initial self-evident propositions or from basic observation statements, although neither position has been entirely vacated. Mathematics is still generated from initial premises; we have just given up the claim that these are necessarily or self-evidently true. Science still depends on observation statements, but we accept as a fact that observation is theory-laden. Philosophers can and do take these positions without being feminists, and some women philosophers believe that a naturalized epistemology as described by Dewey or Quine is entirely adequate for feminist purposes.[9] From this perspective, no special feminist philosophy is required.

Other feminist philosophers argue that the vestiges of Cartesianism are still too strong even in current naturalistic epistemology. For example, some contend that the epistemological emphasis on rational autonomy and on the one acceptable method that accompanies such rationality excludes many who have legitimate claims to knowledge. We noted Naomi Scheman's claim that there is something schizophrenic about the Cartesian model.[10] On the one hand, it purports to elevate the individual knower; it frees knowers from authority and dogma. On the other hand, the individual knower with all her or his desires, allegiances, projects, and concrete history is reduced to a *method*. From the Cartesian perspective, it is not a full-bodied subject who creates knowledge; it is, rather, an epistemological subject—a mental mechanism.

Many feminists deny that knowledge claims are somehow vitiated when they are colored by the personal aims and interests of the knower. Often called "standpoint" epistemologists, these thinkers insist that a certain privilege is acquired by those who experience oppression. Thus, women have access to privileged knowledge with respect to issues of gender, the poor with respect to poverty, blacks and other ethnic minorities with respect to race, and perhaps students with respect to schooling. Notice that whereas many philosophers agree that scientific knowledge can be and probably is contaminated with such influences, standpoint theorists do not believe that we get closer to "truth" by confessing our biases and rooting them out. On the contrary, they claim that such standpoint-laden claims and reports are epistemically richer and more accurate than those generated through traditionally objective methods.

Feminist epistemology also intersects with and may modify postmodernism. In agreement with postmodernists, some feminists reject most claims to universality, the traditional notion of objectivity, the search for universal truth and certainty, and the creation and use of "grand narratives." However, the postmodern rejection of the subject worries many feminists. Although they may agree that the constituting subject growing out of the Cartesian tradition is a myth, many are not ready to speak of a constituted subject or to abandon the concept of a subject entirely.[11] To these feminists, it is ironic that just as women are beginning to claim their subjecthood, some philosophers declare the death of the subject! Of course, this objection is political, not strictly epistemological. But then, these feminists have already argued that there is no epistemology entirely free of the political broadly construed. Thus it seems more prudent to many of us to speak of a partially constituted subject—one who is shaped in large part by her situation in time and place but also at least in part by her own decisions and actions.

Another interesting contribution to epistemology has been made by black feminists. Instead of judging claims—especially claims in the social sciences—by referring them to the traditional criteria of justified true belief, some black feminists prefer to ask who is speaking. This is a variety of standpoint epistemology that puts great emphasis on the experiential credentials of the speaker/knower and correspondingly less on the speaker's argument. Thus, in answer to the question "How do you know?" these feminists expect a narrativelike response emphasizing personal experience. Even when an argument is necessary, its force is judged in part by the passion of expression and the commitment of the speaker, not solely by its internal logic.[12]

A note of caution should be sounded here. The view just mentioned could lead to one in which only the oppressed are allowed to speak on their condition. This is sometimes interpreted to mean that only blacks can speak about the lives of black people, only women on women's oppression, and so on. Standpoint theory does not lead inevitably to this position, and it is easy to show that the position fails the test of internal logic. If, for example, only women can speak credibly on women's condition, then men would either have to remain silent on such issues or merely parrot what women say. But if we insist that objectivity in the best sense is achieved by including all voices that have a stake in a given matter, we would have to include men's voices as well as women's. Men and women, blacks and whites, oppressors and oppressed, speak from different perspectives—different standpoints—but each may contribute something valuable to a discussion of the issues that arise in interaction.

Feminist thinking in epistemology has obvious connections to educational thought and practice. If we consider standpoint epistemology seriously, we will certainly seek out and give more credence to the stories of students and teachers about the phenomena of teaching. For example, students have been telling us for years that social studies is the most boring subject in the high school curriculum. Educators have responded by tinkering with methods and exploring more entertaining modes of presentation. But we have rarely worked with students to help them develop their own themes, and we have done little to raise their consciousness about their own situations. Instead we try to motivate them to study material already designed by others for the purposes of others.[13]

Similarly, we are just awakening to the power of teachers' stories in educational research.[14] Teachers, like students, do not know everything about the phenomena of teaching, but they know some things, and they, too, can be encouraged to develop their own themes and to probe deeply into their own situations. They do not have to be researchers. Instead they should be credited with the special knowledge of teachers, and interaction with researchers should raise the consciousness of both groups.

Philosophy of Social Science

As in epistemology, there is a current trend away from the notion of science as normatively controlled and objective. Many philosophers now construe science as a social practice, one influenced by group biases as well as individual ones. In social science, the biases of both the scientist and the scientific community are further aggravated by the fact that its objects of research are themselves subjects replete with their own biases and idiosyncratic responses. Recognizing the multiplicity of interactions in social science research, Lee Cronbach some time ago advised limiting research claims to what feminist and postmodern thinkers now call "local truth"; that is, educational researchers and other social scientists should seek results that are accurate for particular groups under particular conditions for particular purposes.[15] These "local" truths are, nevertheless, truths. Their recognition echoes Rorty's claim that changes are more often brought about by changes in the candidates for truth-value than changes in truth-value.

Feminist philosophers of science have shown that the group biases of scientists have included a masculinist ideology that objectifies its human subjects and genderizes nature. Its treatment of nature as "she" has expressed the dual desires to control both nature and women—to force nature to disclose her ways and to dominate women.[16] The exposure of masculinist ideology in science, accomplished largely through the analysis of language, has led to a critique of both the methods and results of science. With respect to method, feminists have questioned the sharp separation between subject and object (is total detachment either necessary or desirable?), control as a primary purpose, objectivity as an ideal achievable by an individual investigator, replicability as the main criterion of acceptable method, and the habit of ignoring anomalies and discarding outliers. With respect to results, feminists have challenged, among other conclusions, the notion that "only men have evolved" and that males are inherently more variable than females in intelligence.[17]

Feminists have suggested alternative methods, and, as in epistemology, they have allies who agree that these methods are often preferable. Sociologist John O'Neill recommended some time ago that the subjects of sociological research be treated as authentic subjects and that research be conducted within a relation of trust and cooperation.[18] Similarly, feminist sociologist Dorothy Smith calls for research *for* women, not *on* women.[19]

Evelyn Fox Keller, in her biography of Nobelist Barbara McClintock, shows how attachment to the object of study (a "feeling for the organism") can enhance research.[20] So, too, careful attention to anomalies or outliers can lead to the discovery of significant properties and principles. One does not have to seek general principles in central tendencies, nor does one have to engage in reductionism to investigate complex phenomena. The acceptance of pluralism in the physical sciences has its counterpart in the social sciences, ethics, and theology. In theology, for example, feminist "thealogians" are bringing a new respectability to polytheism.

Feminist philosophers of science, ethics, epistemology, and theology all face a thorny problem. If the masculinist traditions in all of these domains are legitimately criticized for claiming right methods and true conclusions, by what criteria do we pronounce them wrong? If we offer alternatives, by what criteria do we defend the alternatives? Feminist theologians, for example, have accused male theologians of illegitimately positing one god described in the image of men of their own culture. The criticism seems justifiable. However, some feminist theologians go on to describe a god created in the image of women in their own culture. What justifies this move?[21] It may well be that the initial criticism can be justified only by allowing a pluralistic conception of deity. Similarly, an attack on the central methods of traditional science can only be sustained contextually, not by the substitution of an alternative, singular method.[22] Again, these ideas are not unique to current feminism; an argument for a pluralistic universe was made years ago by William James,[23] and it is sometimes made by contemporary mathematicians as well.[24]

What can feminist philosophy of social science contribute to educational research? Perhaps the most important contribution is the warning not to substitute "one right way" for another. Qualitative research is not more right than quantitative; narrative no more right than paradigmatic. Rather, the rightness of a research method must be judged by both the purposes of the participants (researchers *and* subjects) and its effects. Instead of asking merely how a study holds up against preestablished criteria of adequacy, we ask now whether purposes are shared and whether the results are both useful and acceptable.

Ethics

Feminist ethics, like feminist epistemology and philosophy of science, is varied; there is no unitary position called "feminist ethics." Some feminists concentrate on the liberal agenda and what it should mean for women's rights and justice. Some work from a socialist position and focus on oppression and relief from oppression; these theorists are concerned with racism and classism as well as matters of gender. Some are separatists and seek to develop a female culture quite apart from the social order developed by men.[25] Still others of us are working to articulate an ethic of care, and that is the approach I will say more about here.

Carol Gilligan's *In a Different Voice*, which we discussed briefly in Chapter 8, has generated an enormous volume of debate—much of it interesting and important but a lot of it irrelevant to the actual development of an ethic of care.[26] Whether the different voice should be exclusively associated with women (whether it can be empirically so linked) is an interesting question but one I find distracting. The main point to consider is whether an ethic of care can lead us to a less violent, more caring way of life. What is this ethic, and why should we think it has such potential?

First, the ethic of care dismisses the old distinction between *is* and *ought* as a pseudoproblem. We do not have to construct elaborate logical rationales to explain why human beings ought to treat one another as positively as our situation permits. Ethical life is not separate from and alien to the physical world. Because we human beings are *in* the world, not mere spectators watching from outside it, our social instincts and the reflective elaboration of them are also in the world. Pragmatists and care theorists agree on this. The ought—better, the "I ought"—arises directly in lived experience. "Oughtness," one might say, is part of our "isness." Anyone who lives beyond infancy has at least an inkling of having been cared for; that inkling may not be enough to really understand what it means to be cared for, and certainly it is often inadequate to produce a fully caring adult. But it is the root of our responsibility to one another. At least in part because of this rootedness in care, in many common human situations, we respond spontaneously to another's plight. I have called this spontaneous response "natural" caring. Perhaps there is a better, less loaded word for it, but what I mean to convey is that the motive to care in many situations arises on its own; it does not have to be summoned.[27]

In contrast, "ethical" caring does have to be summoned. The "I ought" arises but encounters conflict: An inner voice grumbles, "I ought but I don't want to," or "Why should I respond?" or "This guy deserves to suffer, so why should I help?" On these occasions we need not turn to a principle; more effectively, we turn to our memories of caring and being cared for and a picture or ideal of ourselves as carers. I think Kant was right to distinguish between the acts we do spontaneously out of love and those we do from duty or, I would prefer to say, from faithfulness to an ideal picture of ourselves. I think he was wrong—tragically wrong—to elevate ethical caring over natural caring. Ethical caring's great contribution is to guide action long enough for natural caring to be restored and for people once again to interact with mutual and spontaneous regard.

An interesting debate has arisen over the role of principles in ethics. No one would deny the everyday usefulness of principles as rules of thumb or shortcuts to reliable conclusions. We all learn from experience to respond in certain ways to certain situations, and for the most part these rules or principles save us a great deal of mental labor. But Kantians and rule utilitarians have made principles the very heart of ethics. Kant's categorical imperative has been used (by Kant himself as well as followers) to derive other principles and rules—just as we derive theorems from axioms and postulates in mathematics. Ethical decisions, then, are made on the basis of logico-mathematical reasoning.

In contrast, the ethic of care gives only a minor place to principles and insists instead that ethical discussions must be made in caring interactions with those affected by the discussion. Indeed, it is exactly in the most difficult situations that principles fail us. Thus, instead of turning to a principle for guidance, a carer turns to the cared-for. What does he or she need? Will filling this need harm others in the network of care? Am I competent to fill this need? Will I sacrifice too much of myself? Is the expressed need really in the best interest of the cared-for? If the cared-for is a stranger, I might ask how I would respond to her or him if she or he were a member of my inner circle.

Jean Grimshaw has raised an important question about this kind of thinking.[28] Does it not also proceed from a principle but one of a different sort? Grimshaw imagines her own mother using a principle like this: "Consider whether your behaviour will stand in the way of maintaining care and relationships."[29] The suggestion is that the ethic of care is itself an ethic of principle; its fundamental principle might be: Always act so as to establish, maintain, or enhance caring relations.

On one level, there should be no objection to this. As a descriptive principle, one that describes how carers look to observers outside the caring relation, we hope it will be generally accurate. But it need not be the guiding force behind the carer's response, nor can we derive other principles and rules from it. Kant's moral agent can decide moral questions in solitude. Carers must rub elbows with the recipients of their care. Guiding questions arise, but even these change with the situation, and there are no recipes for caring. Cultural and personal differences will result in different manifestations of care. Thus, at the prescriptive level, there is no universalization—unless it is something so general that it merely reflects the natural tendency mentioned earlier, such as, Do the best you can to keep people from being hurt. But clearly even this cannot be an absolute. The only universals recognized by care theorists are those describing the human condition: the commonalities of birth, death, physical and emotional needs, and the longing to be cared for. This last—whether it is manifested as a need for love, physical care, respect, or mere recognition—is the fundamental starting point for the ethic of care.

Perhaps the greatest contribution of an ethic of care is its emphasis on the relation and the role of the cared-for. Not surprisingly, this is a feature rejected by many traditional ethicists. It insists that caring does not reside entirely in the attitude and intentions of the carer. We must ask about the effects on the cared-for. If A claims to care for B, but B denies that A cares, then the relation between A and B is not one of caring. This does not mean that A is at fault (although she may be), nor does it mean that B is at fault (although she may be). There may be something wrong in the situation.

This insistence on including the cared-for as an active contributor to the caring relation makes it impossible to codify caring. I cannot retreat to my office and figure out logically what I should do—what principle I should invoke to justify my acts. Nor can I rely on calculation of utilities. Nor can I call upon my virtues and heroically display the behaviors most admired by my community. I may, of course, be influenced by any or all of these considerations. However, at bottom, I have to respond to the cared-for who addresses me in a special way and asks me for something concrete and, perhaps, even unique. Thus what I as a carer do for one person may not satisfy another. I take my cues not from a stable principle but from the living other whom I encounter.

Some feminists have raised a concern that an ethic of care might contribute to the continued exploitation of women. Both Barbara Houston and Sarah Hoagland argue that stress on the maintenance of caring relationships can lead carers to neglect their own welfare and, worse, to blame themselves for the shortcomings of those for whom they try to care.[30] This is a very important objection, and it must be answered carefully. The fear expressed by Houston and Hoagland is certainly borne out historically. Women have in fact been expected to maintain relationships even when the relationships are abusive, and until recently, women were often blamed when their husbands and children went wrong. Surely no advocate of an ethic of care wants to endorse such a situation. Does the ethic of care lead logically to this unwanted result? I think the answer is clear that it does not.

First, "carer" and "cared-for" are not permanent labels attached in stable and distinct ways to two different sets of people. They are labels for the parties in an encounter or in a series of encounters in a continuing relationship. Except in structurally unequal relationships (e.g., parent-child, teacher-student, physician-patient), both parties are expected to act as carers when they are so addressed by another. Of course, it can happen that a selfish person will continually make demands on one who tries to respond consistently as carer, but the ethic of care not only allows the carer in such a situation to withdraw, it insists that she must do so to preserve her capacity to care. Houston objects that this way of allowing the carer to escape exploitation does not accord her unconditional respect; it values her only as carer. The cared-for, in contrast, enjoys unconditional care. But the concern is, theoretically, unwarranted because the carer is also a potential cared-for and, in addition, the cared-for does not enjoy unconditional respect, either. Both parties, not just one of them, are constrained by the ethic to care.

Second, the ethic is not meant just for women, and there is surely a danger in labeling it a feminine ethic or women's ethic.[31] When I used the word *feminine* (and I probably will not do so again), I intended to point to centuries of female experience and the tasks and values long associated with that experience. I do believe that the care approach is more likely to arise from experience that includes direct, hands-on responsibility for others than from experience more separated from others. The ethic of care is thus "feminine" in the sense that it represents an articulation of one important facet of female experience, but that experience and the moral thought that grows out of it are no more limited to women than scholarly experience and Kantian thought are limited to men. The pertinent question is, which sort of experience and which moral thought will improve the condition of humankind?

Third, and finally, the ethic of care guards against exploitation by emphasizing moral education. If all children, both girls and boys, are raised to be competent carers and sensitive cared-fors, exploitation should be rare. The ethic of care binds carers and cared-fors in relationships of mutual responsibility. In contrast to the individualism of Kantian ethics wherein every moral agent is wholly responsible for his or her own moral perfection, the ethic of care requires each of us to recognize our own frailty and to bring out the best in one another. It recognizes that we are dependent on each other (and to some degree on good fortune) for our moral goodness. How good I can be depends at least in part on how you treat me. Thus a major aim of the ethic of care is to prevent the very separation that induces the dualisms exploiter/exploited, oppressor/oppressed, moral agent/object, and so on.

An interesting theoretical question about care ethics has arisen. Is the ethic of care a form of virtue ethics? I said very little about virtue ethics in the chapter on ethics and moral education, confining my remarks to its use as a foundation for character education. Contemporary virtue ethicists and care ethicists both rely more on the character, attitudes, and moral resources of moral agents than on the application of principles in making moral decisions. Further, both see a close relationship between human goods and moral virtues.[32] Both, for example, discuss the link between the human desire to be cared for and the moral response of caring. But, as we will see in the discussion of care theory and moral education, there is also a difference; care ethics concentrates more on the relation, virtue ethics on the moral agent.[33]

Care ethics has grown rapidly in the past few decades. Virginia Held notes that "it has given rise to an extensive body of literature and has affected many moral inquiries in many areas."[34] Michael Slote's work attempts "to show that a care-ethical approach makes sense across the whole range of normative moral and political issues that philosophers have sought to deal with."[35] And my own recent work tries to trace care ethics to its earliest evolutionary roots in maternal instinct.[36] Given the scope of current work on care ethics, it probably is no longer appropriate to label it a "feminist" ethic.

Although care theorists are still working on problems centered on human relations within friendships, families, small communities, and schools, interest is growing in its applications to global affairs and justice. There is, for example, lively debate over the primacy of rights or needs in constructing a theory of justice, and care theorists are working to produce a care-driven theory of justice. In the next few years, it is predictable that new work will appear connecting care ethics to peace studies. Indeed, Held closes her book on care ethics with this statement: "A globalization of caring relations would help people of different states and cultures to live in peace, to respect each other's rights, to care together for their environments, and to improve the lives of their children."[37]

Care and Education

Because I have mentioned the centrality of moral education in the ethic of care, it makes sense to start our discussion of care and education with the ethic's approach to moral education. Moral education from the care perspective has four major components: modeling, dialogue, practice, and confirmation.

Modeling is important in most schemes of moral education, but in caring, as in character education, it is especially important. In contrast to cognitive developmentalists, we are not primarily concerned with moral reasoning, although, of course, we do not ignore reasoning. We are mainly concerned with the growth of our students as carers and cared-fors. We have to show in our own behavior what it means to care. Thus we do not merely tell them to care and give them texts to read on the subject; we demonstrate our caring in our relations with them. However, we do not care merely for the purpose of modeling. Our caring must be genuine; the inevitable modeling is a by-product.

In addition to showing what it means to care, we engage our students in *dialogue* about caring. On one level, dialogue is such an essential part of caring that we could not model caring without engaging in it. However, it is also important to talk about our caring, because caring can be manifested in very different ways. Students often need help in interpreting the behavior of adults. Is a tough teacher necessarily caring? Might she be? Is a permissive teacher caring? What does our assessment depend on?

Students can be encouraged to analyze patterns of behavior and reactions to these patterns. If, in the name of fairness, a teacher treats all students exactly alike, do all students feel cared for? Is there a sense of fairness that is compatible with caring? Many students today equate coercion with caring. They believe that a teacher who cares for them will demand that they do certain things. Critical theorists as well as care theorists worry that such thinking may induce a permanent dependency on a strong boss or leader. Thus, one function of dialogue is to help us and our students to reflect upon and critique our own practice. It gives us an opportunity to ask why we are doing certain things and with what effect.

A major difference between virtue ethics and care ethics is revealed in this discussion. As I have described caring, emphasis is on the relation. A person earns the label "caring" by regularly establishing caring relations, and a caring relation requires that the cared-for recognize the caring. But there is a form of caring compatible with virtue ethics but questionable in care ethics. In this form of caring, the main determinant of caring is the motives and conduct of the one said to care. A teacher who acts in what she supposes to be the best interests of her students (whether or not they recognize her conduct as caring) may be said to care. This is a very important difference, and you might want to read more on it.[38] If you, as a teacher, force students to do things they hate because you believe these things are good for them, should you be credited with caring? Can you claim to have established caring relations? Notice that these are two very different questions and may require different answers. To establish caring relations, dialogue is necessary.

Dialogue is implied by the phenomenology of caring. When we care, we receive the other in an open and genuine way. I've called this receptivity "engrossment," but that term is not meant to suggest infatuation, obsession, or single-mindedness. It suggests, rather, a nonselective form of attention that allows the other to establish a frame of reference and invite us to enter it. As dialogue unfolds, we participate in a mutual construction of the frame of reference, but this is always a sensitive task that involves total receptivity, reflection, invitation, assessment, revision, and further exploration.

Dialogue is essential in moral education from the care perspective. It is a means by which we evaluate the effects of our attempts to care. Through dialogue we learn more about the other, and we need this knowledge to act effectively as carers. As we try to care, we are helped in our efforts by the feedback we get from the recipients of our care.

Finally, dialogue contributes to the growth of cared-fors. All sorts of questions, information, points of view, and attitudes are conveyed in dialogue. Teachers engaged in dialogue with their students can invite their students to participate in the "immortal conversation."[39] Here care theorists agree with Socrates (and Adler) that an education worthy of the name must help students to examine their own lives and explore the great questions human beings have always asked. There is a caveat on this, however. Care theorists would not *force* students to grapple with the so-called eternal questions. Rather, we would *invite* such conversation and allow students to codirect the line of investigation. We would not declare that the unexamined life is not worth living, but we would raise questions: Is the unexamined life worth living? Should we decide this for others? How do we feel about our own?

Practice is also vital in moral education. The experiences in which we immerse ourselves tend to produce a "mentality." Much talk of mentalities is a product of stereotyping, but some of it is real and useful. Those who educate business executives, military leaders, and lawyers, for example, often believe that they are teaching far more than a batch of content; they are training minds with a certain outlook. If we want to produce people who will care for one another, then it makes sense to give students practice in caring and reflecting on that practice.

Sometimes practice in care is translated into a specific requirement for community service. Such experience can contribute to a growing competence in caring, but a perfunctorily satisfied requirement does not ensure the desired growth. Children need to participate in caring with adult models who show them how to care, talk with them about the difficulties and rewards of such work, and demonstrate in their own work that caring is important.

Current curriculum recommendations put a great emphasis on cooperative learning, and cooperative learning can be used to promote competence in caring. However, as we saw in our earlier discussion, cooperative learning can be used for a wide variety of purposes, and it can be defined in many different ways. Teachers should be explicit in telling students that a primary purpose of cooperative work is helping one another—to understand, to share, and to support. The aim is not always or primarily academic learning.

The fourth component, *confirmation*, sets caring apart from other approaches to moral education. Martin Buber described confirmation as an act of affirming and encouraging the best in others.[40] When we confirm someone, we identify a better self and encourage its development. To do this, we must know the other reasonably well. Otherwise, we cannot see what the other is really striving for, what ideal he or she may long to make real. Formulas and slogans have no place in confirmation. We do not posit a single ideal for everyone and then announce "high expectations for all." Rather we recognize something admirable, or at least acceptable, struggling to emerge in each person we encounter. The goal or attribute must be seen as worthy both by the person trying to achieve it and by us. We do not confirm people in ways we judge to be wrong.

> Confirmation requires attribution of the best possible motive consonant with reality. When someone commits an act we find reprehensible, we ask ourselves what might have motivated such an act. Often, it is not hard to identify an array of possible motives ranging from the gross and grubby to some that are acceptable or even admirable. This array is not constructed in abstraction. We build it from a knowledge of this particular other and by listening carefully to what she or he tells us. The motive we attribute has to be a real, a genuine, possibility. Then we can open our dialogue with something like, "I know you were trying to help your friend," or "I know what you're trying to accomplish. . . . " It will be clear that we disapprove of this particular act, but it will also be clear to the other that we see a self that is better than this act. Often the other will respond with enormous relief. *Here is this significant and percipient other who sees through the smallness or meanness of my present behavior a self that is better and a real possibility.* Confirmation lifts us toward a vision of a better self.[41]

Trust and continuity are required for confirmation. Continuity is needed because we require knowledge of the other. Trust is required for the carer to be credible and also to sustain the search for an acceptable motive. Because trust and continuity are required, I have suggested that teachers and students should stay together, by mutual consent, for several years. Moral life guided by an ethic of care must attend to the establishment, maintenance, and enhancement of caring relations.

The discussion of moral education can be usefully extended to thinking on multiculturalism. Instead of encouraging an atmosphere in which subgroups compete for time in the curriculum and space for sharply separate political action, we invite dialogue and genuine meetings. Ann Diller has discussed pluralism in education from the perspective of an ethic of care.[42] She calls for reciprocity of understanding, coexploring, and coenjoyment. These aims go well beyond the usual aims of mere coexistence and cooperation. Clearly, these aims reflect our emphasis on authentic dialogue in which both parties are fully receptive; if either turns a deaf ear or listens only to extract words out of context, there can be no reciprocity of understanding. Similarly, to "coexplore" requires both dialogue and practice. Students from different cultures need opportunities to work together not only on intergroup problems and disputes but also on activities with a common aim. Coexploration can reveal common values and interests, and the activities themselves can yield enjoyment.

Often people who are not enthusiastic about multicultural education identify it with ethnic studies. Even some minority scholars express deep reservations about ethnic studies because they believe that there are "higher" human values than those tightly tied to a particular ethnic group. Such scholars speak of "transcendent" values, "higher" values, and "universal" values. Their arguments suggest that people must reach beyond their own ethnic identities toward a higher vision of what it means to be fully human. Most of what they seek is admirable; they want an ethnicity and race-blind civility, respect for persons regardless of origins. They seem to want a new humanism.

Care theorists, along with some postmodernists, wonder whether such transcendence is either necessary or desirable. Do not most cultures recommend civility, kindness to strangers, honesty in interactions, and the like? Is it necessary to get beyond one's ethnic identity to locate and exercise such virtues? The danger in supposing that some kind of transcendence is required is that one group's virtues will be described as universal, and the others will be asked, in the name of some abstract humanism, to assimilate. Their own unique patterns of care, courage, and compassion will be lost in a grand narrative. The coexploration envisioned by Diller can lead instead to a recognition that the virtues we admire can be found in other ways of life, and that the evils we deplore can be found in ours as well as those of others. Coexploration can lead to mutual transformation.

I think the ethic of care has something in common with the ethics of alterity (otherness) described by Jacques Derrida and Emmanuel Levinas.[43] Both call for respect of the other *as* other. Richard Bernstein says this of Derrida:

Few writers have written with such nuanced understanding about the suffering, mourning "other." In one of his most beautiful and loving essays, his homage to Levinas (from whom he appropriates so much), Derrida writes of . . . "the *respect* for the other *as what it is:* other. Without this acknowledgement, which is not a knowledge, or let us say without this 'letting be' of an existent (Other) as something existing outside me in the essence of what is (first in its alterity), no ethics would be possible."[44]

The ethic of care approaches the other in a similar fashion. A newborn child is not just "flesh of my flesh" but a genuine other whose appearance may or may not mirror mine, whose interests may be different, and whose fate is tied up with yet somehow separate from mine. I look at her face not as a reflection but as a genuine, unique subject who gazes back at me. The very heart of this ethic is the receptivity that allows the other to enter my consciousness in all his or her own fullness—not as a set of facts I have gathered. The result of our encounters will not necessarily be love, and we do not start with an impossible commandment to love—one that in essence presupposes that we are all "children of one God." Rather, we are prepared for the whole range of human emotions when we meet the other, but recognizing our mutual otherness, we reject violence. We "stay with" the other and pass beyond the potential violence of a particular moment.[45]

Derrida's "letting the other be" and the confirmation advocated by the ethic of care are often misunderstood. "Letting be" does not imply mere coexistence. It does not mean neglecting the other or abstaining from any intervention or attempt to persuade. Similarly, confirmation does not imply making excuses for the other or pretending that an ill-motivated act was done with good intentions. On the contrary, both attitudes suggest an understanding of the other that respects that other's ideal. As we intervene, as we attempt to persuade, we help the other to do better *as other*, not as a mere shadow of ourselves. Similarly, when we see evil in the other, we withhold judgment long enough to be sure that the evil is in the other and not a projection of evil in ourselves. Thus the receptivity of caring is directed not only outward but inward as well.

Receptivity directed inward suggests a new dimension to critical thinking. Recall that Richard Paul, too, calls for self-understanding as part of critical thinking, but as Barbara Thayer-Bacon points out, Paul's emphasis is on helping critical thinkers to separate themselves from their own biases.[46] Thayer-Bacon wants a more appreciative acceptance of subjectivity and the richness it contributes to critical thinking.

Two goals might be pursued in this extension of critical thinking. First, as both Thayer-Bacon and Jane Roland Martin (see the discussion in

Chapter 5) urge, critical thinking might be turned from its largely negative role to a more generous and positive one. Second, a positive form of critical thinking should lead to greater study and use of interpersonal reasoning. As we understand ourselves better, we may increase our motivation to understand others; similarly, as we engage in caring forms of interpersonal reasoning, we should gain a deeper understanding of ourselves. Thus, the two pursuits should be synergistic.

A positive form of critical thinking would be directed at our own emotional lives and patterns of response, not at just our beliefs and arguments. For example, German youth during the Nazi era might have been helped to understand the effects of martial music and smart uniforms. Youth today might consider what they feel as they watch sporting events, listen to rap music, or view violent films. As we inquire into human behavior and our own in particular, we may find that the reasons for our behavior are rarely beliefs. More often it is something we feel that impels us to action; and what we feel is often triggered, as Rorty said, by language. Traditional views of critical thinking try to overcome this tendency to act on feeling. The result, as Martin pointed out so forcefully, is often a highly rationalized coldness and meanness toward others. Critical thinking guided by an ethic of care encourages us to stay in touch with our own feelings and accept our embodied condition. Such acceptance does not imply approval of every emotional reaction. On the contrary, our hope is that the identification and acceptance of our own emotional states should help us to set them aside (not overcome them) and replace them, first, with a tragic sense that we too are vulnerable to error and evil and, second, with more positive feelings for those we encounter.

As we understand the emotional roots of our own behavior, we may learn when to abandon conventional critical thinking and engage in interpersonal reasoning. There are many occasions in human affairs when argumentation fails to advance negotiation; there are even times when it induces hatred, and, as Richard Bernstein noted, we can rarely agree on the "force of the better argument."

Interpersonal reasoning is concerned primarily with the relationship between participants in conversation or dialogue.[47] It is characterized by an attitude of solicitude or care, and it does not aim to defeat the other or even to keep the other "on the point." As part of a caring encounter, it requires the engrossment or attention described in the phenomenology of care. It asks the other, explicitly or implicitly, What are you going through?[48]

Because the primary aim of interpersonal reasoning is to maintain or to move the relationship in a positive direction, it is flexible. It may exhibit remarks that would be judged non sequiturs in argumentation, but these remarks have a purpose: They defuse anger or irritation, support the partner with reminders of more affectionate or happy times, relieve tension with humor, provide breathing time, and the like. Sometimes such "off the point" remarks are used to gather information about a partner's feelings or mood, and, depending on what is learned, a topic may be explored in the conventional mode of argumentation or postponed indefinitely. Interpersonal reasoning often involves a search for an appropriate response. In the usual pattern of critical thinking, appropriate responses are built into an argument. One uses logic to decide the response. Even in "strong" critical thinking, the response is determined by the logic of the argument or by a challenge to one's own premises. In interpersonal reasoning, one seeks an appropriate response to a living other, not to an argument.

You can see that many of the topics we have explored together could be considerably enlarged if we revisited them from the care perspective. For example, although I have already argued against the establishment of national goals and a national curriculum, we could add to the argument by looking at that program through the lens of care. Genuine education must engage the purposes and energies of those being educated. To secure such engagement, teachers must build relationships of care and trust, and within such relationships, students and teachers construct educational objectives cooperatively.

Of course, there should be standards in any enterprise, and students should be encouraged to achieve mastery in their chosen fields of study. But the key here is choice of enterprise. In both the ethic of alterity and the ethic of care, we seek to enhance the other's growth, but we do not threaten the other's Otherness, and we do not define for another exactly what he or she must do or be. If we are to avoid the dull uniformity described by Rousseau, we must encourage multiple ideals of what it means to be educated. Just as it recognizes the contribution of the cared-for to every caring relation, the ethic of care recognizes the contribution of the student to the teaching relation. The odd notion that establishing national goals will make teachers work harder and more effectively, thereby making students work harder and more effectively, is part of a long, long tradition that assumes an autonomous agent can logically plot a course of action and, through personal competence, somehow carry it out, even if others are intimately involved. Such agents, like Scheman's Cartesian knower, are somewhat schizophrenic, for in claiming their own autonomy, they forget that the human objects of their project must also be autonomous.

The ethic of care rejects the notion of a truly autonomous moral agent and accepts the reality of moral interdependence. Our goodness and our growth are inextricably bound to that of others we encounter. As teachers, we are as dependent on our students as they are on us.

SUMMARY QUESTIONS

1. Is objectivity possible? How should objectivity be defined?
2. What are some arguments in favor of essentialism? What are the arguments against it?
3. Can Rousseau's recommendation for Sophie's education be defended?
4. Is Cartesian epistemology a model of rationality, or is it, as Naomi Scheman suggests, schizophrenic?
5. Does one have to be a woman to speak credibly on women's condition? Does one have to be black to talk about the condition of blacks?
6. Why do some philosophers object to "grand narratives"?
7. What do we mean by "local truth"?
8. Is it reasonable or irrelevant to challenge an argument by asking who is speaking?
9. What might be meant by research *for* women rather than research *on* women?
10. Is detachment a virtue in research?
11. How might feminists argue against a male vision of God and for a female one?
12. Are qualitative research and quantitative research commensurable?
13. Why (and how) might we argue against the concept of moral autonomy?
14. Do we need principles in ethics? For what purpose?
15. What is the contribution of the cared-for in a caring relation?
16. How can women avoid continued exploitation if they embrace an ethic of care?

17. How does moral education in the care perspective differ from other forms of moral education?
18. How does interpersonal reasoning differ from analytical reasoning?
19. How might teachers "confirm" their students?
20. What might it mean to "let the other be"?

INTRODUCTION TO THE LITERATURE

On feminist epistemology, see Sandra Harding, *The Science Question in Feminism*; also Louise Antony and Charlotte Witt, eds., *A Mind of One's Own*; on feminist philosophy of science, see Ruth Bleier, ed., *Feminist Approaches to Science*; and Evelyn Fox Keller, *Reflections on Gender and Science*; on feminist ethics, see Nel Noddings, *Caring: A Feminine Approach to Ethics and Moral Education*; Nel Noddings, *Starting at Home: Caring and Social Policy*; also Jean Grimshaw, *Philosophy and Feminist Thinking*; on caring in education, see Nel Noddings, *The Challenge to Care in Schools*.

NOTES

CHAPTER 1

1. For a substantial discussion of aims, see Chapter 4 of my *Happiness and Education* (Cambridge: Cambridge University Press, 2003).

2. A contemporary philosopher of education who recommends a modified use of the Socratic method is Sophie Haroutunian-Gordon. See her *Turning the Soul: Teaching Through Conversation in the High School* (Chicago: University of Chicago Press, 1991).

3. The account of Socrates' trial, imprisonment, and death is given in the dialogues "Apology," "Crito," and "Phaedo." They are available in many collections. See, for example, Plato, *The Great Dialogues,* trans. and ed. B. Jowett (Roslyn, N.Y.: Walter J. Black, 1942). Most of *Republic* also appears in this collection.

4. *Republic,* Books 2, 3, 5, and 7.

5. See Jane Roland Martin, *Reclaiming a Conversation* (New Haven, Conn.: Yale University Press, 1985).

6. See, for example, Nel Noddings, *The Challenge to Care in Schools* (New York: Teachers College Press, 1992).

7. See Aristotle, *Nicomachean Ethics,* trans. Terence Irwin (Indianapolis: Hackett, 1985).

8. See Alasdair MacIntyre, *After Virtue,* 2d ed. (Notre Dame, Ind.: University of Notre Dame Press, 1984).

9. See Book 10 of *Nicomachean Ethics.* On this sometimes overlooked Aristotelian advice on moral education, see also M. F. Burnyeat, "Aristotle on Learning to Be Good," in *Essays on Aristotle's Ethics*, ed. Amelie Oksenberg Rorty (Berkeley: University of California Press, 1980), pp. 69–92.

10. Lawrence Kohlberg, *The Philosophy of Moral Development* (San Francisco: Harper and Row, 1981).

11. James Terry White, *Character Lessons in American Biography for Public Schools and Home Instruction* (New York: The Character Development League, 1909).

12. For a defense of character education, see Betty A. Sichel, *Moral Education* (Philadelphia: Temple University Press, 1988).

13. See Martha C. Nussbaum, *The Fragility of Goodness* (Cambridge: Cambridge University Press, 1986).

14. See Martin, *Reclaiming a Conversation;* also Susan Moller Okin, *Women in Western Political Thought* (Princeton: Princeton University Press, 1979).

15. Jean-Jacques Rousseau, *Emile,* trans. Allan Bloom (New York: Basic Books, 1974).

16. See Charles E. Silberman, *Crisis in the Classroom: The Remaking of American Education* (New York: Random House, 1970).

17. A. S. Neill, *Summerhill* (New York: Hart Publishing, 1960).

18. See Jean Piaget, *Genetic Epistemology* (New York: Columbia University Press, 1970); also L. S. Vygotsky, *Mind in Society: The Development of Higher Psychological Processes* (Cambridge, Mass.: Harvard University Press, 1978).

19. See Maria Montessori, *The Secret of Childhood*, trans. M. Joseph Costelloe (New York: Ballantine Books, 1966).

20. From *Emile*, quoted in Okin, *Women in Western Thought*, p. 136.

21. For an account of Pestalozzi's approach and its relation to the ideas of Locke, see John Cleverly and D. C. Phillips, *Visions of Childhood* (New York: Teachers College Press, 1986).

22. See Jonathan Kozol, *Savage Inequalities* (New York: Crown Books, 1991).

23. See Lewis Pyenson, *The Young Einstein* (Bristol and Boston: Adam Hilger, Ltd., 1985).

24. John Dewey, *Democracy and Education* (New York: Macmillan, 1916), p. 71.

25. Ibid., pp. 71–72.

26. Ibid., p. 58.

CHAPTER 2

1. See Milton Halsey Thomas, *John Dewey: A Centennial Bibliography* (Chicago: University of Chicago Press, 1962).

2. See the account in Max Eastman, *Heroes I Have Known* (New York: Simon and Schuster, 1942). See also Richard Hofstadter, *Anti-Intellectualism in American Life* (New York: Alfred A. Knopf, 1963); Albert Lynd, *Quackery in the Public Schools* (New York: Grosset and Dunlap, 1953). The suggestion that Dewey might have had a worse influence than Hitler was made by Mortimer Adler in an interview in *Time:* "Fusilier," *Time* 59 (March 17, 1953), p. 77.

3. Quoted in Manley Thompson, *The Pragmatic Philosophy of C. S. Peirce* (Chicago: University of Chicago Press, 1963), p. 80.

4. See S. Morris Eames, *Pragmatic Naturalism* (Carbondale: Southern Illinois University Press, 1977).

5. For more on growth, see Eamonn Callan, "Dewey's Conception of Education as Growth," *Educational Theory* 32, no. 1 (Winter 1982):19–27; also Sidney Hook, "John Dewey: Philosopher of Growth," in Sidney Morgenbesser, ed., *Dewey and His Critics* (New York: Journal of Philosophy, 1977), pp. 9–17.

6. See John Dewey, *Experience and Education* (New York: Collier Books, 1963), p. 36.

7. Richard S. Peters, "Aims of Education: A Conceptual Inquiry," in Richard S. Peters, ed., *The Philosophy of Education* (Oxford: Oxford University Press, 1973), p. 13.

8. Dewey, *Experience and Education*, p. 67.

9. John Dewey, "The Reflex Arc Concept in Psychology," *Psychological Review* 3 (July 1896):357–370.

10. John Dewey, *The School and Society* (Chicago: University of Chicago Press, 1900).

11. For a fuller discussion on warranted assertions, see John Dewey, *Logic: The Theory of Inquiry* (New York: Henry Holt, 1938).

12. John Dewey, *Democracy and Education* (New York: Macmillan, 1916).

13. For a contemporary argument along these lines, see Seymour Sarason, *The Predictable Failure of Educational Reform* (San Francisco: Jossey-Bass, 1990).

14. Dewey, *Democracy and Education*, p. 83.

15. See Arthur M. Schlesinger, Jr., *The Disuniting of America: Reflections on a Multicultural Society* (New York: W. W. Norton, 1992).

16. Dewey, *Democracy and Education*, p. 180.

17. I have argued this point myself. See Nel Noddings, *The Challenge to Care in Schools* (New York: Teachers College Press, 1992).

18. Dewey, *Democracy and Education*, p. 211.

19. Ibid., p. 213.

20. See, for example, George S. Counts, *Dare the School Build a New Social Order?* (New York: Arno Press, 1969).

CHAPTER 3

1. Ludwig Wittgenstein was a philosopher who first worked in the analytic mode of Russell and later created the field of ordinary language analysis. For the former, see his *Tractatus Logico-Philosophicus*, trans. D. F. Pears and B. F. McGuinness (London: Routledge and Kegan Paul, 1971); for the latter, see *Philosophical Investigations*, ed. G.E.M. Anscombe, Rush Rhees, and G. H. von Wright, trans. G.E.M. Anscombe (Oxford: Oxford University Press, 1953).

2. Jonas F. Soltis, *An Introduction to the Analysis of Educational Concepts* (Reading, Mass.: Addison-Wesley, 1968), p. 2.

3. Many fine examples of analytical essays exist, among them B. Paul Komisar and C.J.B. Macmillan, eds., *Analytical Concepts in Education* (Chicago: Rand McNally, 1967); C.J.B. Macmillan and Thomas Nelson, eds., *Concepts of Teaching* (Chicago: Rand McNally, 1968); James E. McClellan, *Philosophy of Education* (Englewood Cliffs, N.J.: Prentice-Hall, 1976); Richard S. Peters, ed., *The Philosophy of Education* (Oxford: Oxford University Press, 1973); B. Othanel Smith and Robert H. Ennis, eds., *Language and Concepts in Education* (Chicago: Rand McNally, 1961).

4. See the essays in Lee S. Shulman and Evan R. Keislar, eds., *Learning by Discovery* (Chicago: Rand McNally, 1966).

5. See, for example, George F. Kneller, ed., *Foundations of Education* (New York: John Wiley and Sons, 1963).

6. See William F. Frankena, "Is the Philosophy of Education Intellectually Respectable?" in *Proceedings of the Seventeenth Annual Meeting of the Philosophy of Education Society*, ed. Robert E. Mason, (Normal, Ill.: Philosophy of Education Society, 1961), pp. 36–45.

7. See Robert Mason's response to Frankena, ibid., pp. 46–48.

8. The prototype work is Wittgenstein's *Philosophical Investigations*.

9. For the distinction between teaching as occupation and act, see B. Paul Komisar, "Teaching: Act and Enterprise," in Macmillan and Nelson, *Concepts*, pp. 63–88.

10. John Dewey, *How We Think* (Chicago: Henry Regnery, 1933), pp. 35–36.

11. Israel Scheffler, *The Language of Education* (Springfield, Ill.: Charles C. Thomas, 1960).

12. Israel Scheffler, "The Concept of Teaching," in Macmillan and Nelson, *Concepts*, p. 27.

13. Komisar, "Teaching: Act and Enterprise," p. 79.

14. Ibid., p. 76.

15. Dewey, *How We Think*, p. 36.

16. See Denis C. Phillips and Jonas F. Soltis, *Perspectives on Learning* (New York: Teachers College Press, 1985).

17. Nel Noddings, "'Reasonableness' as a Requirement of Teaching," in Kenneth A. Strike, ed., *Philosophy of Education* (Urbana, Ill.: Educational Theory, 1976), pp. 181–188.

18. B. Othanel Smith, "A Concept of Teaching," in Smith and Ennis, *Language and Concepts in Education,* p. 93.

19. Gilbert Ryle, *The Concept of Mind* (London: Hutchinson, 1952).

20. B. Othanel Smith, "A Concept of Teaching," in Macmillan and Nelson, *Concepts,* p. 16.

21. Scheffler, "The Concept of Teaching," p. 27.

22. Thomas F. Green, "A Topology of the Teaching Concept," in Macmillan and Nelson, *Concepts,* pp. 28–62.

23. See, for example, I. A. Snook, "The Concept of Indoctrination," *Studies in Philosophy and Education* 7, no. 2 (1970):65–108.

24. C.J.B. Macmillan and James W. Garrison, "An Erotetic Concept of Teaching," *Educational Theory* 33, no. 3–4 (Summer/Fall 1983):157.

25. See Jaakko Hintikka, "Semantics of Questions and the Questions of Semantics," *Ada Philosophica Pennica* 28, no. 4 (1976); also Jaakko Hintikka and Merrill Hintikka, "Sherlock Holmes Confronts Modern Logic: Towards a Theory of Information-seeking Through Questioning," in E. J. Barth and J. Martens, eds., *Theory of Argumentation* (Amsterdam: Benjamins, 1982).

26. Susan Laird, "The Concept of Teaching: *Betsey Brown* vs. Philosophy of Education?" in *Philosophy of Education: 1988,* ed. James Giarelli (Normal, Ill.: Philosophy of Education Society, 1989), pp. 32–45.

27. Ntozake Shange, *Betsey Brown* (New York: St. Martin's Press, 1985); quoted in ibid., p. 33.

28. Laird, "Concept of Teaching," p. 37.

29. Lynda Stone, "Philosophy, Meaning Constructs, and Teacher Theorizing," in E. Wayne Ross, Jeffrey W. Cornett, and Gail McCutcheon, eds., *Teacher Personal Theorizing,* (Albany: State University of New York Press, 1992), p. 20.

CHAPTER 4

1. See Alasdair MacIntyre, "Existentialism" in the *Encyclopedia of Philosophy,* ed. Paul Edwards (New York: Macmillan, 1967), vol. 3, p. 147.

2. For an introduction to the themes of existentialism, see Maurice Friedman, ed., *The Worlds of Existentialism* (Chicago: University of Chicago Press, 1964). See also Jean-Paul Sartre, *Essays in Existentialism,* ed. Wade Baskin (Secaucus, N.J.: Citadel Press, 1977).

3. See Søren Kierkegaard, *Either/Or,* vol. 1, trans. David F. Swenson and Lillian M. Swenson (Princeton: Princeton University Press, 1959).

4. See Martin Buber, *I and Thou,* trans. Ronald Gregor Smith (New York: Scribner's, 1958).

5. See Paul Tillich, *The Courage to Be* (New Haven, Conn.: Yale University Press, 1952).

6. For an introduction to Buber's educational thought, see the essays in his *Between Man and Man* (New York: Macmillan, 1965).

7. The reference is to Jean-Paul Sartre, *Being and Nothingness,* trans. Hazel E. Barnes (New York: Washington Square Press, 1956).

8. Sartre, *Essays in Existentialism,* p. 36.

9. Ibid.

10. Ibid., p. 45.

11. Ibid., p. 51.

12. See Maxine Greene, *Teacher as Stranger* (Belmont, Calif.: Wadsworth, 1973); *Landscapes of Learning* (New York: Teachers College Press, 1978); and *The Dialectic of Freedom* (New York: Teachers College Press, 1988).

13. Greene, *Dialectic of Freedom,* p. 51.

14. See C. A. Bowers, "An Open Letter to Maxine Greene on 'The Problem of Freedom' in an Era of Ecological Interdependence," *Educational Theory* 41, no. 3 (Summer 1981):325–330.

15. Buber, *Between Man and Man,* p. xi.

16. Ibid., p. 98.

17. Ibid.

18. Ibid.

19. See, for example, Alexander M. Sidorkin, *Learning Relations* (New York: Peter Lang, 2002).

20. See, for example, Mary Poplin and J. Weeres, *Voices from the Inside: A Report on Schooling from Inside the Classroom* (Los Angeles: Institute for Education in Transformation at the Claremont Graduate School, 1992); also Robert V. Bullough, Jr., *Life on the Other Side of the Teacher's Desk: Stories of Children at Risk* (New York: Teachers College Press, 2000); and Judith Deiro, *Teaching with Heart* (Thousand Oaks, Calif.: Corwin Press, 1996).

21. See Nel Noddings, *Caring: A Feminine Approach to Ethics and Moral Education* (Berkeley: University of California Press, 1984); also Noddings, *The Challenge to Care in Schools* (New York: Teachers College Press, 1992).

22. See Nicholas Burbules, *Dialogue in Teaching* (New York: Teachers College Press, 1993); also Sophie Haroutunian-Gordon, *Turning the Soul: Teaching Through Conversation in the High School* (Chicago: University of Chicago Press, 1991).

23. For examples of this work, see D. Jean Clandinin, Annie Davies, Pat Hogan, and Barbara Kennard, eds., *Learning to Teach, Teaching to Learn* (New York: Teachers College Press, 1993); also Carol Witherell and Nel Noddings, eds., *Stories Lives Tell: Narrative and Dialogue in Education* (New York: Teachers College Press, 1991).

24. Philip W. Jackson, *Untaught Lessons* (New York: Teachers College Press, 1992).

25. See Edmund Husserl, *Ideas,* trans. W. R. Boyce Gibson (New York: Collier/Macmillan, 1962).

26. See Sartre, *Essays in Existentialism,* especially the introduction by Jean Wahl.

27. Husserl, *Ideas,* p. 6.

28. Noddings, *Caring.*

29. See Iris Murdoch, *The Sovereignty of Good* (London: Routledge and Kegan Paul, 1970); Simone Weil, *Simone Weil Reader,* ed. George A. Panichas (Mt. Kisco, N.Y.: Moyer Bell Limited, 1977).

30. Weil, *Simone Weil Reader,* p. 51.

31. Nancy Fraser, *Unruly Practices: Power, Discourse, and Gender in Contemporary Social Theory* (Minneapolis: University of Minnesota Press, 1989), p. 113.

32. Ibid.

33. Patricia Jagentowicz Mills, *Woman, Nature, and Psyche* (New Haven, Conn.: Yale University Press, 1987), p. xii.

34. See Paulo Freire, *Pedagogy of the Oppressed,* trans. Myra Bergman Ramos (New York: Herder and Herder, 1970).

35. See Henry A. Giroux, *Schooling and the Struggle for Public Life* (Minneapolis: University of Minnesota Press, 1988).

36. Mary Daly, *Beyond God the Father* (Boston: Beacon Press, 1974), p. 8.

37. See, for example, Samuel Bowles and Herbert Gintis, *Schooling in Capitalist America* (New York: Basic Books, 1976); also Martin Carnoy and Henry Levin, *Schooling and Work in the Democratic State* (Stanford, Calif.: Stanford University Press, 1985).

38. See Paul Willis, *Learning to Labour* (Farnborough, England: Saxon House, 1977).

39. See Mortimer J. Adler, *The Paideia Proposal* (New York: Macmillan, 1982).

40. For a discussion of school knowledge and privilege, see Michael W. Apple and Lois Weis, eds., *Ideology and Practice in Schooling* (Philadelphia: Temple University Press, 1983).

41. See Noddings, *The Challenge to Care in Schools*.

42. It could also be tragic for the society because some vital skills might be lost in the misguided attempt to teach the same material to everyone. See Jane Roland Martin, *Cultural Miseducation* (New York: Teachers College Press, 2002); see also Mike Rose, *The Mind at Work: Valuing the Intelligence of the American Worker* (New York: Penguin, 2005).

43. See Jane Roland Martin, *The Schoolhome: Rethinking Schools for Changing Families* (Cambridge, Mass.: Harvard University Press, 1992); and John White, *Education and the Good Life* (New York: Teachers College Press, 1991).

44. Richard Rorty, *Philosophy and the Mirror of Nature* (Princeton: Princeton University Press, 1979), p. 318.

45. Ibid., p. 319.

46. Interestingly, even physicists have started to question their reliance on reductionism. They talk now of "emergent" phenomena. See Robert B. Laughlin, *A Different Universe* (New York: Basic Books, 2005).

47. Dewey quoted in Richard J. Bernstein, *The New Constellation* (Cambridge, Mass.: MIT Press, 1992), p. 50. The Dewey quote is from "From Absolution to Existentialism," in Richard J. Bernstein, ed., *John Dewey: On Experience, Nature, and Freedom* (New York: Library of Liberal Arts, 1960), p. 13.

48. See, for example, Ernst von Glasersfeld, "An Introduction to Radical Constructivism," in P. Watzlawick, ed., *The Invented Reality* (New York: Norton, 1984), pp. 17–40; Robert B. Davis, Carolyn A. Maher, and Nel Noddings, eds., *Constructivist Views on the Teaching and Learning of Mathematics*, JRME Monograph 4 (Reston, Va.: National Council of Teachers of Mathematics, 1990).

49. See Sandra Harding, *The Science Question in Feminism* (Ithaca, N.Y.: Cornell University Press, 1986).

50. Bernstein, *The New Constellation*, pp. 220–221.

51. See the chapters on Derrida in ibid.

52. See the discussion in Susan J. Hekman, *Gender and Knowledge* (Boston: Northeastern University Press, 1990).

CHAPTER 5

1. See Noam Chomsky, *Language and Mind* (New York: Harcourt Brace Jovanovich, 1968); Jean Piaget, *Genetic Epistemology* (New York: Columbia University Press, 1970); for a discussion of competence theories in education, see Nel Noddings, "Competence Theories and the Science of Education," *Educational Theory* 24, no. 4 (1974):356–364.

2. Patrick Suppes, *Introduction to Logic* (New York: Van Nostrand Reinhold, 1957), p. xv.

3. Ibid., p. xvi.

4. See Michael Scriven, *Reasoning* (New York: McGraw-Hill, 1976). See also the discussion in John E. McPeck, *Critical Thinking and Education* (Oxford: Martin Robertson, 1981).

5. See Gila Hanna, *Rigorous Proof in Mathematics Education* (Toronto: OISE Press, 1983).

6. Martin Gardner, *The Annotated Alice* (Lewis Carroll) (New York: World Publishing, 1963).

7. Ibid., p. 76.

8. Ibid., p. 95.

9. See I. A. Richards, *The Meaning of Meaning* (New York: Harcourt, Brace, 1956).

10. Robert H. Ennis, "A Concept of Critical Thinking," *Harvard Educational Review* 32, no. 1 (1962):83–111.

11. Robert H. Ennis, "A Conception of Rational Thinking," in Jerrold R. Coombs, ed., *Philosophy of Education* (Normal, Ill.: Philosophy of Education Society, 1974), pp. 3–30.

12. Ibid., p. 10.

13. See McPeck, *Critical Thinking*.

14. See Richard Paul, *Critical Thinking: What Every Person Needs to Survive in a Rapidly Changing World* (Rohnert Park, Calif.: Center for Critical Thinking and Moral Critique, 1990).

15. See Robert Gagne, "Psychological Issues in Science: A Process Approach," in Gagne, ed., *The Psychological Eases of Science: A Process Approach* (Washington, D.C.: American Association for the Advancement of Science, 1965).

16. Harvey Siegel, *Educating Reason: Rationality, Critical Thinking, and Education* (New York: Routledge, 1988), pp. 12–13.

17. Siegel elaborates on Paul's view on this in note 26, pp. 143–144, ibid.

18. Mark Weinstein, "Critical Thinking: The Great Debate," *Educational Theory* 43, no. 1 (1993):99–117.

19. Ibid., p. 117.

20. Ibid., p. 117 and note 29.

21. See Siegel, *Educating Reason*.

22. McPeck argues for this claim in *Critical Thinking* and in "Thoughts on Subject Specificity," in Stephen P. Norris, ed., *The Generalizability of Critical Thinking* (New York: Teachers College Press, 1992), pp. 198–205.

23. Refer to the discussion in Chapter 4.

24. See, for example, Sandra S. Harding, *The Science Question in Feminism* (Ithaca, N.Y.: Cornell University Press, 1986); also Naomi Scheman, "Though This Be Method, Yet There Is Madness in It: Paranoia and Liberal Epistemology," in Louise M. Antony and Charlotte Witt, eds., *A Mind of One's Own* (Boulder, Colo.: Westview Press, 1993), pp. 145–170.

25. McPeck, "Thoughts on Subject Specificity," p. 201.

26. For a discussion of five prominent definitions, see Ralph H. Johnson, "The Problem of Defining Critical Thinking," in Norris, *Generalizability*, pp. 38–53.

27. Robert H. Ennis, "The Degree to Which Critical Thinking Is Subject Specific: Clarification and Needed Research," in Norris, *Generalizability*, pp. 21–37.

28. Siegel, *Educating Reason*, p. 21.

29. Jane Roland Martin, "Critical Thinking for a Humane World," in Norris, *Generalizability*, pp. 163–180.

30. Ibid., p. 164.

31. See the discussion of African American women's ways of presenting their arguments in Patricia Hill Collins, "The Social Construction of Black Feminist Thought," *Signs* 14, no. 41 (1989):745–773.

32. McPeck, "Thoughts on Subject Specificity," p. 201.

33. See, for example, Michael Oakeshott, *Rationalism in Politics and Other Essays* (London: Methuen, 1962); also Mortimer J. Adler, *The Paideia Proposal* (New York: Macmillan, 1982).

34. See Donald Vandenberg, *Human Rights in Education* (New York: Philosophical Library, 1983).

CHAPTER 6

1. *Theaetetus* is in any of several collections; see, for example, *The Works of Plato,* trans. B. Jowett, ed. Irwin Edman (New York: Modern Library, 1956).

2. For a readable account of the two basic ideas on foundations, see W.V.O. Quine and Robert Ullian, *The Web of Belief* (New York: Random House, 1970).

3. See Keith Lehrer, *Theory of Knowledge* (Boulder, Colo.: Westview Press, 1990). This is also a good reference for coherence theories.

4. See Simon Blackburn, *Truth* (Oxford: Oxford University Press, 2005); also Michael P. Lynch, *True to Life* (Cambridge, Mass.: MIT Press, 2005).

5. See Karl Popper, *Objective Knowledge* (Oxford: Clarendon Press, 1972).

6. See W.V.O. Quine, "Epistemology Naturalized," in Quine, *Ontological Relativity and Other Essays* (New York: Columbia University Press, 1969).

7. See the account in Lehrer, *Theory of Knowledge.*

8. See John Dewey, *The Quest for Certainty* (New York: G. P. Putnam's Sons, 1929); see also Section 3, "The Experience of Knowing," in John J. McDermott, ed., *The Philosophy of John Dewey* (New York: G. P. Putnam's Sons, 1973).

9. The notion of cognitive structure aroused considerable debate in educational philosophy and theory; see for example, D. C. Phillips, "On Describing a Student's Cognitive Structure," *Educational Psychologist* 18, no. 2 (1983):59–74.

10. See Jean Piaget, *Genetic Epistemology* (New York: Columbia University Press, 1970); also Piaget, *Biology and Knowledge* (Chicago: University of Chicago Press, 1971).

11. Jean Piaget, *Insights and Illusions of Philosophy* (New York: World Publishing, 1971), pp. 57–58.

12. Possibly the most influential contemporary work on power is that of Michel Foucault, *Discipline and Punish: The Birth of the Prison,* trans. Alan Sheridan (New York: Vintage, 1979); also Foucault, *The Archaeology of Knowledge,* trans. A. M. Sheridan Smith (New York: Pantheon, 1972).

13. See, for example, Sandra S. Harding, *The Science Question in Feminism* (Ithaca, N.Y.: Cornell University Press, 1986); also Nancy Hartsock, "The Feminist Standpoint: Developing the Grounds for a Specifically Feminist Historical Materialism," in Sandra Harding and Merrill B. Hintikka, eds., *Discovering Reality: Feminist Perspectives on Epistemology, Metaphysics, Methodology, and Philosophy of Science* (Dordrecht, Holland: D. Reidel, 1983).

14. Naomi Scheman, "Though This Be Method, Yet There Is Madness in It: Paranoia and Liberal Epistemology," in Louise M. Antony and Charlotte Witt, eds., *A Mind of One's Own* (Boulder, Colo.: Westview Press, 1993), p. 148.

15. See, for example, Louise M. Antony, "Quine as Feminist: The Radical Import of Naturalized Epistemology," in Antony and Witt, *A Mind of One's Own,* pp. 185–226.

16. See J. J. White, "Searching for Substantial Knowledge in Social Studies," *Theory and Research in Social Education* 16 (1988):115–140.

17. See Stephen J. Thornton, "The Social Studies Near Century's End: Reconsidering Patterns of Curriculum and Instruction," in Linda Darling-Hammond, ed., *Review of Research in Education* 20 (Washington, D.C.: American Educational Research Association, 1994), pp. 223–254.

18. An impressive amount of philosophical work was devoted to the structure of the disciplines and the organization of curriculum. See, for example, Paul Hirst, *Knowledge and the Curriculum* (London: Routledge, 1974); D. C. Phillips, *Philosophy, Science, and Social Inquiry* (Oxford: Pergamon, 1987); Joseph J. Schwab, *Science, Curriculum, and Liberal Education: Selected Essays* (Chicago: University of Chicago Press, 1978).

19. See Nel Noddings, "Theoretical and Practical Concerns About Small Groups in Mathematics," *Elementary School Journal* 89, no. 5 (1989):607–623; see also Thomas L. Good, Catherine Mulryan, and Mary McCaslin, "Grouping for Instruction in Mathematics: A Call for Pragmatic Research on Small-Group Processes," in Douglas A. Grouws, ed., *Handbook of Research on Mathematics Teaching and Learning* (New York: Macmillan, 1992), pp. 165–196; also Linda Darling-Hammond and John Bransford, eds., *Preparing Teachers for a Changing World* (San Francisco: Jossey-Bass, 2005).

20. See the discussions in Michael W. Apple, *Ideology and Curriculum* (Boston: Routledge and Kegan Paul, 1979); Apple, *Education and Power* (Boston: Routledge and Kegan Paul, 1982); Henry Giroux, *Schooling and the Struggle for Public Life* (Minneapolis: University of Minnesota Press, 1988).

21. See Nel Noddings, "Does Everybody Count?" *Journal of Mathematical Behavior* 13, no. 1 (1994):89–104. For an important argument that questions the value of the traditional disciplines, see Mike Rose, *Possible Lives: The Promise of Public Education in America* (Boston: Houghton Mifflin, 1995); also Rose, *The Mind at Work: Valuing the Intelligence of the American Worker* (New York: Penguin, 2005).

22. See Nel Noddings, *The Challenge to Care in Schools* (New York: Teachers College Press, 1992).

23. See Robert B. Davis, Carolyn A. Maher, and Nel Noddings, eds., *Constructivist Views on the Teaching and Learning of Mathematics,* Journal for Research in Mathematics Education Monograph 4 (Reston, Va.: National Council of Teachers of Mathematics, 1990); also Paul Ernest, "Constructivism, the Psychology of Learning, and the Nature of Mathematics: Some Critical Issues," *Science and Education* 2, no. 1 (1993):87–94; also Ernest, *Social Constructivism as a Philosophy of Mathematics* (Albany: State University of New York Press, 1998); Brent Davis and Dennis Sumara, "Constructivist Discourses and the Field of Education: Problems and Possibilities," *Educational Theory* 52, no. 4 (2002):409–428; and D. L. Schwartz and J. D. Bransford, "A Time for Telling," *Cognition and Instruction* 16, no. 4 (1998):475–522.

24. See the accounts of classroom practice in Davis, Maher, and Noddings, *Constructivist Views;* also Maughn Rollins Gregory, "Constructivism, Standards, and the Classroom Community of Inquiry," *Educational Theory* 52, no. 4 (2002): 397–408.

25. See Paul Cobb, Terry Wood, and Erna Yackel, "Classrooms as Learning Environments for Teachers and Researchers," in Davis, Maber, and Noddings, *Constructivist Views,* pp. 125–146.

26. Gerald Goldin, "Epistemology, Constructivism, and Discovery," in Davis, Maher, and Noddings, *Constructivist Views,* p. 39.

27. Michael R. Matthews, "A Problem with Constructivist Epistemology," in H. A. Alexander, ed., *Philosophy of Education* (Urbana: University of Illinois Press, 1993), p. 305.

28. Ernst von Glasersfeld, "An Exposition of Constructivism: Why Some Like It Radical," in Davis, Maher, and Noddings, *Constructivist Views,* p. 23.

29. Ibid., p. 24.

30. See Ludwig Wittgenstein, *Tractatus Logico-Philosophicus,* trans. D. F. Pears and B. F. McGuinness (London: Routledge and Kegan Paul, 1971).

31. W. A. Suchting, "Constructivism Deconstructed," *Science and Education* 1, no. 3 (1992):223–254.

CHAPTER 7

1. See Ian Hacking, *The Social Construction of What?* (Cambridge, Mass.: Harvard University Press, 1999).

2. See D. C. Phillips, *Philosophy, Science, and Social Inquiry* (Oxford: Pergamon, 1987).

3. Thomas S. Kuhn, *The Structure of Scientific Revolutions* (Chicago: University of Chicago Press, 1962).

4. Ibid., p. 10.

5. Ibid., p. 102.

6. Ibid., pp. 108–109.

7. See William A. Firestone, "Alternative Arguments for Generalizing from Data as Applied to Qualitative Research," *Educational Researcher* 22, no. 4 (1993):16–23; also Alan Peshkin, "The Goodness of Qualitative Research," *Educational Researcher* 22, no. 2 (1993):24–30.

8. See Elliot Eisner, *The Enlightened Eye: Qualitative Inquiry and the Enhancement of Educational Practice* (New York: Macmillan, 1991).

9. See Lee J. Cronbach, *Designing Evaluations of Educational and Social Programs* (San Francisco: Jossey-Bass, 1982).

10. See D. C. Phillips, "Telling It Straight," *Educational Psychologist* 29, no. 1 (1994):13–21.

11. See Nel Noddings, *Educating for Intelligent Belief or Unbelief* (New York: Teachers College Press, 1993).

12. See Richard Shavelson and Lisa Towne, eds., *Scientific Research in Education* (Washington, D.C.: National Academies Press, 2002).

13. See ibid.

14. See Nel Noddings, *The Challenge to Care in Schools* (New York: Teachers College Press, 1992).

15. See Linda Darling-Hammond and John Bransford, eds., *Preparing Teachers for a Changing World* (San Francisco: Jossey-Bass, 2005); also Ellen Condliffe Lagemann and Lee Shulman, eds., *Issues in Education Research* (San Francisco: Jossey-Bass, 1999). See also the symposium on education science in *Educational Theory* 55, no. 3 (2005).

16. See the exchange between Glasersfeld and Suchting in *Science and Education* 1, no. 3–4, and 2, no. 1 (1992).

17. See Nel Noddings, "Theoretical and Practical Concerns About Small Groups in Mathematics," *Elementary School Journal* 89, no. 5 (1989):620–621.

CHAPTER 8

1. See Aristotle, *Nicomachean Ethics,* trans. Terence Irwin (Indianapolis: Hackett, 1985).

2. See Martha Nussbaum, "Non-Relative Virtues: An Aristotelian Approach," *Midwest Studies in Philosophy* 13 (1988):32–53.

3. Alasdair MacIntyre, *Whose Justice? Which Rationality?* (Notre Dame, Ind.: University of Notre Dame Press, 1988), p. 403.

4. See Alasdair MacIntyre, *After Virtue,* 2d ed. (Notre Dame, Ind.: University of Notre Dame Press, 1984).

5. See, for example, David Rasmussen, ed., *Universalism vs. Communitarianism: Contemporary Debates in Ethics* (Cambridge, Mass.: MIT Press, 1990); Michael Sandel, *Liberalism and the Limits of Justice* (Cambridge: Cambridge University Press, 1982); Charles Taylor, *Philosophy and the Human Sciences,* Philosophical Papers 2 (Cambridge: Cambridge University Press, 1985); Michael Walzer, *Spheres of Justice: A Defense of Pluralism and Equality* (New York: Basic Books, 1983).

6. See, for example, Crane Brinton, *A History of Western Morals* (New York: Harcourt, Brace, 1959).

7. See Nel Noddings, *Educating for Intelligent Belief or Unbelief* (New York: Teachers College Press, 1993).

8. See Brinton, *History of Western Morals.*

9. See Alasdair MacIntyre, *Whose Justice? Which Rationality?*

10. An eminently readable version of the classic work on utilitarianism is John Stuart Mill, *Utilitarianism,* ed. George Sher (Indianapolis: Hackett, 1979, 1861).

11. Some of Anne Perry's Victorian mysteries are *Highgate Rise, The Face of a Stranger, A Dangerous Mourning,* and *Defend and Betray.*

12. See Mill, *Utilitarianism.*

13. See Henry Sidgwick, *The Methods of Ethics* (Indianapolis: Hackett, 1981, 1874).

14. John Kenneth Galbraith, *The Culture of Contentment* (Boston: Houghton Mifflin, 1992).

15. See John Dewey, *Human Nature and Conduct* (New York: Modern Library, 1930).

16. Virginia Held, *Feminist Morality* (Chicago: University of Chicago Press, 1993), p. 25.

17. Ibid., p. 24. See also the concerns I have raised in "Thoughts on John Dewey's 'Ethical Principles Underlying Education,'" *Elementary School Journal* 98, no. 5 (1998):479–488.

18. See Larry P. Nucci, ed., *Moral Development and Character Education* (Berkeley: Mc-Cutchan, 1989); and Betty A. Sichel, *Moral Education* (Philadelphia: Temple University Press, 1988).

19. James Terry White, *Character Lessons in American Biography* (New York: The Character Development League, 1909).

20. A widely popular work is Thomas Lickona, *Educating for Character: How Our Schools Can Teach Respect and Responsibility* (New York: Bantam Books, 1991).

21. The classic studies are Hugh Hartshorne and Mark A. May, *Studies in the Nature of Character;* see vol. 1, *Studies in Deceit* (New York: Macmillan, 1928), and vol. 2, *Studies in Self-Control* (New York: Macmillan, 1929).

22. Alice Miller, *For Your Own Good,* trans. Hildegarde Hannun and Hunter Hannun (New York: Farrar, Straus, and Giroux, 1983).

23. See Lawrence Kohlberg, *The Philosophy of Moral Development* (San Francisco: Harper and Row, 1981).

24. See the exchange between Lawrence Walker and Diana Baumrind in Mary Jeanne Larrabee, ed., *An Ethic of Care* (New York and London: Routledge, 1993).

25. Carol J. Gilligan, *In a Different Voice* (Cambridge, Mass.: Harvard University Press, 1982).

26. Some, of course, affirm this Kantian position. See, for example, Gertrud Nunner-Winkler, "Two Moralities: A Critical Discussion of an Ethic of Care and Responsibility Versus an Ethic of Rights and Justice," in Larrabee, *Ethic of Care,* pp. 143–156.

27. See D. C. Phillips, *Philosophy, Science, and Social Inquiry* (Oxford: Pergamon, 1987).

28. See ibid., Chapter 14.

29. See Lawrence Walker, "Sex Differences in the Development of Moral Reasoning: A Critical Review," in Larrabee, *Ethic of Care,* pp. 157–176.

30. See Nel Noddings, *Educating Moral People* (New York: Teachers College Press, 2002).

31. See Robert E. Carter, *Dimensions of Moral Education* (Toronto: University of Toronto Press, 1984).

32. See the analysis in Barry Chazan, *Contemporary Approaches to Moral Education* (New York: Teachers College Press, 1985).

33. For many examples, see Joseph Kahne, *Neglecting Alternatives: An Assessment of the Status and Implications of Varied Social Theories in Educational Policy* (unpublished doctoral dissertation, Stanford University, 1993).

34. Louis Raths, Merrill Harmin, and Sidney Simon, *Values and Teaching* (Columbus, Ohio: Charles E. Merrill, 1966; 2d ed., 1978).

35. See Chazan, *Contemporary Approaches*, on this.

36. See John Dewey, *Experience and Education* (New York: Collier Books, 1963).

CHAPTER 9

1. John Rawls, *A Theory of Justice* (Cambridge, Mass.: Harvard University Press, 1971), p. 4.

2. Ibid., p. 60.

3. For an important and readable critique, see Michael Sandel, *Liberalism and the Limits of Justice* (Cambridge: Cambridge University Press, 1982).

4. John Dewey, *The Public and Its Problems* (New York: Henry Holt, 1927), p. 158.

5. See Nel Noddings, *The Challenge to Care in Schools* (New York: Teachers College Press, 1992).

6. John Dewey, *The School and Society* (Chicago: University of Chicago Press, 1900), p. 3.

7. Jonathan Kozol, *Savage Inequalities* (New York: Crown Books, 1991).

8. See John Kenneth Galbraith, *The Culture of Contentment* (Boston: Houghton Mifflin, 1992).

9. Rawls, *Theory of Justice*, p. 75.

10. Ibid., p. 60.

11. Ibid., p. 101.

12. Ibid.

13. See Kenneth A. Strike, "Liberal Discourse and Ethical Pluralism: An Educational Agenda," in H. A. Alexander, ed., *Philosophy of Education 1992* (Champaign, Ill.: Philosophy of Education Society, 1993), pp. 226–236.

14. Kenneth Baker's review of Stephen Shute and Susan Hurley, eds., *On Human Rights: The Oxford Amnesty Lectures* (New York: Basic Books, 1993), *San Francisco Chronicle*, Sunday, January 16, 1994, p. 8.

15. See the chapter "The Eclipse of the Public" in Dewey, *The Public and Its Problems*.

16. Nel Noddings, "For All Its Children," *Educational Theory* 43, no. 1 (1993):17.

17. Ibid., p. 26.

18. Urie Bronfenbrenner, "Who Needs Parent Education?" *Teachers College Record* 74 (1978):774.

19. Martin Buber, *Between Man and Man* (New York: Macmillan, 1965), p. 98.

20. Ibid.

21. Ibid.

22. See, for example, James G. Henderson, *Reflective Teaching* (New York: Macmillan, 1992); Carol Witherell and Nel Noddings, eds., *Stories Lives Tell: Narrative and Dialogue in Education* (New York: Teachers College Press, 1991); for a good review of such work, see Suzanne Rice, "Teaching and Learning Through Story and Dialogue," *Educational Theory* 43, no. 1 (1993):85–97.

23. See Thomas J. Sergiovanni, *Building Community in Schools* (San Francisco: Jossey-Bass, 1994); see also Mary Anne Raywid, "Community and Schools: A Prolegomenon," in James Giarelli, ed., *Philosophy of Education: 1988* (Normal, Ill.: Philosophy of Education Society, 1989), pp. 2–17.

24. See the discussion in David Rasmussen, ed., *Universalism vs. Communitarianism: Contemporary Debates in Ethics* (Cambridge, Mass.: MIT Press, 1990).

25. David Horowitz, "The Decline of Academic Discourse: The MLA Fiasco," *Heterodoxy* 2, no. 5 (1994):13.

26. See my discussion of the dark side of community in Nel Noddings, "On Community," *Educational Theory* 4, no. 3 (1996):245–267.

27. Besides Buber, see the work of Emmanuel Levinas, *The Levinas Reader*, ed. Sean Hand (Oxford: Blackwell, 1989).

28. Howard Gardner refers to these talents as "intelligences." See Gardner, *Frames of Mind* (New York: Basic Books, 1983).

29. Dewey, *School and Society*, p. 3.

30. Dewey, *Democracy and Education* (New York: Macmillan, 1916), p. 116.

31. Michael W. Apple, "The Politics of Official Knowledge: Does a National Curriculum Make Sense?" *Discourse* 14, no. 1 (1993):1.

32. Ibid., p. 2.

33. Ibid., p. 8. The embedded quotation is from Richard Johnson, "A New Road to Serfdom?" in *Education Limited*, ed. Education Group II (London: Unwin Hyman, 1991).

34. See Noddings, *The Challenge to Care in Schools*.

CHAPTER 10

1. See J. B. Watson, *Behaviorism* (New York: W. W. Norton, 1924).

2. Quoted in Herbert Kliebard, *Schooled to Work: Vocationalism and the American Curriculum 1876–1946* (New York: Teachers College Press, 1999), p. 43.

3. See Kenneth Howe, *Understanding Equal Educational Opportunity* (New York: Teachers College Press, 1997).

4. See Jonathan Kozol, *Savage Inequalities* (New York: Crown Books, 1991). For an introduction to the great educational critics of the 1960s, see Beatrice Gross and Ronald Gross, eds., *Radical School Reform* (New York: Simon and Schuster, 1969).

5. See Ira Katznelson, *When Affirmative Action Was White* (New York: W. W. Norton, 2005).

6. See Isaiah Berlin, *Four Essays on Liberty* (Oxford: Oxford University Press, 1969).

7. See Richard Rothstein, *Class and Schools* (Washington, D.C.: Economic Policy Institute, 2004); see also David K. Shipler, *The Working Poor: Invisible in America* (New York: Alfred A. Knopf, 2004).

8. For an elaboration on this argument, see Nel Noddings, "For All Its Children," *Educational Theory* 43, no.1 (1993):15–22.

9. See the discussion in Howe, *Understanding Equal Educational Opportunity*.

10. On the possibilities for intelligent vocational education, see Mike Rose, *Possible Lives: The Promise of Public Education in America* (Boston: Houghton Mifflin, 1995); also Rose, *The Mind at Work: Valuing the Intelligence of the American Worker* (New York: Penguin, 2005).

11. See Eamonn Callan, *Creating Citizens: Political Education and Liberal Democracy* (Oxford: Oxford University Press, 1997).

12. The quotation and a discussion appear in Nel Noddings, *Happiness and Education* (Cambridge: Cambridge University Press, 2003), p. 77; also in Herbert Kliebard, *The Struggle for the American Curriculum: 1893–1958* (New York: Routledge, 1995), p. 98.

13. See George Orwell, "Such, Such Were the Joys," in Orwell, *A Collection of Essays* (San Diego: Harcourt Brace, 1981).

14. See Roger Shattuck, "The Shame of the Schools," *New York Review of Books*, April 7, 2005.

15. See Diane Ravitch, *National Standards in American Education* (Washington, D.C.: Brookings Institution Press, 1995). For a different view, see Nel Noddings, "Thinking About Standards," *Phi Delta Kappan* 79, no. 3 (1997):184–189.

16. For a description of behavioral objectives, see Robert Mager, *Preparing Instructional Objectives* (San Francisco: Fearon Press, 1962); for an introduction to the debate over such objectives, see the *AERA Monograph Series on Curriculum Evaluation* 3 (Chicago: Rand McNally, 1969).

17. Richard Rorty, *Contingency, Irony, and Solidarity* (Cambridge: Cambridge University Press, 1989), pp. 47–48.

18. See Nel Noddings, "What Does It Mean to Educate the Whole Child?" *Educational Leadership* 63, no. 1 (2005): 8–13. See also other articles in the same issue.

CHAPTER 11

1. Valerie Ooka Pang, *Multicultural Education: A Caring-Centered, Reflective Approach* (New York: McGraw-Hill, 2001), p. 53.

2. Ibid.

3. Joel Spring, *American Education* (Boston: McGraw-Hill, 2000), p. 146.

4. Ibid., p. 166.

5. Arthur M. Schlesinger, Jr., *The Disuniting of America: Reflections on a Multicultural Society* (New York: W. W. Norton, 1992), p. 16.

6. See Jean Bethke Elshtain, *Jane Addams and the Dream of American Democracy* (New York: Basic Books, 2002).

7. See the account in Jon Schaffarzick and Gary Sykes, eds., *Value Conflicts and Curriculum Issues* (Berkeley: McCutchan, 1979).

8. Quoted in ibid., p. 10.

9. See Spring, *American Education;* also Sonia Nieto, *The Light in Their Eyes: Creating Multicultural Learning Communities* (New York: Teachers College Press, 1999).

10. See Rita M. Kissen, *The Last Closet: The Real Lives of Lesbian and Gay Teachers* (Portsmouth, N.H.: Heinemann, 1996); also Nel Noddings, *Critical Lessons: What Our Schools Should Teach* (Cambridge: Cambridge University Press, 2006).

11. See Susan Jacoby, *Freethinkers* (New York: Metropolitan Books, 2004).

12. See David T. Hansen, "Chasing Butterflies Without a Net: Interpreting Cosmopolitanism," *Studies in Philosophy of Education* 29 (2010):151–166.

13. See Jacoby, *Freethinkers;* also Michael True, *An Energy Field More Intense Than War* (Syracuse, N.Y.: Syracuse University Press, 1995).

14. Martha Nussbaum, *For Love of Country?* ed. Joshua Cohen (Boston: Beacon Press, 1996).

15. Benjamin Barber, "Constitutional Faith," in ibid., p. 33.

16. Ibid., p. 33.

17. For a vigorous attack on the view that America's destiny is to lead and police the whole world, see Andrew J. Bachevich, *Washington Rules: America's Path to Permanent War* (New York: Metropolitan Books, 2010).

18. See Jean Bethke Elshtain, *Women and War* (New York: Basic Books, 1987).

19. Early concerns about multicultural education appear in Charles Taylor, *Multiculturalism and "The Politics of Recognition"* (Princeton, N.J.: Princeton University Press, 1992).

20. See other writers in Nussbaum, *For Love of Country?* For example, Sissela Bok, "From Part to Whole," pp. 38–44.

21. See Nel Noddings, ed., *Educating Citizens for Global Awareness* (New York: Teachers College Press, 2005).

CHAPTER 12

1. Jane Roland Martin, *Reclaiming a Conversation* (New Haven, Conn.: Yale University Press, 1985).

2. Nel Noddings, *The Challenge to Care in Schools* (New York: Teachers College Press, 1992).

3. See, for example, M. Esther Harding, *Woman's Mysteries* (New York: Harper Colophon Books, 1976).

4. Foremost here is Ruth Hubbard. See Ruth Hubbard, Mary Sue Henifin, and Barbara Fried, eds., *Biological Woman: The Convenient Myth* (Cambridge, Mass.: Schenkman, 1982); and Hubbard, *The Politics of Women's Biology* (New Brunswick, N.J.: Rutgers University Press, 1990).

5. Rousseau quoted in Susan Moller Okin, *Women in Western Political Thought* (Princeton, N.J.: Princeton University Press, 1979), pp. 163–164.

6. Ibid., p. 164.

7. Mary Wollstonecraft, *A Vindication of the Rights of Woman,* ed. Carol H. Poston (New York: W. W. Norton, 1975).

8. Sara Blaffer Hrdy, for example, extols the craftiness evolution has conferred on women. Similarly, many nineteenth-century feminists called on women, thought to be morally superior to men, to save both men and themselves. See Hrdy, *The Woman That Never Evolved* (Cambridge, Mass.: Harvard University Press, 1981).

9. On Quine, see, for example, Louise Antony, "Quine as Feminist: The Radical Import of Naturalized Epistemology," in Louise Antony and Charlotte Witt, eds., *A Mind of One's Own* (Boulder, Colo.: Westview Press, 1993), pp. 185–226.

10. Naomi Scheman, "Though This Be Method, Yet There Is Madness in It," in ibid., pp. 145–170.

11. See the discussion in Susan J. Hekman, *Gender and Knowledge* (Boston: Northeastern University Press, 1990).

12. See Patricia Hill Collins, *Black Feminist Thought* (Boston: Unwin Hyman, 1990).

13. For a discussion of the generation of themes in education, see Paulo Freire, *Pedagogy of the Oppressed,* trans. Myra Bergman Ramos (New York: Herder and Herder, 1970). For an alternative view of what might be taught in schools, see Nel Noddings, *Critical Lessons: What Our Schools Should Teach* (Cambridge: Cambridge University Press, 2006).

14. See D. Jean Clandinin, Annie Davies, Pat Hogan, and Barbara Kennard, eds., *Learning to Teach, Teaching to Learn* (New York: Teachers College Press, 1993).

15. See Lee J. Cronbach, "The Logic of Experiments on Discovery," in Lee S. Shulman and Evan R. Keislar, eds., *Learning by Discovery* (Chicago: Rand McNally, 1966), pp. 77–92.

16. See, for example, Ruth Bleier, ed., *Feminist Approaches to Science* (New York: Pergamon Press, 1988); Ruth Hubbard, M. S. Henefin, and B. Fried, eds., *Women Look at Biology Looking at Women* (Cambridge, Mass.: Schenkman, 1979); Evelyn Fox Keller, *A Feeling for the Organism: The Life and Work of Barbara McClintock* (New York: Freeman, 1983); also Keller, *Reflections on Gender and Science* (New Haven, Conn.: Yale University Press, 1985).

17. On evolution, see Ruth Hubbard, "Have Only Men Evolved?" in Hubbard, Henefin, and Fried, *Women Look at Biology,* pp. 17–46; on variability, see Nel Noddings, "Variability: A Pernicious Hypothesis," *Review of Educational Research* 62, no. 1 (1992): 85–88.

18. John O'Neill, *Making Sense Together: An Introduction to Wild Sociology* (London: Heinemann, 1975).

19. Dorothy E. Smith, *The Everyday World as Problematic: A Feminist Sociology* (Boston: Northeastern University Press, 1987).

20. See Keller, *Feeling for the Organism.*

21. See Sheila Greeve Davaney, "Problems with Feminist Theory: Historicity and the Search for Sure Foundations," in Paula M. Cooey, Sharon A. Farmer, and Mary Ellen Ross,

eds., *Embodied Love: Sexuality and Relationship as Feminist Values* (San Francisco: Harper and Row, 1987), pp. 79–96.

22. On this, see Helen Longino, "Essential Tensions—Phase Two: Feminist, Philosophical, and Social Studies of Science," in Antony and Witt, *A Mind of One's Own*, pp. 257–272.

23. William James, *The Varieties of Religious Experience* (New York: Mentor, 1958, 1902).

24. See Rudy Rucker, *Infinity and the Mind* (Boston: Birkhauser, 1982).

25. For a description of these views, see Alison M. Jaggar, *Feminist Politics and Human Nature* (Totowa, N.J.: Rowman and Allanheld, 1983).

26. See Carol J. Gilligan, *In a Different Voice* (Cambridge, Mass.: Harvard University Press, 1982); also Mary Jeanne Larrabee, ed., *An Ethic of Care* (New York and London: Routledge, 1993).

27. See Nel Noddings, *Caring: A Feminine Approach to Ethics and Moral Education* (Berkeley: University of California Press, 1984).

28. Jean Grimshaw, *Philosophy and Feminist Thinking* (Minneapolis: University of Minnesota Press, 1986).

29. Ibid., p. 209.

30. See the symposium on caring in *Hypatia* 5, no. 1 (Spring 1990):101–126.

31. See Joan Tronto, "Beyond Gender Difference to a Theory of Care," *Signs* 12, no. 4 (1987):644–663.

32. See Michael Slote, *Morals from Motives* (Oxford: Oxford University Press, 2001).

33. See Michael Slote, "Caring Versus the Philosophers," in Randall Curren, ed., *Philosophy of Education: 1999* (Champaign, Ill.: Philosophy of Education Society, 2000), pp. 25–35. See also my response: Nel Noddings, "Two Concepts of Caring," pp. 36–39.

34. Virginia Held, *The Ethics of Care: Personal, Political, and Global* (Oxford: Oxford University Press, 2006), p. 3.

35. Michael Slote, *The Ethics of Care and Empathy* (London and New York: Routledge, 2007), p. 1.

36. Nel Noddings, *The Maternal Factor: Two Paths to Morality* (Berkeley: University of California Press, 2010).

37. Held, *Ethics of Care*, p. 168.

38. See Nel Noddings, "Caring as Relation and Virtue in Teaching," in P. J. Ivanhoe and Rebecca Walker, eds., *Working Virtue: Virtue Ethics and Contemporary Moral Problems* (Oxford: Oxford University Press, 2006).

39. See Nel Noddings, "Conversation as Moral Education," *Journal of Moral Education* 23, no. 2 (1994):107–118.

40. Martin Buber, "Education," in Buber, *Between Man and Man* (New York: Macmillan, 1965).

41. Noddings, *Challenge to Care in Schools*, p. 25.

42. See Ann Diller, "Pluralisms for Education: An Ethics of Care Perspective," in H. A. Alexander, ed. *Philosophy of Education* (Champaign, Ill.: Philosophy of Education Society, 1993), pp. 22–29.

43. For a lucid account of Derrida's ethical position, see Richard J. Bernstein, *The New Constellation* (Cambridge, Mass.: MIT Press, 1992); for an introduction to Levinas, see *The Levinas Reader*, ed. Sean Hand (Oxford: Blackwell, 1989).

44. Bernstein, *New Constellation,* pp. 184–185; the embedded Derrida quotation is from "Violence and Metaphysics," p. 138.

45. For a discussion of staying with and holding, see Sara Ruddick, *Maternal Thinking: Towards a Politics of Peace* (Boston: Beacon Press, 1989).

46. Barbara J. Thayer-Bacon, *Transforming Critical Thinking* (New York: Teachers College Press, 2000).

47. See Nel Noddings, "Stories in Dialogue: Caring and Interpersonal Reasoning," in Carol Witherell and Nel Noddings, eds., *Stories Lives Tell* (New York: Teachers College Press, 1991), pp. 157–170.

48. See Simone Weil, "Reflections on the Right Use of School Studies with a View to the Love of God," in *Simone Weil Reader,* ed. George A. Panichas (Mt. Kisco, N.Y.: Moyer Bell Limited, 1977), pp. 44–52.

BIBLIOGRAPHY

Adler, Mortimer J. *The Paideia Proposal.* New York: Macmillan, 1982.

AERA. *AERA Monograph Series on Curriculum Evaluation* 3. Chicago: Rand McNally, 1969.

Antony, Louise M., and Charlotte Witt, eds. *A Mind of One's Own.* Boulder, Colo.: Westview Press, 1993.

Apple, Michael W. *Ideology and Curriculum.* Boston: Routledge and Kegan Paul, 1979.

———. *Education and Power.* Boston: Routledge and Kegan Paul, 1982.

———. "The Politics of Official Knowledge: Does a National Curriculum Make Sense?" *Discourse* 14, no. 1 (1993): 1.

Apple, Michael W., and Lois Weis, eds. *Ideology and Practice in Schooling.* Philadelphia: Temple University Press, 1983.

Aristotle. *Nicomachean Ethics.* Translated by Terence Irwin. Indianapolis: Hackett, 1985.

Atkinson, Carroll, and Eugene Maleska. *The Story of Education.* New York: Bantam Books, 1961.

Bachevich, Andrew J. *Washington Rules: America's Path to Permanent War.* New York: Metropolitan Books, 2010.

Baron, J. B., and Robert J. Sternberg, eds. *Teaching Thinking Skills: Theory and Practice.* New York: Freeman, 1987.

Berlin, Isaiah. *Four Essays on Liberty.* Oxford: Oxford University Press, 1969.

Bernstein, Richard J. *The New Constellation.* Cambridge, Mass.: MIT Press, 1992.

———, ed. *John Dewey: On Experience, Nature, and Freedom.* New York: Library of Liberal Arts, 1960.

Blackburn, Simon. *Truth.* Oxford: Oxford University Press, 2005.

Bleier, Ruth, ed. *Feminist Approaches to Science.* New York: Pergamon Press, 1988.

Bowles, Samuel, and Herbert Gintis. *Schooling in Capitalist America.* New York: Basic Books, 1976.

Brinton, Crane. *A History of Western Morals.* New York: Harcourt, Brace, 1959.

Buber, Martin. *I and Thou.* Translated by Ronald Gregor Smith. New York: Scribner's, 1958.

———. *Between Man and Man.* New York: Macmillan, 1965.

Bullough, Robert V., Jr. *Life on the Other Side of the Teacher's Desk: Stories of Children at Risk.* New York: Teachers College Press, 2000.

Burbules, Nicholas. *Dialogue in Teaching.* New York: Teachers College Press, 1993.

Callan, Eamonn. "Dewey's Conception of Education as Growth." *Educational Theory* 32, no. 1 (Winter 1982): 19–27.

———. *Creating Citizens: Political Education and Liberal Democracy.* Oxford: Oxford University Press, 1997.

Carnoy, Martin, and Henry Levin. *Schooling and Work in the Democratic State.* Stanford, Calif.: Stanford University Press, 1985.

Carter, Robert E. *Dimensions of Moral Education.* Toronto: University of Toronto Press, 1984.

Chazan, Barry. *Contemporary Approaches to Moral Education.* New York: Teachers College Press, 1985.

Chisholm, Roderick M. *Theory of Knowledge.* 3d ed. Englewood Cliffs, N.J.: Prentice-Hall, 1989.

Clandinin, D. Jean, Annie Davies, Pat Hogan, and Barbara Kennard, eds. *Learning to Teach, Teaching to Learn.* New York: Teachers College Press, 1993.

Cleverly, John, and D. C. Phillips. *Visions of Childhood.* New York: Teachers College Press, 1986.

Collins, Patricia Hill. *Black Feminist Thought.* Boston: Unwin Hyman, 1990.

Counts, George S. *Dare the School Build a New Social Order?* New York: Arno Press, 1969.

Cronbach, Lee J. *Designing Evaluations of Educational and Social Programs.* San Francisco: Jossey-Bass, 1982.

Curren, Randall, ed. *Philosophy of Education: 1999.* Champaign, Ill.: Philosophy of Education Society, 2000.

Daly, Mary. *Beyond God the Father.* Boston: Beacon Press, 1974.

Darling-Hammond, Linda, ed. *Review of Research in Education* 20. Washington, D.C.: American Educational Research Association, 1994.

Darling-Hammond, Linda, and John Bransford, eds. *Preparing Teachers for a Changing World.* San Francisco: Jossey-Bass, 2005.

Davis, Philip J., and Reuben Hersh. *The Mathematical Experience.* Boston: Birkhauser, 1981.

Davis, Robert B., Carolyn A. Maher, and Nel Noddings, eds. *Constructivist Views on the Teaching and Learning of Mathematics.* JRME Monograph 4. Reston, Va.: National Council of Teachers of Mathematics, 1990.

Deiro, Judith. *Teaching with Heart.* Thousand Oaks, CA: Corwin Press, 1996.

Dewey, John. *The School and Society.* Chicago: University of Chicago Press, 1900.

———. *The Child and the Curriculum.* Chicago: University of Chicago Press, 1902.

———. *Democracy and Education.* New York: Macmillan, 1916.

———. *The Public and Its Problems.* New York: Henry Holt, 1927.

———. *The Quest for Certainty.* New York: G. P. Putnam's Sons, 1929.

———. *Human Nature and Conduct.* New York: Modern Library, 1930.

———. *How We Think.* Chicago: Henry Regnery, 1933.

———. *Logic: The Theory of Inquiry.* New York: Henry Holt, 1938.

———. *Experience and Education.* New York: Collier Books, 1963. (Originally printed in 1938.)

———. *Reconstruction in Philosophy and Essays 1920.* Edited by Jo Ann Boydston. Carbondale: Southern Illinois University Press, 1988.

Diller, Ann. "Pluralisms for Education: An Ethics of Care Perspective." Pp. 22–29 in *Philosophy of Education,* edited by H. A. Alexander. Champaign, Ill.: Philosophy of Education Society, 1993.

Eisner, Elliot. *The Enlightened Eye: Qualitative Inquiry and the Enhancement of Educational Practice.* New York: Macmillan, 1991.

Elshtain, Jean Bethke. *Women and War.* New York: Basic Books, 1987.

———. *Jane Addams and the Dream of American Democracy.* New York: Basic Books, 2002.

Ennis, Robert. "A Concept of Critical Thinking." *Harvard Educational Review* 32, no. 1 (1962): 83–111.

———. "Critical Thinking and Subject Specificity: Verification and Needed Research." *Educational Researcher* 18, no. 3 (1989): 4–10.

Ernest, Paul. *Social Constructivism as a Philosophy of Mathematics.* Albany: State University of New York Press, 1998.

Foucault, Michel. *Discipline and Punish: The Birth of the Prison.* Translated by Alan Sheridan. New York: Vintage, 1979.

Fraser, Nancy. *Unruly Practices: Power, Discourse, and Gender in Contemporary Social Theory.* Minneapolis: University of Minnesota Press, 1989.

Freire, Paulo. *Pedagogy of the Oppressed.* Translated by Myra Bergman Ramos. New York: Herder and Herder, 1970.

Friedman, Maurice, ed. *The Worlds of Existentialism.* Chicago: University of Chicago Press, 1964.

Galbraith, John Kenneth. *The Culture of Contentment.* Boston: Houghton Mifflin, 1992.

Gardner, Howard. *Frames of Mind.* New York: Basic Books, 1983.

Gardner, Martin. *The Annotated Alice.* (Lewis Carroll.) New York: World Publishing, 1963.

Gilligan, Carol J. *In a Different Voice.* Cambridge, Mass.: Harvard University Press, 1982.

Giroux, Henry A. *Schooling and the Struggle for Public Life.* Minneapolis: University of Minnesota Press, 1988.

Gordon, Mordechai, ed. *Hannah Arendt and Education.* Boulder, Colo.: Westview Press, 2001.

Green, Thomas. "A Topology of the Teaching Concept." Pp. 28–62 in *Concepts of Teaching,* edited by C. J. B. Macmillan and Thomas Nelson. Chicago: Rand McNally, 1968.

Greene, Maxine. *Teacher as Stranger.* Belmont, Calif.: Wadsworth, 1973.

———. *Landscapes of Learning.* New York: Teachers College Press, 1978.

———. *The Dialectic of Freedom.* New York: Teachers College Press, 1988.

Grimshaw, Jean. *Philosophy and Feminist Thinking.* Minneapolis: University of Minnesota Press, 1986.

Gross, Beatrice, and Ronald Gross, eds. *Radical School Reform.* New York: Simon and Schuster, 1969.

Hacking, Ian. *The Social Construction of What?* Cambridge, Mass.: Harvard University Press, 1999.

Hand, Sean, ed. *The Levinas Reader.* Oxford: Blackwell, 1989.

Hanna, Gila. *Rigorous Proof in Mathematics Education.* Toronto: OISE Press, 1983.

Hansen, David T. "Chasing Butterflies Without a Net: Interpreting Cosmopolitanism." *Studies in Philosophy of Education* 29 (2010): 151–166.

Harding, M. Esther. *Woman's Mysteries.* New York: Harper Colophon Books, 1976.

Harding, Sandra S. *The Science Question in Feminism.* Ithaca, N.Y.: Cornell University Press, 1986.

Harding, Sandra, and Merrill B. Hintikka, eds. *Discovering Reality: Feminist Perspectives on Epistemology, Metaphysics, Methodology, and Philosophy of Science.* Dordrecht, Netherlands: D. Reidel, 1983.

Haroutunian-Gordon, Sophie. *Turning the Soul: Teaching Through Conversation in the High School.* Chicago: University of Chicago Press, 1991.

Hartshorne, Hugh, and Mark A. May. *Studies in the Nature of Character.* Vol. 1, *Studies in Deceit.* New York: Macmillan, 1928. Vol. 2, *Studies in Self-Control.* New York: Macmillan, 1929.

Hekman, Susan J. *Gender and Knowledge.* Boston: Northeastern University Press, 1990.

Held, Virginia. *Feminist Morality.* Chicago: University of Chicago Press, 1993.

———. *The Ethics of Care: Personal, Political, and Global.* Oxford: Oxford University Press, 2006.

Hirst, Paul. *Knowledge and the Curriculum.* London: Routledge, 1974.

Hofstadter, Richard. *Anti-Intellectualism in American Life.* New York: Alfred A. Knopf, 1963.

Howe, Kenneth. *Understanding Equal Educational Opportunity.* New York: Teachers College Press, 1997.

Hubbard, Ruth. "Have Only Men Evolved?" Pp. 17–46 in *Women Look at Biology Looking at Women,* edited by Ruth Hubbard, M. S. Henefin and B. Fried. Cambridge, Mass.: Schenkman, 1979.

———. *The Politics of Women's Biology.* New Brunswick, N.J.: Rutgers University Press, 1990.

Hubbard, Ruth, M. S. Henefin, and B. Fried, eds. *Women Look at Biology Looking at Women.* Cambridge, Mass.: Schenkman, 1979.

———. *Biological Woman: The Convenient Myth.* Cambridge, Mass.: Schenkman, 1982.

Ivanhoe, P. J., and Rebecca Walker, eds. *Working Virtue: Virtue Ethics and Contemporary Moral Problems.* Oxford: Oxford University Press, 2006.

Jackson, Philip W. *Untaught Lessons.* New York: Teachers College Press, 1992.

Jacoby, Susan. *Freethinkers.* New York: Metropolitan Books, 2004.

Jaggar, Alison M. *Feminist Politics and Human Nature.* Totowa, N.J.: Rowman and Allanheld, 1983.

James, William. *The Varieties of Religious Experience.* New York: Mentor, 1958, 1902.

Kant, Immanuel. *Grounding for the Metaphysics of Morals.* Translated by James W. Ellington. Indianapolis: Hackett, 1981.

Katznelson, Ira. *When Affirmative Action Was White.* New York: W. W. Norton, 2005.

Keller, Evelyn Fox. *A Feeling for the Organism: The Life and Work of Barbara McClintock.* New York: Freeman, 1983.

———. *Reflections on Gender and Science.* New Haven, Conn.: Yale University Press, 1985.

Kierkegaard, Søren. *Either/Or.* Vol. 1. Translated by David F. Swenson and Lillian M. Swenson. Princeton, N.J.: Princeton University Press, 1959.

Kliebard, Herbert. *The Struggle for the American Curriculum: 1893–1958.* New York: Routledge, 1995.

———. *Schooled to Work: Vocationalism and the American Curriculum 1876–1946.* New York: Teachers College Press, 1999.

Kneller, George F., ed. *Foundations of Education.* New York: John Wiley and Sons, 1963.

Kohlberg, Lawrence. *The Philosophy of Moral Development.* San Francisco: Harper and Row, 1981.

Kohn, Alfie. *The Case Against Standardized Testing.* Portsmouth, N.H.: Heinemann, 2000.

Komisar, B. Paul, and C. J. B. Macmillan, eds. *Analytical Concepts in Education.* Chicago: Rand McNally, 1967.

Kozol, Jonathan. *Savage Inequalities.* New York: Crown Books, 1991.

Kuhn, Thomas. *The Structure of Scientific Revolutions.* Chicago: University of Chicago Press, 1962.

Lagemann, Ellen Condliffe, and Lee Shulman, eds. *Issues in Education Research*. San Francisco: Jossey-Bass, 1999.

Laird, Susan. "The Concept of Teaching: *Betsey Brown* vs. Philosophy of Education?" Pp. 32–45 in *Philosophy of Education: 1988,* edited by James Giarelli. Normal, Ill.: Philosophy of Education Society, 1989.

Larrabee, Mary Jeanne, ed. *An Ethic of Care*. New York and London: Routledge, 1993.

Laughlin, Robert B. *A Different Universe*. New York: Basic Books, 2005.

Lehrer, Keith. *Theory of Knowledge*. Boulder, Colo.: Westview Press, 1990.

Lickona, Thomas. *Educating for Character: How Our Schools Can Teach Respect and Responsibility*. New York: Bantam Books, 1991.

Lynch, Michael P. *True to Life*. Cambridge, Mass.: MIT Press, 2005.

MacIntyre, Alasdair. *After Virtue*. 2d ed. Notre Dame, Ind.: University of Notre Dame Press, 1984.

———. *Whose Justice? Which Rationality?* Notre Dame, Ind.: University of Notre Dame Press, 1988.

Macmillan, C. J. B., and James W. Garrison. "An Erotetic Concept of Teaching." *Educational Theory* 33, no. 3–4 (1983): 157–166.

Macmillan, C.J.B., and Thomas Nelson, eds. *Concepts of Teaching*. Chicago: Rand McNally, 1968.

Mager, Robert. *Preparing Instructional Objectives*. San Francisco: Fearon Press, 1962.

Martin, Jane Roland. *Reclaiming a Conversation*. New Haven, Conn.: Yale University Press, 1985.

———. *The Schoolhome: Rethinking Schools for Changing Families*. Cambridge, Mass.: Harvard University Press, 1992.

———. *Cultural Miseducation*. New York: Teachers College Press, 2002.

McClellan, James E. *Philosophy of Education*. Englewood Cliffs, N.J.: Prentice-Hall, 1976.

McDermott, John J., ed. *The Philosophy of John Dewey*. New York: G. P. Putnam's Sons, 1973.

McPeck, John E. *Critical Thinking and Education*. Oxford: Martin Robertson, 1981.

Mill, John Stuart. *Utilitarianism*. Edited by George Sher. Indianapolis: Hackett, 1979, 1861.

Miller, Alice. *For Your Own Good*. Translated by Hildegarde Hannun and Hunter Hannun. New York: Farrar, Straus, and Giroux, 1983.

Montessori, Maria. *The Secret of Childhood*. Translated by M. Joseph Costelloe. New York: Ballantine Books, 1966.

Morgenbesser, Sidney, ed. *Dewey and His Critics*. New York: Journal of Philosophy, 1977.

Murdoch, Iris. *The Sovereignty of Good*. London: Routledge and Kegan Paul, 1970.

Neill, A. S. *Summerhill*. New York: Hart Publishing, 1960.

Nieto, Sonia. *The Light in Their Eyes: Creating Multicultural Learning*. New York: Teachers College Press, 1999.

Noddings, Nel. *Caring: A Feminine Approach to Ethics and Moral Education*. Berkeley: University of California Press, 1984.

———. *The Challenge to Care in Schools*. New York: Teachers College Press, 1992.

———. *Educating for Intelligent Belief or Unbelief*. New York: Teachers College Press, 1993.

———. "For All Its Children." *Educational Theory* 43, no. 1 (1993): 17.

———. "Does Everybody Count?" *Journal of Mathematical Behavior* 13, no. 1 (1994): 89–104.

———. "On Community." *Educational Theory* 4, no. 3 (1996): 245–267.

———. "Thinking About Standards." *Phi Delta Kappan* 79, no. 3 (1997): 184–189.

———. *Starting at Home: Caring and Social Policy*. Berkeley: University of California Press, 2002.

———. *Educating Moral People*. New York: Teachers College Press, 2002.

———. *Happiness and Education*. Cambridge: Cambridge University Press, 2003.

———. "What Does It Mean to Educate the Whole Child?" *Educational Leadership* 63, no. 1 (2005): 8–13.

———. *Critical Lessons: What Our Schools Should Teach*. Cambridge: Cambridge University Press, 2006.

———. *The Maternal Factor: Two Paths to Morality*. Berkeley: University of California Press, 2010.

———, ed. *Educating Citizens for Global Awareness*. New York: Teachers College Press, 2005.

Norris, Stephen R. *The Generalizability of Critical Thinking*. New York: Teachers College Press, 1992.

Nucci, Larry P., ed. *Moral Development and Character Education*. Berkeley: McCutchan, 1989.

Nussbaum, Martha C. *The Fragility of Goodness*. Cambridge: Cambridge University Press, 1986.

———. *For Love of Country?* Edited by Joshua Cohen. Boston: Beacon Press, 1996.

Oakeshott, Michael. *Rationalism in Politics and Other Essays*. London: Methuen, 1962.

Okin, Susan Moller. *Women in Western Political Thought*. Princeton, N.J.: Princeton University Press, 1979.

O'Neill, John. *Making Sense Together: An Introduction to Wild Sociology*. London: Heinemann, 1975.

Orwell, George. *A Collection of Essays*. San Diego: Harcourt Brace, 1981.

Pang, Valerie Ooka. *Multicultural Education: A Caring-Centered, Reflective Approach*. New York: McGraw-Hill, 2001.

Paul, Richard. "Teaching Critical Thinking in the Strong Sense: A Focus on Self-Deception, World Views, and a Dialectical Mode of Analysis." *Informal Logic Newsletter* 4, no. 2 (1982): 2–7.

———. *Critical Thinking: What Every Person Needs to Survive in a Rapidly Changing World*. Rohnert Park, Calif.: Center for Critical Thinking and Moral Critique, 1990.

Peters, Richard S., ed. *The Philosophy of Education*. Oxford: Oxford University Press, 1973.

Phillips, D. C. "On Describing a Student's Cognitive Structure." *Educational Psychologist* 18, no. 2 (1983): 59–74.

———. *Philosophy, Science, and Social Inquiry*. Oxford: Pergamon, 1987.

———. "Telling It Straight." *Educational Psychologist* 29, no. 1 (1994): 13–21.

Phillips, Denis, and Jonas Soltis. *Perspectives on Learning*. New York: Teachers College Press, 1985.

Piaget, Jean. *Genetic Epistemology*. New York: Columbia University Press, 1970.

———. *Biology and Knowledge*. Chicago: University of Chicago Press, 1971.

———. *Insights and Illusions of Philosophy*. New York: World Publishing, 1971.

Plato. *The Great Dialogues*. Translated and edited by B. Jowett. Roslyn, N.Y.: Walter J. Black, 1942.

———. *The Republic of Plato*. Translated with notes and an "Interpretive Essay" by Allan Bloom. New York: Basic Books, 1968.

Poplin, Mary, and J. Weeres. *Voices from the Inside: A Report on Schooling from Inside the Classroom*. Los Angeles: Institute for Education in Transformation at the Claremont Graduate School, 1992.

Popper, Karl. *Objective Knowledge*. Oxford: Clarendon Press, 1972.

Quine, W.V.O., and Robert Ullian. *The Web of Belief*. New York: Random House, 1970.

Rasmussen, David, ed. *Universalism vs. Communitarianism: Contemporary Debates in Ethics*. Cambridge, Mass: MIT Press, 1990.

Raths, Louis, Merrill Harmin, and Sidney Simon. *Values and Teaching*. Columbus, Ohio: Charles E. Merrill, 1966; 2d ed., 1978.

Ravitch, Diane. *National Standards in American Education*. Washington, D.C.: Brookings Institution Press, 1995.

———. *Left Back: A Century of Battles over School Reform*. New York: Simon and Schuster, 2000.

Rawls, John. *A Theory of Justice*. Cambridge, Mass.: Harvard University Press, 1971.

Raywid, Mary Anne. "Community and Schools: A Prolegomenon." Pp. 2–17 in *Philosophy of Education: 1988*, edited by James Giarelli. Normal, Ill.: Philosophy of Education Society, 1989.

Richards, I. A. *The Meaning of Meaning*. New York: Harcourt, Brace, 1956.

Rorty, Amelie Oksenberg, ed. *Essays on Aristotle's Ethics*. Berkeley: University of California Press, 1980.

Rorty, Richard. *Philosophy and the Mirror of Nature*. Princeton, N.J.: Princeton University Press, 1979.

———. *Contingency, Irony, and Solidarity*. Cambridge: Cambridge University Press, 1989.

Rose, Mike. *Possible Lives: The Promise of Public Education in America*. Boston: Houghton Mifflin, 1995.

———. *The Mind at Work: Valuing the Intelligence of the American Worker*. New York: Penguin, 2005.

Rothstein, Richard. *Class and Schools*. Washington, D.C.: Economic Policy Institute, 2004.

Rousseau, Jean-Jacques. *Emile*. Translated by Allan Bloom. New York: Basic Books, 1974.

Ruddick, Sara. *Maternal Thinking: Towards a Politics of Peace*. Boston: Beacon Press, 1989.

Ryle, Gilbert. *The Concept of Mind*. London: Hutchinson, 1952.

Sandel, Michael. *Liberalism and the Limits of Justice*. Cambridge: Cambridge University Press, 1982.

Sarason, Seymour B. *The Predictable Failure of Educational Reform*. San Francisco: Jossey-Bass, 1990.

Sartre, Jean-Paul. *Being and Nothingness*. Translated by Hazel E. Barnes. New York: Washington Square Press, 1956.

———. *Essays in Existentialism*. Edited by Wade Baskin. Secaucus, N.J.: Citadel Press, 1977.

Schaffarzick, Jon, and Gary Sykes, eds. *Value Conflicts and Curriculum Issues*. Berkeley: McCutchan, 1979.

Scheffler, Israel. *The Language of Education*. Springfield, Ill.: Charles C. Thomas, 1960.

Scheman, Naomi. "Though This Be Method, Yet There Is Madness in It: Paranoia and Liberal Epistemology." Pp. 145–170 in *A Mind of One's Own*, edited by Louise M. Antony and Charlotte Witt. Boulder, Colo.: Westview Press, 1993.

Schlesinger, Arthur M., Jr. *The Disuniting of America: Reflections on a Multicultural Society*. New York: W. W. Norton, 1992.

Schwab, Joseph J. *Science, Curriculum, and Liberal Education: Selected Essays*. Chicago: University of Chicago Press, 1978.

Scriven, Michael. *Reasoning*. New York: McGraw-Hill, 1976.

Sergiovanni, Thomas J. *Building Community in Schools*. San Francisco: Jossey-Bass, 1994.

Shavelson, Richard, and Lisa Towne, eds. *Scientific Research in Education*. Washington, D.C.: National Academies Press, 2002.

Shipler, David K. *The Working Poor: Invisible in America*. New York: Alfred A. Knopf, 2004.

Shulman, Lee S., and Evan R. Keislar, eds. *Learning by Discovery*. Chicago: Rand McNally, 1966.

Sichel, Betty A. *Moral Education*. Philadelphia: Temple University Press, 1988.

Sidgwick, Henry. *The Methods of Ethics*. Indianapolis: Hackett, 1981, 1874.

Sidorkin, Alexander M. *Learning Relations*. New York: Peter Lang, 2002.

Siegel, Harvey. *Educating Reason: Rationality, Critical Thinking, and Education*. New York: Routledge, 1988.

Silberman, Charles E. *Crisis in the Classroom: The Remaking of American Education*. New York: Random House, 1970.

Singer, Peter, ed. *A Companion to Ethics*. Oxford: Basil Blackwell, 1991.

Slote, Michael. *Morals from Motives*. Oxford: Oxford University Press, 2001.

———. *The Ethics of Care and Empathy*. London and New York: Routledge, 2007.

Smith, B. Othanel, and Robert H. Ennis, eds. *Language and Concepts in Education*. Chicago: Rand McNally, 1961.

Smith, Dorothy E. *The Everyday World as Problematic: A Feminist Sociology*. Boston: Northeastern University Press, 1987.

Snook, I. A. "The Concept of Indoctrination." *Studies in Philosophy and Education* 7, no. 2 (1970): 65–108.

Soltis, Jonas. *An Introduction to the Analysis of Educational Concepts*. Reading, Mass.: Addison-Wesley, 1968.

Spring, Joel. *American Education*. Boston: McGraw-Hill, 2000.

Suppes, Patrick. *Introduction to Logic*. New York: Van Nostrand Reinhold, 1957.

Taylor, Charles. *Philosophy and the Human Sciences*. Philosophical Papers 2. Cambridge: Cambridge University Press, 1985.

———. *Multiculturalism and "The Politics of Recognition."* Princeton, N.J.: Princeton University Press, 1992.

Thayer-Bacon, Barbara J. *Transforming Critical Thinking*. New York: Teachers College Press, 2000.

Thomas, Milton Halsey. *John Dewey: A Centennial Bibliography*. Chicago: University of Chicago Press, 1962.

Tillich, Paul. *The Courage to Be*. New Haven, Conn.: Yale University Press, 1952.

Tronto, Joan. "Beyond Gender Difference to a Theory of Care." *Signs* 12, no. 4 (1987): 644–663.

———. *Moral Boundaries: A Political Argument for an Ethic of Care*. New York: Routledge, 1993.

True, Michael. *An Energy Field More Intense Than War*. Syracuse, N.Y.: Syracuse University Press, 1995.

Vandenberg, Donald. *Human Rights in Education*. New York: Philosophical Library, 1983.

Vygotsky, L. *Mind in Society: The Development of Higher Psychological Processes*. Cambridge, Mass.: Harvard University Press, 1978.

Walzer, Michael. *Spheres of Justice: A Defense of Pluralism and Equality*. New York: Basic Books, 1983.

Watson, J. B. *Behaviorism*. New York: W. W. Norton, 1924.

Weil, Simone. *Simone Weil Reader.* Edited by George A. Panichas. Mt. Kisco, N.Y.: Moyer Bell Limited, 1977.

Weinstein, Mark. "Critical Thinking: The Great Debate." *Educational Theory* 43, no. 1 (1993): 99–117.

Westbrook, Robert. *John Dewey and American Democracy.* Ithaca, N.Y.: Cornell University Press, 1991.

White, James Terry. *Character Lessons in American Biography for Public Schools and Home Instruction.* New York: The Character Development League, 1909.

White, John. *Education and the Good Life.* New York: Teachers College Press, 1991.

Willis, Paul. *Learning to Labour.* Farnborough, England: Saxon House, 1977.

Winch, Peter. *The Idea of a Social Science.* London: Routledge, 1967.

Witherell, Carol, and Nel Noddings, eds. *Stories Lives Tell: Narrative and Dialogue in Education.* New York: Teachers College Press, 1991.

Wollstonecraft, Mary. *A Vindication of the Rights of Woman.* Edited by Carol H. Poston. New York: W. W. Norton, 1975.

INDEX